Reward Management in Context

Angela Wright

Chartered Institute of Personnel and Development

First published 2004

© Chartered Institute of Personnel and Development, 2004

Designed and typeset by Fakenham Photosetting, Fakenham, Norfolk
Printed in Great Britain by The Cromwell Press, Trowbridge, Wiltshire

British Library Cataloguing in Publication Data
A catalogue of this manual is available from the British Library

ISBN 0 85292 993 5

The views expressed in this manual are the author's own and may not necessarily reflect those of the CIPD.

The CIPD has made every effort to trace and acknowledge copyright holders. If any source has been overlooked, CIPD Enterprises would be pleased to redress this for future editions.

Chartered Institute of Personnel and Development, CIPD House,
Camp Road, London, SW19 4UX
Tel: 020 8971 9000   Fax: 020 8263 3333
E-mail: cipd@cipd.co.uk   Website: www.cipd.co.uk
Incorporated by Royal Charter.   Registered Charity No. 1079797
The catalogue of all CIPD titles can be viewed on all the CIPD website:
www.cipd.co.uk/bookstore

Contents

List of tables and figures

Tables

Figures

Acknowledgements

I would like to express my thanks to the organisations and individuals who have kindly allowed me to use their material as examples in this book. I am particularly grateful to Jenny Bell and Alastair Hatchet at Incomes Data Services, to Jim Mathewman, Steve French, John Purcell, Maeve Quaid, Ian Kessler and Robert Elliot, as well as to the various publishers who agreed to our reproducing material from their published works.

Pay information is often sensitive; and the case studies in the work are anonymous, since, while they represent real organisational issues and problems, in most instances the experiences from several organisations have been melded together to provide a (hopefully) cohesive whole.

I am also grateful to the anonymous reviewers, who provided practical advice on how I might improve the draft text. In this context, I would also like to thank Ruth Lake, the CIPD Commissioning Editor, for her invaluable help and patience. Any errors in this work, though, are mine.

Finally, I would like to express my grateful thanks to my colleagues at the Universities of Westminster and Coventry, who have encouraged me and provided moral support – as, last but not least, has my family.

Angela Wright, January 2004

Reward in context

CHAPTER 1

INTRODUCTION

Pay is full of paradoxes. On the one hand, all forms of reward – from pay through to praise – can be viewed as an integral and vitally important part of the fabric of an organisation. On the other hand, there is little consistent evidence to suggest which are the critical aspects of reward design and management, which ones can directly affect organisational health. This book attempts to span what is at times a wide divide between academic and practitioner perspectives. In this subject area, the texts hitherto available tend either to have an academic orientation or to offer practitioner insights – sometimes with a marked difference in view from the two 'camps'. In some aspects of reward this is because there is little in-depth research; in others, while there is evidence, it is not in an accessible format. Practitioner insights may be considered by academics to lack rigour, while academics may seem to practitioners to lack grounding in the realities of corporate life.

The following chapters contribute to spanning this divide by examining reward in context. They aim to meet the needs of students of the CIPD employee reward module, seeking to satisfy the professional standards in that field.

This chapter contributes to the following standards of the CIPD employee reward module.
Operational indicators – Practitioners must be able to:

- contribute to the identification of an appropriate employee-reward strategy from an analysis of an organisation's corporate strategy, and take part in the preparation of reward plans
- contribute to the administration of employee-reward policies and processes, and evaluate effectiveness and value for money
- assist in preparing an employee-reward policy statement and specify a process for ensuring its continuous review.

Knowledge indicators – Practitioners must understand and be able to explain:

- the role of reward strategies and policies in an organisation, and their potential for supporting change when integrated with personnel and organisational strategies and policies
- the key economic, psychological and motivational theories that influence reward policies and practices
- the part that financial and non-financial rewards play in attracting, retaining and motivating people
- the factors that influence levels of employee satisfaction with their rewards and with the reward system – such as equity and fairness.

BUSINESS CONTEXTS

Contingency theory (which is not itself unchallenged – see below) suggests that the varied business contexts for reward practice are crucial in determining what is appropriate in different circumstances. There is less guidance on what that means in practice. Poole and Jenkins (1998) identify the following 'structural factors' that affect reward in different organisational settings:

- whether an organisation is in the public or the private sector, although with some reward approaches – notably performance pay – there is evidence of 'convergence'
- the size of the organisation, with evidence that reward systems are more sophisticated in larger enterprises
- whether or not the firm is expanding or contracting in size, with expanding firms more likely to emphasise pay for skills and competencies and the ability to recruit and retain high-quality employees.

An earlier study that more practically sought to give a framework for assessing fit between organisational attributes and type of pay system was contained in the early 'socio-technical' work of Lupton and Gowler (1969). However, while useful in its time this work is most relevant to the collectively bargained manual-worker pay structures of the 1960s and has less practical relevance in the modern context. The value of this work relies on its approach and its ambition to formulate a framework for decision-making – an achievement that has not subsequently been updated in a systematic way.

The case studies within this book reflect varying organisational settings – public, private and voluntary sectors; small organisations; large companies; and mature as well as growing businesses.

Reflecting current organisational settings is important when structuring appropriate reward practices, but equally important are future plans and strategic direction. Lawler (1990) argues that reward approaches should be tailored to fit the business strategic 'compass' of a specific organisation. This is certainly easier said than done. Kessler (2001) points to the paucity of evidence for a relationship between reward and strategic business issues. There is a difficult set of relationships to unpack and research. Nonetheless it has become commonplace to assert that reward decisions must fit business strategy and circumstances.

The first problem is to identify what actually *is* the business strategy of the organisation. Different conceptualisations of what constitutes 'strategy' notwithstanding, it has been argued in the HRM context that in much of the literature notions about strategy are too simplistic (Legge 1989). Definitional problems seem to increase rather than diminish if we take as a starting point a broader definition of strategy as a 'consistent pattern' in decision-making (drawing on Mintzberg 1987).

A study by Gomez-Mejia and Balkin (1992) compared the pay and business strategies of more than 200 US manufacturing companies. Dividing these into 'algorithmic' organisations in generally stable market situations and 'experiential' companies in growth sectors, Gomez-Mejia suggested that the former category was most suited to traditional grading structures, job-based (as distinct from person-based) approaches and service-related pay progression. The growth-sector companies would be more suited to devoting a relatively high proportion of employee earnings to 'variable' pay, such as performance pay. The study showed an association between the identified business and pay strategies, but even when closely allied, the linkages did not explain the observed differences in relative corporate financial performance.

Drawing on the work of Schuler and Jackson (1987) – see Table 1 (page 4) – may help to provide a broad framework for analysing modern organisational strategic contexts and the associated pay strategies. In this work there are three categories of business strategy – innovation, quality enhancement and cost minimisation. The model seeks to identify the generalised employee behaviours required to support such strategies and the consequential reward policies.

STUDENT REVIEW TASK

In groups, discuss which of the three strategic business-context perspectives put forward by Schuler and Jackson your own organisations seem to resemble. Students without an employing organisation should search out recruitment advertisement information for graduates from major employers. Look for information – from careers services, company websites, the national press, TV etc – that gives a reasonable picture of the type of organisation. Identify whether the reward practices mentioned in Table 1 are present (or if there is evidence that they are practised).

From salary administration to strategic management

There are signs that pay is shedding its Cinderella status and making the transformation from the turgid, unimaginative and inflexible world of wage and salary administration to a brave new world where integration with the organisation's goals and other personnel practices typifies the rhetoric, if not always actual practice.

Lewis (2000)

Heneman *et al* (2000) sought to identify the ways in which the field of salary management is moving in a strategic direction and what that might mean in practice (see Table 2, page 5).

The 'new pay'
The new pay agenda ideas, developed by Schuster and Zingheim (1992) and by Lawler (1995), focus on identifying pay practices that enhance the organisation's strategic effectiveness. Lawler contends that reward systems are too rigid to meet the needs of modern organisational challenges. He makes the case that a person-based rather than a job-based approach to pay is necessary in modern knowledge-based organisations. Competency-based pay (see page 78) and skill-based pay encourage individuals to expand their knowledge and skills and are preferential to traditional job-evaluated systems that tend to emphasise organisational rigidity and hierarchy (see Chapter 3, page 70). Emphasis is also placed on encouraging co-operative and teamworking behaviour. Lawler sees the introduction of any particular pay practices as contingent on the business context.

Lewis (2000) explores the application of Lawler's views in the context of a major financial-sector company. He concludes that the Lawler model (see page 5):

Business strategy	Required employee behaviour	HR and reward policies
Innovation	Creative employees, focused on the long-term Need employees to be co-operative with each other and with others Quality fairly important Quantity of output fairly important Equal emphasis on process and results Tolerance of risk-taking and ambiguity	Job design that stresses co-operation and team work Performance management looks to the long term and rewards group-based achievements Reward systems emphasise internal equity as more important than external/market-related pay Broader career paths Emphasise the development of skills
Quality enhancement	Predictablity of employee behaviour, could emphasise compliance High concern for quality of output or service Less emphasis on quantity of output No risk, process important and commitment of employees to organisation's goals important	Competencies may be used to identify 'high-performance' employee behaviours Performance management is short term in focus Emphasis on results Extensive development and training
Cost reduction/minimisation	Repetitive and predictable behaviour Short-term focus Emphasis on the individual High concern for quantity of output, less concern for quality Stability, emphasis on results, low risk-taking	Jobs are clearly and narrowly defined, with little scope for ambiguity Career paths encourage employees to specialise in a narrow range of tasks to encourage efficiency Minimal training and development Pay rates are geared to (low-level) market rates
Adapted from Schuler and Jackson (1987)		

Table 1   *The business context for employee reward*

Administrative focus	Strategic focus
Job-based systems	Person
Individual emphasis	Team emphasis
Time-based pay	Output-based pay
Lag system	Lead system
Top-down	Bottom-up
Centralised	Decentralised
Status-driven	Dynamic
Internal equity emphasised	External equity/market emphasis
Fixed	Variable pay systems
Adapted with full acknowledgement from Heneman *et al* (2000)	

Table 2   *Pay system focus: administrative v strategic*

- oversimplifies the process of strategy formulation, assuming that it is a top-down process
- assumes that there can be a fairly straightforward link between a top-down reward strategy and employee behaviour when the relationship is 'extremely complex' in practice
- gives equal weight to values, structure and process, while in practice process was of greatest significance
- is unitarist (see page 16), while the degree of employee opposition to the reward strategy in practice raises doubts about the validity of unitarist assumptions.

Performance and HRM strategy – best practice, best fit ... or best process?

The potential of reward positively to influence organisational performance is a most attractive idea, but it lacks substance at present. One of the key problems is that it is difficult for researchers wanting to see cause and effect at work to unpick the interrelationships between reward and other HR practices. Gerhart (2000) summarises various studies that assess the influence that reward might have on a firm's performance: he concludes that there is evidence of relationships between organisational performance and pay strategy but that it is difficult to disentangle what these are. While key outcomes such as job satisfaction, recruitment/retention and employee performance seem to be associated with reward, the many (US) studies completed so far fall short because they tend not to be longitudinal (taking a view over time) and because they do not permit reward as an influence on organisational performance to be isolated from other causes.

While there are significant gaps in our understanding of how and why reward contributes to business performance, there has been some progress in research on the links between HRM practices generally and corporate performance. More depth is needed (Marchington and Grugulis 2000), but the research provides some useful starting points. Putting some flesh on the bones of the largely quantitative, positivist (survey-based) methodologies of the US studies, J Purcell *et al* (2003) are engaged in case study research. The results to date in the cases studied suggest that pay does not feature strongly in the picture of high-performance management. A model of the interrelationships at work has been put forward – see Figure 1 (page 6).

Within the HRM strategy and corporate performance debate there are various schools of thought, which may be variously categorised, but broadly the categories may be summarised as follows.

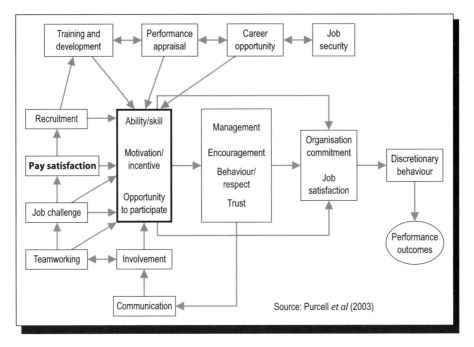

Figure 1   *The Bath People and Performance Model*

Best practice

The 'best practice' school of thought is based on the notion that there are some HR practices that will lead an organisation to success, regardless of its business context or strategy. Pfeffer (1999) is a forthright exponent of this approach. He suggests there are seven key HR practices (see Table 3) which, if all practised in the organisation, will lead to better organisational performance. Huselid's (1995a) work was based on survey work comparing the financial business performance of US private-sector companies with HR practices. Further work (for example MacDuffie, 1995) suggests there are 'bundles' of HR practices that help to drive organisational performance, but that the elements in the bundles may vary according to business sector. There is little evidence of particular pay or reward practices consistently appearing in these 'bundles', but in all the US studies performance-related pay tends to feature. The rationale for the universal applicability of these practices is that they lead to superior performance, as they tap the discretionary effort of individual workers (MacDuffie 1995; Pfeffer 1999). The validity of such work has been challenged because of the lack of rigorous academic analysis (for example Marchington and Grugulis 2000). In this context mention should also be made of the ideas of Purcell (1999), who has proposed there may be a basic level of (good) management practice – 'table stakes' – that may be needed in order for organisational performance to be affected positively.

Pfeffer (1998a) suggests there are 'golden rules' in reward policy and practice that hold good across all organisations. in crafting a reward strategy, remember the following rules:

- include 'large-dose' collective reward
- accept that pay is not a substitute for a 'high-trust' environment, 'fun' and 'meaningful work'

- ensure openness and transparency, with a positive message about equity
- use other means than pay to signal company values and focus behaviour
- use pay as only one element in building employee commitment.

Although Pfeffer bases his conclusions on case studies, the validity of this list has not been independently put to the test.

Best fit

Contingency theory underpins the 'best-fit' approach, which is seemingly common sense – suggesting there is not one best way, but a variety of HR practices that will suit different circumstances. Thorpe and Green (2002) criticise this approach – as exemplified in much of the prescriptive literature – because it is too simplistic, begs too many questions and as a theory is a 'chimera'. It also fails to acknowledge research, which identifies approaches that self-evidently do not work.

Best process

Cox (2000) puts forward this idea. The emphasis in this approach is on employee involvement and participation. The key assumption here is that many different reward practices might work in different settings, but the difference between success and failure relies more on the quality of relationships between management and employees than on the actual practice applied. The extent of employee involvement is crucial.

Employee commitment and trust

Trust between employees and employer is central to the tenets of high-commitment management, also referred to as 'high-involvement' or 'high-performance' human resource practices. '*If you were to ask me what you could do to inflict the most damage on an organisation, I would answer: tamper with its pay system, and do so following the current "conventional wisdom about pay"*' (Pfeffer 1998b). Pfeffer argues that a poorly designed or managed pay arrangement is likely to reduce commitment and trust.

But what of the more positive potential of pay to contribute to the promotion of a high-commitment climate? Wood (1996), in his study of the ingredients of high-commitment management, found little connection with pay practices. There is considerable uncertainty as to the nature of pay management in organisations seen to be in the high-performance league. Kessler (2001) comments: '*It is fundamentally misconceived to try to label any pay practice intrinsically high-commitment oriented*'.

---

1. Employment security
2. Selective hiring of new personnel
3. Self-managed teams and decentralisation of decision-making as the basic principles of organisation design
4. Comparatively high compensation contingent on organisational performance
5. Extensive training
6. Reduction in status distinctions and barriers across levels – including dress, language, office arrangements and wage differences
7. Extensive sharing of financial and performance information throughout the organisation.

Source: Pfeffer (1998b)

Table 3 *Pfeffer's seven best HR practices*

Reward strategy

Reward strategy has been broadly defined as *'the intentions of the organisation on how its reward policies and processes should be developed to meet business requirements'* (Armstrong 1996). The notion that organisations can use reward in a strategic way has gained some ground in recent years.

An Industrial Society survey (1997) examined the reasons that organisations wanted to set up a formal reward strategy. In contrast with Heneman *et al* (2000), the motive for UK managers seems to have been related to the wish of senior managers to introduce individual performance pay, not team-based rewards.

It is therefore important that line managers 'buy in' to the new approach and that as far as possible employees share in the development of the scheme. While all pay systems have faults, the failure of particular pay systems or schemes can lie as much in how they are managed as in the basic design of a particular scheme. Line managers in many ways hold the key.

One of the hallmarks of the reward-strategy approach is that it starts from asking the question 'What makes sense for *this* organisation?', not 'What does everybody else do?'

Much of the evidence to date shows that it is extremely difficult fully to integrate reward into the overall human resources strategy, particularly in large and diverse organisations. Pay and reward practices are often the result of incremental as well as major changes plus a series of compromises made over a period of time and there well may be a time lag or 'drag' effect in aligning them with the human resources strategy, if we assume this is achievable in the first place.

Contents of written reward strategy

The Industrial Society's 1997 survey indicated that organisations with formal reward strategies have tended to concentrate on relatively few aspects of reward – notably linking levels of pay to performance and to external pay survey data. The survey found the following concepts or elements in use in formal reward strategies:

- statement of corporate values/mission
- objectives for reward policies/practices
- culture change
- reorganisation/business restructuring
- corporate policy in relation to pay levels in other organisations, external pay survey data and decentralisation/devolution of decision-making
- internal equity/fairness
- clear link between reward strategy and business plan
- pay related to individual performance
- pay related to corporate/business unit performance
- equal pay for work of equal value
- communication with employees on reward issues
- recruitment and retention

- reward in relation to skill or competency development
- employee involvement
- link between reward and working practices (eg teamwork)
- how the effectiveness of the reward strategy will be measured, monitored or evaluated.

Communicating the reward strategy

Many organisations give their employees too little information about the reward/pay/benefits that apply to them. A new pay system that makes a miraculous appearance as a conjuror produces a rabbit from a hat may not fulfil its potential. The general principle of openness and transparency of pay policies and practices is also a requirement under equal pay legislation (see page 161).

In addition to the purely legal rationale, Milkovich and Newman (1996) suggest that there are three main reasons employers should think seriously about being more open with employees about pay:

- Pay delivers a strong message. If time and expense have gone into designing a reward system, then employees must understand it if it is to influence their behaviour.
- Some studies have shown that employees misperceive pay relationships – for instance, they tend to overestimate the pay of lower-level jobs and underestimate the pay of those in higher-level jobs. If differentials are underestimated their motivational value is reduced.
- Employees whose organisations are open about pay tend to express greater satisfaction with their pay and the system used to determine it.

Employees' involvement – written out of the script?

Employees are not normally included in developing a reward strategy (CIPD 2003 and Industrial Society 1997). It appears that the development of a reward strategy is largely an HR initiative, with the active involvement of the chief executive and other directors. While there may be rhetoric about the importance of reward policies being managed and 'owned' by line managers, in practice they too (according to the Industrial Society's survey) are excluded from influencing the development of reward systems.

Influence of consultants

The Industrial Society's 1997 survey shows that external consultants are more likely to be involved in the setting up of a reward strategy than employees. Clearly there can be a need for additional expertise to be brought into the organisation when making major changes to reward. However, there are indications that the influence of consultants may not always be positive. Pfeffer (1998b) is vehement in his critique of the role of consultants. Identifying 'six dangerous myths about pay' (see Table 4, page 11), he claims that consultants keep the myths alive because they persuade top managers that 'tinkering' with the pay system is a quick and easier way of solving corporate problems than changing the company's culture. In addition, he says: 'changes in pay systems bring their own predicaments ... the consultants will continue to have work solving the problems that the tinkering has caused in the first place'.

Evaluating effectiveness

There is little evidence (Kessler 1995) of pay being a significant driver of strategic change in organisations, although as Gerhart (2000) discusses there is a potential for pay to be of benefit to the organisation at a strategic level. The CIPD's 2003 survey sought managers' perspective, asking if their reward strategies were effective. Nearly three-quarters (74%) of employer respondents contended that they have an effective reward strategy, with private-sector employers more positive (77%) than their public-sector counterparts (57%).

Concerned that such responses might represent no more than a 'gut feeling' about their reward strategies in practice, the CIPD survey asked about measuring effectiveness. Around three-quarters (76%) said they measure the effectiveness of their reward strategy, with the most common measures cited being exit interviews and external benchmarking. About two-thirds of employers (63%) also ask staff what they think about their reward strategy.

In other work the use of exit interviews has been shown to lack robustness (Taylor *et al* 2002). Taylor's research questions how strong the link is between pay and staff turnover. He shows that when asked for their reasons for leaving an organisation, people tend to overstate within the exit interview the importance of pay in their decision to leave – preferring the fiction they are leaving for more money over the more accurate reason that the decision is related to poor working relationships with managers.

In many organisations, evaluation processes are at an early stage – if they exist at all (see also page 32). The review methods revealed by the Industrial Society 1997 survey include periodic reviews solely by senior managers or by personnel staff; using attitude surveys or other research among employees/line managers; and analysis of internal financial and HR data. Consultation with employee representatives or the use of internal working groups are potentially valuable sources on the effectiveness of particular reward practices, but appear to be little used.

STUDENT REVIEW EXERCISE

Consider how the effectiveness of your organisation's reward strategy and/or of pay/benefits policies and practices can be monitored and evaluated. Identify the data sources that might be used.

EMPLOYMENT AND LABOUR MARKET CONTEXT

In the UK the structure of employment has undergone change as the economy becomes predominately based on service industries. Many traditional reward approaches have been developed at a time when manual workers were more numerous than they currently are, when mothers stayed home and workplaces were largely 'male', when collective bargaining was strong, when managers were poorly educated and trained and when there was more apparent stability in organisational forms. In the 1980s the restructuring of industry and rising unemployment levels marked a pronounced change, the ramifications of which are still being felt.

Myth	Reality
1. Pay rates or levels and labour costs are the same thing.	Productivity is the key difference. Labour costs are related to productivity – how much a company pays its employees in relation to how much they produce.
2. You can lower labour costs by cutting pay rates.	Reducing labour costs entails addressing both productivity and pay. In some circumstances lowering pay rates increases labour costs because lowering employee morale can lead to a reduction in productivity. Similarly, increasing pay can lead to higher productivity and hence to a reduction in unit labour costs.
3. Labour costs constitute a significant proportion of total organisational costs.	In some sectors – for example, the public sector and services – labour costs can be as much as 80% of total costs. However, this proportion varies widely by industry and company. Labour costs may not be the biggest item of corporate expenditure, but it may be perceived by managers as the most immediately malleable expense.
4. Low labour costs are a potent and sustainable source of competitive advantage.	Minimising labour costs is perhaps the least sustainable way to compete. Many leading organisations have found it more effective to achieve competitive advantage through quality or customer service improvements. If competitive advantage is achieved through this means – or through product, process, service innovation; or through technology – it is much more difficult for competitors to imitate than to merely cutting costs.
5. Individual incentive pay improves performance.	5. Individual incentive pay, in reality, undermines performance – of both the individual and the organisation. Many studies strongly suggest that this form of reward undermines teamwork, encourages a short-term focus, and leads people to believe that pay is not related to performance at all but to having the 'right' relationships and an ingratiating personality.
6. People work for money.	6. People do work for money – but they work even more for meaning in their lives. In fact, they work to have fun. Companies that ignore this fact are essentially bribing their employees and will pay the price in a lack of loyalty and commitment.

Adapted from Pfeffer (1998a)

Table 4   *Pfeffer's six dangerous myths about pay*

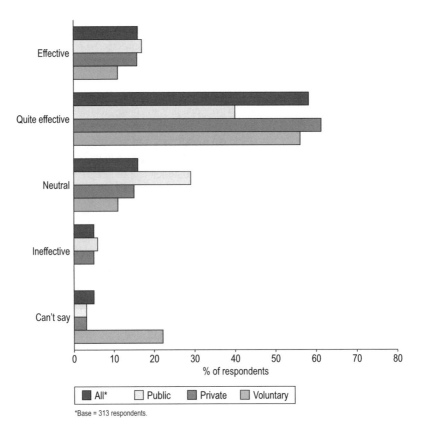

Figure 2 *Effectiveness of employer reward strategies by sector*

Changes in UK workforce

Demographic trends (DTI 2002) show that the UK has:

- an ageing workforce
- more women/working mothers
- fewer older people working until formal retirement age.

One of the most pronounced trends in the past two decades has been the growth in the part-timer workforce. Labour Force Survey data (DTI 2002) reveal the following:

- In the UK 7 million people work part-time (one in four of the workforce). About four-fifths of UK part-timers are women. In Europe as a whole (including the UK) the proportion of women working part-time is about the same in all age groups. Men, on the other hand, tend only to work part-time when they are young (students).
- The UK has the second highest proportion of part-timers in its national workforce in the European Union (EU). The Netherlands has the highest proportion.
- Increasing regulation protects the rights of part-time workers.

	Distribution of workplaces by sector (%)	Workplaces with no part-time employees (%)	Workplaces with most employees part-time (%)	Low-paying workplaces (%)	High productivity growth workplaces (%)
Manufacturing	18	36	1	5	34
Electricity, gas, water	0	51	0	0	55
Construction	4	39	0	1	49
Wholesale and retail	18	14	43	8	51
Hotels and restaurants	6	3	55	48	29
Transport and communications	5	23	4	0	60
Financial services	3	20	5	0	62
Other business services	9	23	7	10	34
Public administration	6	9	1	0	42
Education	14	0	40	2	42
Health	13	1	50	17	34
Other community services	4	8	51	19	23
All workplaces	100	16	26	9	41

Base: all workplaces with 25 or more employees, except column 5, where it is all workplaces five or more years old with 25 employees
Figures are weighted and based on responses form 1,929 managers for column 1, 1,914 for columns 2 and 3, 1,890 for column 4 and 1,668 for column 5.
Source: Cully et al (1998)

Table 5 *Employment, pay and productivity by sector*

- In the EU there are moves to promote the value of part-time work, mainly with a view to increase overall employment opportunities and to create jobs.

Across Europe in all age groups, more men than women are in paid employment, but the UK has one of the highest rates of employment of women in the EU. One of the main labour-market trends during the last three decades of the 20th century was the steep rise in the numbers of women working, with a particularly sharp increase in the proportion of mothers in the workforce. More than 70 per cent of UK women of working age were working in 2002, compared with just 57 per cent in 1971. Labour force survey data (DTI 2002) show that for both women and men the rates of economic activity are highest between the ages of 25 and 49.

If the UK has comparatively high rates of participation in employment, it also has comparatively poor productivity. Peter Nolan (2001) argues that the UK has a very poor productivity record compared with other countries largely because the UK's recent growth in employment has principally been in the service sector. Added value per employee tends to be higher in manufacturing industry than in the service sector, where there are also methodological problems in measuring productivity. Nolan highlights the fact that the fastest-growing occupations are hairdressers, software engineers and educational assistants and refers to this as an 'hourglass economy'. At the top of the hourglass are knowledge-based workers, with high added value – such as in the high-tech sector. At the bottom of the hourglass are routine service-sector jobs – such as hairdressing and cleaning – and these are typically in organisations that compete in the market on the basis of cost minimisation. Amongst other implications of this and related research is that a business case for measures to increase diversity and to introduce more balance between life and work may well be easier to make in the 'added-value' organisations than in 'cost minimisation areas'.

THEORETICAL PERSPECTIVES

The following summary of relevant theoretical perspectives for reward draws on the main subject disciplines that have fed into the subject of reward:

- economics
- sociology
- psychology
- industrial relations
- organisation and management.

That the subject is multidisciplinary is not in question. However, as Thorpe and Green (2002) argue, some writers believe there is a notable *'fragility of classical concepts'*, which suggests that the *'entire framework behind reward systems'* is highly questionable. Some theoretical perspectives have been used more readily by researchers to analyse reward practice than others.

Economic perspectives

Economic concepts and perspectives relevant to reward include those of classical theory, efficiency wage theory, human capital theory, principal-agent theory and transaction costs.

Classical theory

Classical theory in economics relates to the laws of supply and demand. In essence this assumes that employers pay enough to recruit and retain employees, but avoid paying too much since that adds unnecessarily to labour costs and may make a business uncompetitive in the market place.

Efficiency wage theory

Efficiency wage theory assumes that the paying of higher wages or salaries can be justified on the basis of the higher productivity it brings from the more diligent and better-skilled employees. Therefore high productivity in effect means unit labour costs are reduced, as there are fewer people engaged in the work.

Human capital theory

Concepts of human capital are significant to reward managers since the focus is switched from viewing pay and benefits as costs to be minimised to one in which the organisation is seen to invest in the employee. Hence, it is in the interests of both employee and employer to increase skill levels and to retain these in the business. In an analysis based on the 1998 Workplace Employee Relations Survey, Forth and Millward (2000) find some evidence that pay increases are larger when there is evidence of 'some form of up-skilling' of the workforce. However, the evidence is not clear-cut.

Principal-agent theory

Under agency theory the goals of employees (agents) are assumed to diverge from those of employers (principals). The theory assumes that employers want high levels of effort relative to pay from employees, while employees want the reverse. Managers may want employees to comply with their plans and instructions, and employees may want to exercise freedom of choice. There may also be considerable overlaps in the goals of principal and agent, but it is assumed that managers wish employees to put in more work effort than employees would find preferable.

The principal-agent theory applies in practice both to relationships between shareholders and senior managers as well as to that between managers and employees at all levels. It is assumed that inevitable conflicts of interest between principal and agent may arise.

Agency and efficiency wage theory are applied most frequently to incentive pay (especially for executives – see page 135). Agency theory also assumes that the principal is less well informed than the agent about the agent's actions. The employee knows how hard he or she has worked, but the employer can only make indirect inferences from performance evidence. A criticism of agency theory is that it tends to overemphasise efficiency and neglect the institutional context.

Transaction costs

Transaction costs may be defined as the costs of negotiating, monitoring and evaluating an exchange or of setting up and running a market-based operation. The concept can be used to analyse the costs of reward policies, which might emphasise market rates as against internal equity or policies that require a lot of administrative work to give a more individualised approach to reward. Organisations are assumed to use reward systems to retain skilled employees – arguably assuming that pay rates that are internal are generally lower than those in the market place.

The concept has potentially wide implications and uses in reward management, including in the case of an organisation individualising pay practices. The transaction costs in such circumstances include the time of HR/personnel managers (and also of employees) in negotiating what is to be included in the contracts and the extra time taken in monitoring their application in practice. As Brown *et al* (1999) point out, an acknowledgement of the extent of transaction costs might encourage employers to offer more open, longer-term employment contracts rather than individually tailored short-term contracts, since the time commitment for HR staff and managers would be reduced. When potentially high transaction costs are recognised this tends to lead to a degree of standardisation of terms and conditions (see also page 45).

STUDENT REVIEW EXERCISE

Consider a job or role that has a highly transferable set of skills and for which there is significant mobility for individuals between organisations – some examples might be secretarial or IT staff. Analyse how far economic theories explain what affects pay in practice in your organisation for such occupations. Decide if the law of supply and demand seems to work and what the constraints are on the operation of a 'perfect market'.

Industrial relations perspectives

Reward might once have been thought of as an integral part of industrial relations. However, in the UK the steep decline in the incidence of collective bargaining since the political era of prime minister Margaret Thatcher beginning in the early 1980s has changed the nature of reward. No longer are most pay rises set by bargaining (see Chapter 2, page 44), and there is evidence that not just union representatives but also employees as a whole are largely excluded from decisions affecting their pay. Irrespective of whether pay is set on a collective or individualised basis, some key theoretical concepts drawn from industrial relations continue to have relevance.

Labour process theory
Labour process theory draws on Marxist perspectives and sees 'labour' pitted against 'capital'. The assumption is that there are inevitable conflicts of interest between employee and employer. The ideas associated with this highly political perspective are criticised, inter alia, for a deterministic and mechanistic approach that leaves little scope for individuals or groups of employees to shape developments in the organisation. Some of the key work in the area is that of Braverman (1974), who argued that the scientific management approach of FW Taylor has a political dimension.

Unitarist and pluralist perspectives
Unitarism assumes that employees and employers have similar goals and can work together harmoniously to achieve an organisation's goals. *Pluralism* assumes that there are inevitable differences and potentially conflicting interests within an organisation, and acknowledges that there will be different interest groups.

The development of human resource management has been associated with more emphasis on unitarist perspectives, whereas traditionally much of industrial relations theory and practice has been founded on pluralist notions.

Wage-effort bargaining

Drawing on the work of Baldamus (1961), the wage-effort bargain is seen as the informal contract that employees have with an employer. The theory assumes that employers establish an administrative system to control employees.

Level of bargaining and decentralisation

The level of pay bargaining has become less centralised in the UK since around 1980. The decentralisation of pay and working-time determination has widely been seen as marking a shift to organisation-based arrangements, and away from multi-employer or national-level bargaining. The nature of the changes at organisational level was investigated by Arrowsmith and Sisson (1999). Their survey of more than 300 workplaces in four sectors – printing, engineering, retail and health – found that a strong sector effect is demonstrated whether or not there are national arrangements in place. Even when they are not required to keep in step with others in their sector – in terms of the type of pay settlement agreed – employers tend to move like 'ships in a convoy'. Particularly when making major changes to pay arrangements, employers in the same sectors tended to echo the practices of others, in part because they were seeking 'legitimacy in a context of growing uncertainty'. The product markets, use of technology and labour market contexts were also seen as significant for organisations in keeping with the rest of their sector's 'convoy'.

Organisation and management perspectives

Organisation and management perspectives include those of scientific management, human relations and 'new' forms of organisation.

Scientific management

FW Taylor's scientific management concepts were related to his belief in 'economic man', which assumes that people are primarily motivated by economic gain and that, therefore, the prospect of more pay is sufficient to bring about an increase in the desired behaviour. Scientific management is the basis for much traditional practice, not just in reward but more broadly in management practices. Indeed, the more modern creation of forms of working – such as that evident in call centres – has promoted suggestions that Taylorism lives on. The reward practice implicit in Taylorism is that of piecework – with employees carrying out a narrow range of prescribed tasks, being paid per task or 'piece' of work (see also page 136).

Human relations school

The human relations approach to management may be summarised as entailing the following. (See Huczynski and Buchanan 2001.)

- People are motivated by more than just pay and conditions.
- Work is a group activity, and individuals should be seen as group members and not in isolation.
- The need for recognition, security and a sense of belonging is more important in determining employee morale and productivity than the physical conditions under which they work.
- Through their development of 'unofficial' norms and sanctions, informal groups exercise strong controls over the work habits and attitudes of individual group members.

■ Supervisors need to be aware of both individuals' social needs and the power of the informal group, if they wish to align these to formal corporate objectives.

'New' forms of organisation

It can be argued that reward practices need to fit with organisational forms. A pay structure that suits a bureaucratic organisation may be substantially different from one that would suit a small entrepreneurial company. Changes in organisation structure have been wide-ranging in recent years (Sisson and Storey 2000). Storey identifies seven features of such developments:

■ decentralisation and divisionalisation of organisations

■ devolvement of managerial decision-making

■ de-layering of tiers of management

■ emphasis on lateral communication, reducing functional hierarchies

■ cross-'boundary' working, internally and externally

■ self-organising teamwork

■ customer responsiveness, with empowerment of front-line staff.

Sociological and cultural perspectives

Sociological and cultural perspectives include those of power and politics, institutional theory and organisational culture.

Power and politics

It would be very strange if reward policies and practices did not have a political dimension. As Huczynski and Buchanan (2001) point out, power and politics in organisations are inextricably linked: *'power concerns the capacity of individuals to exert their will over others, while political behaviour is the practical domain of power in action'*. Hatch (1997) summarises the main aspects of power and political behaviour in modern organisations (see Table 6). Being able to control resources such as money (budgets), technology and skills gives an individual or group an important source of power. Where a valued resource is scarce, greater power is possessed by those who control it. Wright and McMahan (1992) have argued that pay decisions are strongly influenced by organisational politics, departmental power and individual power.

STUDENT REVIEW EXERCISE

Power to the line!
Discuss which of the strategies listed in Table 6 opposite might be used by an HR manager asked by her chief executive to develop a plan to devolve more responsibility for pay decision-making on individuals to a rather reluctant set of line managers.

COMMON STRATEGIES FOR DEVELOPING AND USING POWER WITHIN ORGANISATIONS

Develop power by:
Creating dependence in others
■ work in areas of high uncertainty
■ cultivate centrality by working in critical areas
■ develop non-substitutable skills
Coping with uncertainty on behalf of others
■ prevention, forecasting, absorption
Developing personal networks
Developing and constantly augmenting your expertise
 	
Use power to:
Control information flows to others
Control agendas
■ issue definition
■ order of issues
■ issue exclusion
Control decision-making criteria
■ long- v. short-term considerations
■ return v. risk
■ choose criteria that favour your abilities and contributions
Co-optation and coalition-building
■ external alliances (eg, networks of reward specialists)
■ internal alliances
   ■ promote loyal subordinates
   ■ appoint commitees, working groups or project teams
   ■ gain representation on important committees
Bring in outside experts (eg, consultants) to bolster your position
 	
Adapted from Hatch (1997)

Table 6 *Power and politics in organisations*

Institutional perspective or theory

As developed by Wright and McMahan (1992), institutional theory suggests that organisations will adopt an innovation, even if it is inefficient for them to do so, in order to gain legitimacy or to conform to accepted standards of 'best practice'. For example, organisations may adopt practices used in other organisations to appear to be 'modern' or 'professional' – a tendency some might call following fads or fashion. Proponents of this theory distinguish between early or 'preinstitutional' adopters of the innovation, who introduce it because of its capacity to improve organisational performance, and later adopters, who change to meet what is seen as prevailing practice. The theory has been used to explain the growth of executive pay. Critics of the theory say that it fails to take into account the importance of an organisation's strategic goals.

Organisational culture

Company culture and management style may be significant in influencing organisational performance. They are also potentially significant in assessing the effectiveness of reward practices (Gerhart 2000). The growth of 'symbolic management', which identified the potential of managers tapping into organisational myths, rituals and customs to direct employee behaviour (Huczynski and Buchanan 2001), may have some relevance for reward – if we accept that pay has a strong symbolic aspect to it. Kessler and Purcell's work (1992) on performance-related pay (PRP) showed that employers who moved towards PRP (see also Chapter 5) wanted to change organisational culture – they saw the PRP initiative as an important part of that change. The debate over whether there are linkages between strong organisational culture and performance has spawned much prescriptive literature, but this is difficult to use specifically in analysing the part reward plays in corporate culture.

One practical attempt to provide an analytical model which might be useful in assessing the cultural climate for reward practice was that of ACAS (2001), contrasting a 'control' organisational culture with a 'quality of working life' (QWL) involvement culture (see Table 7).

'Control' culture	QWL involvement culture
Emphasis on rules, procedures; precedent	Emphasis on core values; mission statements
Emphasis on control and compliance; co-ordination and control via rules and procedures	Emphasis on commitment; co-ordination and commitment via shared goals, values and traditions
Power and decision-making centralised at the top (position authority)	Power and decision-making devolved throughout organisation
Top-down controls (authoritarian)	Mutual influence systems (participative)
A culture of inferiority; assumes people cause problems and therefore have to be controlled	A culture of pride; taps people's problem-solving skills; assumes people are the greatest asset
Individuality suppressed and systems dominate; assumes 'one best way'	Individuals are trusted and can question systems; seeks to develop 'appropriate way'
Human resource issues of secondary consideration in strategic business decisions	Human resource issues are a primary concern in strategic business decisions
A closed system, highly resistant to change; stressing stability	Open flexible system; stressing adaptability
Internal orientation, boundary problems, political conflict and demarcations	External orientation, market-led, close to the customer and the environment
Adapted from Advisory, Conciliation and Arbitration Service (2001)	

Table 7 *Characteristics of two distinct organisational cultures*

ACAS (2001) argues that reward approaches consistent with a QWL culture would include:

■ broader jobs, with wider responsibilities and skill requirements
■ teamworking and the need to reward group rather than individual performance
■ rewards for skills and knowledge acquired rather than specific job content
■ fewer grade levels.

ACAS also suggests that reward policies that support greater employee involvement include principles of harmonisation and single status. These are discussed in Chapter 3. They also advocate:

■ payments based on value added
■ profit-sharing
■ share ownership
■ skill-based pay.

Psychological perspectives

Concepts and theories drawn from psychology have become prominent in reward. Both needs-driven and cognitive process psychological theories have become prominent in managerial writing. This development seems to be related to beliefs held by managers that they can take measures capable of solving the motivational problems they perceive among their workforce.

Both *intrinsic* rewards (for example, self-fulfilment) and *extrinsic* rewards (such as pay, promotion) are important in any discussion of motivation.

Motivated behaviour is goal-directed behaviour. The assumption is that an individual will engage in behaviour that will lead to the attainment of goals and reward of individual values. For managers to plan reward schemes with motivational value they need information on what individuals in their organisations value and they need to deliver the reward.

Two-factor theory

Using Herzberg's (1968) 'two-factor theory' we can consider the extent to which pay and benefits can positively motivate employees. The theory was developed from an analysis of 'critical incident' narratives supplied by Pittsburgh engineers and accountants who had been asked to recall events that made them feel good or bad about their work. Herzberg's division of factors into those that might motivate people and those that are contextual or 'hygiene' factors has become well-known. Both pay and aspects such as status and security are in the 'hygiene' list in Table 8 overleaf – and are not motivators according to Herzberg. Recognition, though, is a motivator, if you accept his theory.

Herzberg argued that pay was not a motivator, and that motivation could only come from structuring jobs in such a way that the work itself provided achievement, responsibility and growth. Herzberg's theory has been criticised on the grounds of faulty data and because the work seems to imply that job satisfaction and motivation are synonymous.

Motivator factors (content)	Hygiene factors (context)
Achievement	Pay
Advancement	Company policy
Growth	Supervisory style
Recognition	Status
Responsibility	Security
Nature of work	Working conditions
Adapted from Herzberg (1968)	

Table 8 *Motivator and hygiene factors*

Expectancy theory and desirable rewards

Expectancy theory (Vroom 1964), a process theory of motivation, may have special relevance to pay. The theory puts forward the idea that an individual will be motivated to perform a task if the reward for so doing is valued by that individual, and he or she believes that the effort expended will result in the reward being obtained. Vroom suggested that the strength of an individual's motivation to perform well is expressed as the product of the *valence* or value of the anticipated outcome, the *expectancy* that effort will lead to good performance and the *instrumentality* of good performance leading to valued outcomes.

The following formula is used to summarise the theory. Note that the formula is a multiplication – so that if any of the elements is zero then the level of motivation will also be zero.

$F = V \times I \times E$
F is the Force of the individual's motivation
V is the Valence or value the individual perceives the outcome to have
I is Instrumentality – the extent to which performance is seen to be linked to valued rewards.
E is Expectancy – the extent to which individuals think that their effort will be rewarded.

Porter and Lawler's (1968) extension of Vroom's expectancy theory of motivation (as redrawn by Marsden *et al* (2002) – see Figure 3) provides a useful model for analysing the relationship between reward, motivation and performance. This model shows that managers should first strive to identify how much workers desire a particular reward. Thereafter, workers assess the extent to which they have to exert themselves in order to gain the 'desired' reward. Under this model, if the effort needed to gain the reward is perceived by individuals to be too great, they are unlikely to exert themselves – resulting in no change to performance. A similar situation may arise where organisations use team-based rewards in which 'free-riders' are able to maintain existing levels of performance while benefiting from reward provided to team members. The implication is that controls are needed to curb free-riding if team pay is to succeed (see also page 129). Whatever the nature of the reward system, for motivation to be sustained it needs to provide rewards that are desirable to the individual. In addition, employees need to consider the rewards to be equitably distributed, taking into account the level of their performance. The extent to which the rewards received meet or exceed this perceived equitable level will affect how satisfied employees are.

Expectancy theory has relevance to all aspects of reward but has been especially used in analysing performance pay (see Chapter 5).

Equity theory

Adams's (1963) equity theory is also a cognitive process motivation theory, and is based on people's perceptions about what fair treatment is. As such it is potentially critical in reward practice. One of the basic tenets of the theory is that individuals will act to keep their effort-reward relationship in line with the ratio they perceive in the work of other employees they choose to compare themselves with. Adams said that people react differently to 'over-reward' and 'under-reward'. Whereas people tend to put any apparent over-reward down to being lucky, perceived under-reward (even of fairly modest proportions) is on the other hand seen as demotivating.

Attribution theory

Attribution theory suggests that motivation in the present depends on how individuals have rationalised success or failure in the past. For example, an individual who attributes success to his or her own ability or effort will be motivated to try to repeat the success. However, as Guest (1992) highlights, individuals' perceptions are subject to error and distortion, and there is a role for managers 'to influence attributions through feedback, communications, appraisal and guidance'.

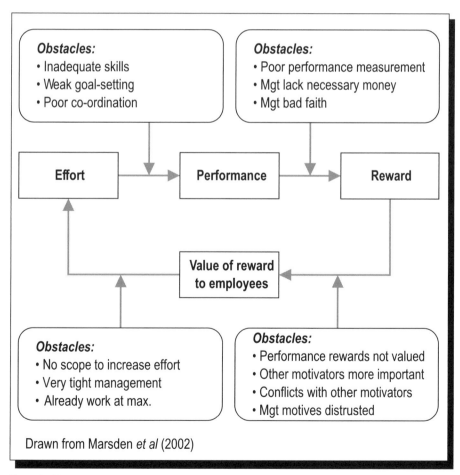

Drawn from Marsden et al (2002)

Figure 3   *Model of expectancy theory*

Goal theory and goal-setting

Locke (1968) argued that setting goals is a valuable motivational technique. His goal theory has four main propositions:

- goals should be clear and specific
- goals should provide a challenge
- goals should be agreed
- feedback or information on past performance should be provided.

Goal theory led to the development of the SMART performance management technique, in which managers and employees agree objectives that the employee will work towards for the coming year – and this will lead (potentially at least) to their variable end of year pay rise (see Chapter 5).

STUDENT REVIEW EXERCISE

Review the arguments on the objective of fairness and equity in reward and the imperative to focus on the business. To what extent can you see these two aims in conflict in your own organisation or an organisation you know well?

The psychological contract

The psychological contract is the term for the mutual expectations between employees and employer. The term began to be used during the 1960s; it has gained prominence because it offers a framework to help understand the impact of changes in the employment relationship, especially from the perspective of employees (Thompson and Heron 2001).

A body of research is building up in this field. Guest and Conway (1998) show that 'employers are cautious in making promises about rewards', which are broadly defined to include opportunities for promotion as well as current pay and benefits packages. Kessler and Undy (1996) show that in terms of the influence employees would like to have in the workplace compared with the level of influence they believe they actually exert, pay issues demonstrate the widest gap between achieved and desired influence.

Case study – International Manufacturing Company

International Manufacturing Co is a large manufacturing company, with international operations. It has a stable workforce and its tradition of strong unionisation and collective bargaining is important in influencing its current reward practices. It has begun experiencing problems in retaining the approximately 25 graduates it recruits to its UK operations each year. It experiences fewer problems recruiting the graduates than retaining them – and graduates from all disciplines are considered for work in all areas of the business. The company is clear about the requirements it has and the attributes it seeks in these graduate recruits. It is looking for top quality in terms of general intelligence, commercial acumen and interpersonal skills. The company stipulates that the graduates it recruits must have the essential attributes to be future senior managers.

An initial analysis within the company suggested there may be problems with recruitment, motivation and communication with the graduates. Reward practices may not be contributing as positively as is needed to retaining the graduates. The HR director is convinced that the difficulties her company has in recruiting and retaining graduates are related to deficiencies in reward practices.

The director looks at the costs and benefits of recruiting graduates in her company and also consults Association of Graduate Recruiters data. She finds that the typical cost of recruiting and developing a graduate over five years is more than £200,000. At the end of five years the benefit to the organisation of its investment begins to pay off. But company turnover data show that it is precisely at that time that graduates tend to leave the company. Therefore in cost-benefit terms the current reward and employment practices are quite simply not working well.

Her reading of various surveys and reports on graduates generally leads her to summarise the following points as relevant to her company's situation.

- Changes in the 'psychological contract' mean that graduates nationally are less loyal to their employers than in previous generations – various surveys indicating that fewer than one in 20 graduates intend to stay with their first employer for more than 18 months.
- The graduate market is markedly different from other recruitment markets as most students now graduate with an average debt of more than £12,000 from their student loan.
- The best graduates are looking to work with a glamorous company or to have a glamorous job.
- By seeking the best talent, most of the largest employers of graduates are trying, in effect, to recruit the same graduates, leading to significant competition. This has led to some high salaries being offered by other companies.
- Survey data of final-year undergraduates shows that students rated salary as the most important factor in choosing an employer and that this was the aspect of the various job offers they received that was most influential in their final decision.

The HR director looks at the salary policy for graduates. The critical pay progression pattern for them is over a five-year period. She summarises the main issues as follows.

- The salary policy for graduates integrates them into a general staff pay structure, but not with managers, for whom there is a separate structure.
- Pay rises are performance-related because the company wants to show that the company recognises and rewards performance and wishes also to reward competency development.
- Overall pay progression for graduates is slower than in competitor companies.
- Pay rises are on average higher for graduates than for other staff, but there is little evidence of a pay-back to the employer from the extra costs incurred.

- Both graduates and staff tend to complain about a lack of transparency in how pay rises are arrived at.
- Discussions with a group of graduate trainees revealed they did not believe their effort was being rewarded, nor did they feel their potential was recognised or valued.

STUDENT REVIEW EXERCISE

Imagine you are an HR officer in the above company asked by the HR director to conduct research in order to find out what the problems are, and to recommend solutions. She would like you to say how you might research this issue further and identify the nature of the psychological contract for graduates in this company both on recruitment and after five years.

You are asked to provide an initial analysis and a set of outline recommendations as to how you could rebalance the reward package to achieve better value for the company. Consider:

- what would be the best research approaches and methods
- which theories and concepts might be most appropriate as a framework for the analysis.

LONG-TERM PAY TRENDS

Since around 1980 pay trends have been characterised by a considerable widening-out of pay differentials – the top levels of pay have been increasing at a faster rate than lower rates of pay. Incomes Data Services (2003) shows that this trend, begun in 1980, has continued. Their data show that after 1990 pay rises for the top earners continued to outstrip those for the rest of the workforce to such an extent that the average wage has been pulled upwards, leaving more and more employees earning beneath it. Figure 4 shows the effect on below-average earners, the proportion of which has been rising – from 61.2 per cent of earners in 1990 to 64.6 per cent in 2002. The strongest rise has been in the years since 1997.

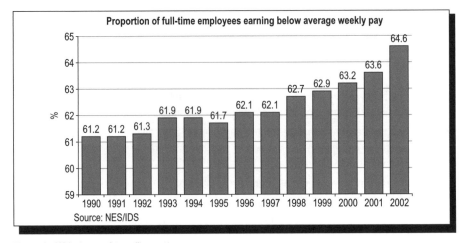

Figure 4 *Widening pay inequality*

At other end of the scale, top earnings have been rising at a much faster rate than for lower-level earners. PIRC (2003) report that between 1993 and 2002 the reported annual remuneration of the 'highest-paid director' in FTSE 100 companies rose by 92 per cent, while over the same period average earnings rose by 44 per cent and inflation increased by 25 per cent. The TUC has also highlighted what is seen as a widening gap at organisational level between top and lower levels of pay. Figure 5 shows the rise in the ratio of 'highest-paid director' pay to average earnings in the same companies rising from a median ratio of 11.5:1 in 1994 to 18:1 in 2001.

Incomes Data Services' analysis of New Earnings Survey data shows that since around 1990, in the economy as a whole, the top decile in the national earnings distribution (the level above which 10 per cent of employees earn) has risen by 53.7 per cent, while the lowest earnings decile has grown by just 45.6 per cent. Employees at the highest decile earned £752.40 a week in 2002, 3.49 times the income of those at the lowest decile, who earned £215.60 a week. It should be noted that New Earnings Survey data, while representing a 1 per cent sample of the UK workforce, probably understates very high earnings.

TOTAL REWARD CONCEPTS AND APPROACHES

Reward can be understood to go beyond basic pay and benefits. In recent years increasing attention has been paid to the concept of 'total reward'. This potentially widens out the definition of reward to include other aspects of the working environment or conditions that affect the quality of an individual's working life. Even if the definition is more limited than this, Sisson and Storey (2000) show how the traditional pay bargaining agenda has become one that increasingly integrates pay with working time.

The concept of total reward, previously associated with top executive reward, if used at all, is achieving a greater degree of currency. The notion is founded in strategic HR concepts, but

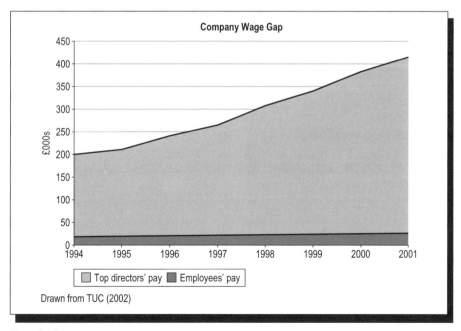

Figure 5   *Company wage gap*

as the CIPD (2002a) comments, it is a concept that is 'rarely implemented'. The value of it lies in acknowledging that pay is not set in isolation and reward practices work best when they fit closely in the overall context of work and other HR/management practices.

Total reward views pay and benefits as only one part of the reward picture, bringing in other aspects that affect the quality of an individual's working life – for example, learning and development opportunities, work environment/leadership styles in the organisation and employee involvement. The two following examples show how the concept has been put into practice.

Examples of total reward in practice

AstraZeneca is an example of a company seeking to operationalise total reward in its reward/HR practices (CIPD 2002b). The company has a three-pronged total reward strategy with the following elements.

1 Competitive and flexible reward

- broad-banded salary structure
- flexible benefits plan
- share schemes.

2 Excellent development opportunities

- active performance management
- coaching, challenging management style
- greater clarity about learning and progression opportunities
- mentoring
- e-learning
- on-the-job learning and further education.

3 Energised working environment

- effective leadership
- communications
- physical environment
- recognition by peers as well as managers
- work-life balance policies.

Nortel is another leading company to have tried to adopt a total reward strategy. Its approach has four elements (Walker 1999).

1 Total cash

- performance pay
- long-term incentives.

2 Benefits

- total compensation
- work-life balance policies.

3 Development

- leadership development
- career development
- performance management
- lateral and vertical opportunities
- 360-degree feedback.

4 Work environment

- challenging work
- respect
- collaboration
- innovation
- learning opportunities
- leadership
- teleworking
- diversity
- flexi-time
- risk-taking.

Problems in operation

'New pay' proponents Zingheim and Schuster (2000) argue that in the US both 'old and new style' companies are taking on board total reward strategies. However, the same authors comment that '*too often, when companies talk about "total reward" they simply mean providing generous benefits and a positive place to work*'.

They also warn that '*Guaranteeing jobs, supporting an attractive work-life balance, adding pay and incentives, encouraging personal development and making the workplace appealing all make poor business sense without an understanding of the need for high performance ... we feel most existing solutions ignore performance and encourage entitlement.*'

If such concepts encourage managers to view traditional reward in a more holistic way than hitherto, total reward notions may have a value even if they seem to encourage employees to focus more on their entitlements than on their contribution to corporate performance. Equally they present something of a challenge to the purely market-based ideas of reward in which individuals are seen as working for the market 'price' of their labour.

STUDENT DISCUSSION POINT

To what extent is reward in your organisation thought by managers or employees in broader terms than pay and benefits?
What implications would you anticipate if the total reward concept were to be adopted?

EXAMINING THE MAKE-UP OF THE 'PAY PACKAGE'

Notwithstanding total reward concepts, the practicalities of what is included in the conventional pay and benefits package has complexities of its own. Chapter 7 discusses some of the current issues and concerns in benefits provisions, while below are examined the principal cash elements in the package that most employee groups will receive. Executive remuneration packages are examined in Chapter 5.

There are few sources of data that permit an assessment of the breadth of the reward package for different groups of employees. One such source is the New Earnings Survey. However, the definitions used in the survey tend to reflect the influence of manual workers' pay. Nevertheless, as Table 9 shows, basic or base pay is the most significant element in the package.

Hours of work

According to the OECD, in most countries the decline in hours of work evident during the 1980s and 1990s has slowed in the first years of the 21st century. Decreases have occurred following negotiated reductions in full-timers' hours of work – for example, the agreement that cut the maximum working week in France to 35 hours. Legislation also had an effect in Europe, where the EU Working Time Directive prescribed a maximum 48-hour working week. In the UK the terms of the directive were implemented in the Working Time Regulations 1998. The UK is said to have a 'long hours' culture as it, uniquely in Europe (DTI 2002), still has a considerable number of employees, mostly men, who continue to work more than the 48-hour maximum working week prescribed under the Regulations.

Some sectors were excluded from the Working Time Regulations 1998 and individuals could voluntarily decide to opt out of the maximum limit, deciding to work longer hours. A review of the Working Time Directive implemented in August 2003 resulted in certain transport-sector employees who were previously excluded now being covered.

In addition to the 48-hour limit, the Regulations also make provision for rest breaks in the working day, as follows (page 31):

| % of earnings from: | Men | | Women | | Men & Women | | |
	Manual	Non-manual	Manual	Non-manual	Manual	Non-manual	ALL
Basic pay & allowances including performance pay consolidated into base pay, but excluding the following:	81.9	92.4	89.4	95.3	83.0	93.5	91.1
Overtime pay	11.8	2.3	5.5	1.5	11.0	2.0	4.0
Payment by results	3.3	4.6	2.4	2.4	3.1	3.8	3.7
Shift pay	3.0	0.7	2.7	0.8	2.9	0.7	1.2
Source: New Earnings Survey, 2002 nationalstatistics.gov.uk							

Table 9   *Make-up of pay – UK workforce 2002*

- a minimum of 11 consecutive hours' rest each working day and a minimum of 35 hours' uninterrupted rest each week
- a maximum of eight hours' work at night
- in-work rest breaks of 20 minutes when working time is more than six hours.

Overtime and overtime pay

As Table 9 shows, paid overtime is most prevalent among male manual workers, for whom it represents about 12 per cent of average weekly gross earnings. Unpaid overtime is most common for managers and professionals. While the incidence of paid overtime has fallen in recent years, the phenomenon of increases in unpaid overtime among non-manual men in particular is also being challenged.

Payment by results

Bonus and profit-sharing payments (Chapter 5), however calculated, are included in the New Earnings Survey definition of payment by results (see Table 9). It should be noted that performance pay that is consolidated into wages or salaries – and is not a payment additional to salary – is included in the definition of basic pay. As can be seen from Table 9, bonus payments for most employees are of fairly modest proportions – averaging around 4 per cent of earnings. The proportion of earnings accounted for by bonuses is much higher for executives (see page 137) – but this is difficult to see in the overall workforce averages given in the New Earnings Survey.

Shift premiums

Premium payments for working unsocial hours are also typically paid as additions to basic pay. As with overtime pay, the amount of pay for working unsocial hours has fallen in recent years, as employers have sought to buy out additional premiums and allowances, in the context of a more flexible labour market. Just 3 per cent of earnings are now accounted for by shift premiums – and this is a pay element almost wholly restricted to manual workers.

Gender implications

New Earnings Survey data (see Table 9) indicate that certain additions to basic pay – for example, payment by results or bonus payments and overtime pay – are more likely to be earned by men than women. In any organisation if there is a systematically different distribution of, say, bonuses between male- and female-dominated occupations, then equal pay cases can arise (see also Chapter 6).

TAKING THE LONG VIEW – ASSESSING REWARD SYSTEM SUCCESS OR FAILURE

Purcell comments on the generally poor durability of pay systems (*People Management*, 2001) that '*no pay system can be effective for more than five years*'. ACAS (1990) and Incomes Data Services (1998) research suggests that the most durable pay systems may be the simplest, most easily understood ones. Lincoln Electric, a widely quoted and lauded US company, has at the heart of its long-standing approach to pay a piecework bonus scheme. However, there is more to the reasons for Lincoln Electric's success than mere reliance on a Taylorist bonus scheme (Pfeffer 1999). Incomes Data Services (1998) summarises the critical aspects of Lincoln Electric's approach to pay as follows.

- The piecework scheme is tightly controlled, with no payment for downtime, but it is also aimed at encouraging people to improve working practices.

■ An additional profit-sharing scheme is focused on individual as well as company performance with six-monthly merit ratings, which are biased towards quality and employee commitment.

■ Trust and commitment underscore the company's employee relations climate – the management style is characterised as 'paternalism combined with participation'.

■ Employment is secure and there is a strong emphasis on the value of seniority and experience of employees.

■ Top management salaries are low in comparison with other companies'.

Incomes Data Services (1998) paint a picture of continuous review and modification by leading companies, but make the point that some forward-looking long-term pay approaches such as profit-sharing have greater longevity than 'more fashionable' approaches, like competency-based pay.

There is a need for more research in this area, and as yet there is little evidence of a more reflective approach by organisations. Corby et al (2002) search for evidence of evaluation frameworks that could assist in answering the key question – does the pay system work? They find little in the literature or reward consultancy approaches save those devoted to evaluating performance pay schemes (Chapter 5, page 142). Although the organisations Corby and colleagues studied routinely collected a considerable amount of HR data, they used only some of the data to measure the impact of their pay system against the stated aims. The exceptions to this general picture were HM Customs & Excise and Royal Mail. At HM Customs & Excise a new pay arrangement was treated as if it was being operated on a trial basis, and the organisation used 'control groups' to evaluate staff attitudes and financial performance.

Pay satisfaction studies

There is a body of research developing in the area of pay satisfaction, drawing on both equity theory and expectancy theory (see page 117). Clearly, such studies can be a useful element within a broader evaluation of any particular reward system. Heneman and Judge (2000) discuss the progress in developing some standardisation of pay satisfaction research. However, methodological problems remain – for example, it is difficult at present to carry out robust research comparing employees' attitudes to various types of pay systems because such research invariably asks employees to hypothesise how they would react to certain systems, some of which they have not experienced in practice.

Kessler and Heron (2002) illustrate how the clarity of the link between effort and reward and an understanding of the criteria determining pay influence pay satisfaction (see Figure 6, page 34).

Case study – People's Insurance and Bank UK

People's Insurance and Bank UK was until about a year ago an independent, wholly UK-based insurance business with some other financial products and services aimed at its target market – principally people living in the North of England. In 1999 a multinational German bank, Volksbank, took over the smaller People's Insurance and Bank UK, which had been experiencing problems in maintaining its market share.

People's Insurance and Bank UK has about 2,000 employees and is now a small subsidiary in the much larger Volksbank group, which has interests in each main EU country and wishes to expand its services both in the countries in which it currently operates and within Eastern European countries. One of Volksbank's reasons for seeking to acquire People's Insurance and Bank UK was to consolidate Volksbank's market position in the UK, as the financial services sector in the UK was notably stronger than in other EU countries. Volksbank's main board felt an acquisition of People's Insurance and Bank UK would be of value to them for the following reasons.

- It would stall the attempts of arch-rival DeutschVolk Bank to gain an extensive foothold in the UK market; DeutschVolk Bank had, according to reports in the *Financial Times*, a strong wish to buy People's Insurance and Bank UK.

- People's Insurance and Bank UK had a good reputation among its customers for honest dealings and practical services for working people with steady but modest incomes.

- The firm had potential as a base from which to 'grow' and market new services to mainland Europe, particularly since it was much cheaper to employ staff in the UK than in Germany or France.

People's Insurance and Bank UK's reputation for straightforward and honest dealing had been made in the wake of the pensions mis-selling scandals that had led to a substantial tightening of the law on pensions marketing. People's Insurance and Bank UK had been the first pensions provider to announce that it was no longer going to be using a 'commission-based' pay system for its staff selling pensions – it was instead going to be paying straight salary, with 'no strings'. The employer bought out the commission scheme, which had previously yielded an average of 20 per cent of base salary to the pensions sales staff, on generous terms. The result is that even the most conservative estimate based on pay survey data puts these sales staff about 30 per cent ahead of the median salary market position for similar jobs.

Other staff within People's Insurance and Bank UK are paid:

- close to the lower quartile level of staff in other finance-sector companies
- within a grading structure with salary scales that are still partially based on service-related increments, up to a performance 'bar', after which progression through the higher portion of the scale is performance-based.

Jobs are assigned to one of eight grades created 15 years before, using a process of 'slotting-in'.

Almost all staff are eligible for inclusion in a profit-sharing scheme that has yielded high payments in recent years. The benefits package, which covers all staff, is generous, particularly in respect of subsidised loans, free high-quality medical insurance and a very good pension scheme.

A new HR manager has been appointed from within the Volksbank group to the newly expanded HR team at People's Insurance and Bank UK, with a brief to handle the reward planning that needs to take place following the merger. She has been asked to consider, in particular, some innovative ways in which the firm's reward systems can be focused more to meet business expansion plans. These expansion plans entail, initially, a new initiative to market new pension products to small and medium-sized companies; but also to seek more organic ways of expanding the business.

The HR manager has also been given the following instructions by the financial director, herself also newly appointed from within the Volksbank group:

■ She must contain salary costs – any revised reward system must not be more costly to run than the status quo, although a transition budget worth 2 per cent of the salary bill can be used for a maximum of two years.

■ She will have to justify any recommended pay or benefits provision that is markedly above the 'norm' for the (financial) 'industry'.

The HR director, who has been with People's Insurance and Bank UK for 10 years, has briefly described to you that the culture of the firm is that of a 'family operation' and that teamworking is good, staff turnover exceptionally low and absence rates also on the low side. He has considered introducing a competency scheme to support employee development but has yet to get his plans off the ground.

There is a basic performance appraisal scheme, which is used by managers to assess development needs and to provide the performance 'marks' that govern salary progression above the performance bars in the salary scales.

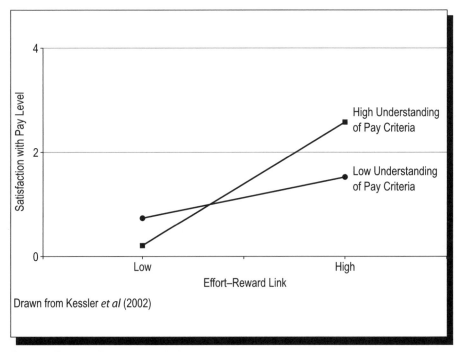

Drawn from Kessler et al (2002)

Figure 6 *Employee effort and pay satisfaction*

STUDENT REVIEW TASK

Consider some optional ways in which you could redesign the company's reward system to encourage innovation, within the given constraints and with the facts that you have on the firm, making any other reasonable assumptions in arriving at your recommendations.

You should identify the options and the business issues. Some of the factors you need to consider are:

- cost constraints
- expansion
- a framework that will encourage innovation
- post-merger problems
- maintaining the firm's 'credibility' within the sector
- maintaining customer confidence and focus.

Consider how reward research can help to understand the underlying issues.

Is a change in pay system really necessary?

Consider the strategic issues. Consider the aftermath of the sales commission scheme. (See Chapter 5.)

Consider how the company can develop its reward structures in the post-merger situation. (See Chapter 4.)

Since there is a structureless position at present, is a job evaluation scheme needed? (See Chapter 2.)

QUESTIONS FOR DISCUSSION

1   Much emphasis has been placed on motivation theories in the context of reward. How far does an understanding of motivation help in planning reward practices?

2   How should pay systems be evaluated?

3   Dilbert (Adams 1997) offers his definition of *virtual hourly compensation'* as including – in addition to the usual pay and benefits – items such as 'inflated travel reimbursement claims', 'stolen office supplies', 'personal phone calls', 'illegitimate sick days' and 'office sex'. Do you agree that broadening out what we mean by reward – as in the total reward concept – can help organisations to manage reward practices more effectively?

REFERENCES

Adams, S (1963) Toward an understanding of inequity. *Journal of Abnormal and Social Psychology.* Vol 67, no 4, pp422–436.

Adams, Scott (1997) *The Dilbert principle.* Boxtree, 1997.

Advisory, Conciliation and Arbitration Service (1990) *Developments in payment systems: the 1988 ACAS survey.* Occasional Paper No 45, ACAS.

Advisory, Conciliation and Arbitration Service (1997) *Motivating and rewarding employees.* ACAS.

Advisory, Conciliation and Arbitration Service (2001) *Effective organisations: the people factor.* ACAS.

Armstrong, M (1996) *Employee reward.* IPD.

Arrowsmith, J and Sisson, K (1999) Pay and working time: towards organization-based systems? *British Journal of Industrial Relations.* Vol 37, no 1, pp51–75.

Baldamus, W (1961) *Efficiency and effort: an analysis of industrial administration.* Tavistock.

Bevan, S, Barber, L and Robinson, D *Keeping the best: a practical guide to retaining key employees.* Institute for Employment Studies Report 337.

Bowey, A (1982) *Effects of incentive payment systems: United Kingdom 1977–80.* Department of Employment Research Paper 36.

Braverman, H (1974) *Labor and monopoly capital: the degradation of work in the twentieth century.* Monthly Review Press.

Brown, W, Deakin, S, Hudson, M, Pratten, C and Ryan, P (1999) *The individualisation of employment contracts in Britain.* Research paper for the Department of Trade and Industry, Centre for Business Research, Department of Applied Economics, University of Cambridge.

Capelli, P (1995) Rethinking employment. *British Journal of Industrial Relations.* Vol 33, no 4, pp563–602.

Capelli, P, Bassie, L, Katz, H, Knoke, D, Osterman, P and Useem, M. (1997) *Change at work.* Oxford University Press.

Chartered Institute of Personnel and Development (2002a) *Total reward.* Quick Fact Sheet. December. CIPD.

Chartered Institute of Personnel and Development (2002b) *Total reward.* Executive Briefing. CIPD.

Chartered Institute of Personnel and Development (2003) *Reward Management Survey: survey report.* January. CIPD.

Corby, S, White, G, Dennison, P, Douglas, F, Druker, J and Meerabeau, E (2002) *Does it work? Evaluating a new pay system.* University of Greenwich Working Paper, available at www.gre.ac.uk/schools/business/publishing

Cox, A (2000) The importance of employee participation in determining pay system effectiveness. *International Journal of Management Reviews.* Vol 2, no 4, pp357–375.

Cully, M, O'Reilly, A and Millward, N (1998) *The 1998 Workplace Employee Relations Survey: first findings.* Department of Trade and Industry.

DTI (2002) *Full and fulfilling employment.* Departmental White Paper, available at www.dti.gov.uk

Forth, J and Millward, N (2000) *The determinants of pay levels and fringe benefit provision in Britain.* Discussion Paper 171. National Institute of Economic and Social Research.

Gerhart, B (2000*)* Compensation strategy and organizational performance. In Rynes, S and

Gerhart, B (eds) *Compensation in organizations: current research and practice.* Jossey-Bass.

Gomez-Mejia, L and Balkin, D (1992) *Compensation, organizational strategy and firm performance.* Southwestern Publishing.

Guest, D (1992) *Motivation for results – incentives now.* Personnel Management publications.

Guest, D (1997) Human resource management and performance: a review and research agenda. *International Journal of Human Resource Management.* Vol 8, no 3, pp263–276.

Guest, D (1999) Human resource management – the workers' verdict. *Human Resource Management Journal.* Vol 9, no3, pp5–25.

Guest, D and Conway, N (1998) *Fairness at work and the psychological contract: the fourth annual IPD survey of the state of the employment relationship.* Institute of Personnel and Development.

Hatch, MJ (1997) *Organisation theory: modern, symbolic and postmodern perspectives.* Oxford University Press.

Heneman, H and Judge, T (2000) Compensation attitudes. In Rynes, S and Gerhart, B (eds) *Compensation in organizations: current research and practice.* Jossey-Bass.

Heneman, R, Ledford, G and Gresham, M (2000) The changing nature of work and its effects on compensation design and delivery. In Rynes, S and Gerhart, B (eds) *Compensation in organizations: current research and practice.* Jossey-Bass.

Herzberg, F (1968) One more time: how do you motivate employees? *Harvard Business Review.* Jan–Feb, pp53–62.

Huczynski, A and Buchanan, D (2001) *Organizational behaviour: an introductory text.* FT/Prentice Hall, 4th edition.

Huselid, M (1995a) The impact of human resource management: an agenda for the 1990s. *International Journal of Human Resource Management.* Vol 1, pp17–43.

Huselid, M (1995b) The impact of human resource management practices on turnover, productivity and corporate financial performance. *Academy of Management Journal.* Vol 38, no 3, pp635–672.

Incomes Data Services (1998) Pay: the test of time. *IDS Focus* 85.

Incomes Data Services (2003) Rising trend in inequality revealed as more earn below the average. *IDS Report* 874. February.

Industrial Society (1997) *Reward strategy.* Managing Best Practice 31. January.

Kessler, I (1995) Reward systems. In J Storey (ed) *Human resource management: a critical text.* Open University Press.

Kessler, I (2001) Remuneration systems. In Bach, S and Sisson, K (eds) *Personnel management: a comprehensive guide to theory and practice.* Blackwell Business, 3rd edition.

Kessler, I and Purcell, J (1992) Performance-related pay: objectives and application. *Human Resource Management Journal.* Vol 2, no 3, pp16–23.

Kessler, I and Undy, R (1996) The new employment relationship: examining the psychological contract. *Issues in People Management* 12, IPD.

Kessler, I, Gagnon, S and Heron, P (2002) The fragmentation of pay determination in the Civil

Service: the employee perspective. Paper presented at the Performance and Reward Conference, Manchester Metropolitan University, 9 April.

Lawler, E (1990) *Strategic pay: aligning organizational strategies and pay systems*. Jossey-Bass.

Lawler, E (1995) The new pay: a strategic approach. *Compensation and Benefits Review*. July–August, pp14–22.

Lazear, E (1995) *Personnel Economics*. MIT Press.

Ledford, G (1995) Designing nimble reward systems. *Compensation and Benefits Review*. July–August, pp46–54.

Legge, K (1989) Human resource management: a critical analysis. In Storey, J (ed) *Perspectives in human resource management*. Routledge.

Lewis, P (2000) Exploring Lawler's new pay theory through the case of Finbank's reward strategy. *Personnel Review*. Vol 29, no 1, pp10–28.

Locke, E (1968) Towards a theory of task performance and incentives. *Organizational Behaviour and Human Performance*. Vol 3, no 2, pp157–189.

Lupton, T and Gowler, D (1969) *Selecting a wage payment system.* Engineering Employers Federation.

MacDuffie, J (1995) Human resource bundles and manufacturing performance: organisational logic and flexible production systems in the world auto industry. *Industrial and Labor Relations Review*. Vol 48, no 2, pp197–221.

Marchington, M and Grugulis, I (2000) 'Best practice' human resource management: perfect opportunity or dangerous illusion? *International Journal of Human Resource Management*. Vol 11, no 6, pp1104–1124.

Marsden, D, French, S and Kubo, K (2002) Why does performance pay demotivate? Financial incentive versus performance appraisal, in Global integration and challenges for industrial relations and human resource management in the 21st century. *Selected papers from the 12th IIRA World Congress, Tokyo 2000*. JIL Report, No 9.

Milkovich, G and Newman, J (1996) *Compensation.* Irwin, 5th edition.

Mintzberg, H (1987) Crafting strategy. *Harvard Business Review*. Vol 65, no 4, pp65–75.

Moss Kanter, R (1987) The attack on pay. *Harvard Business Review*. March–April, pp60–67.

Nolan, P (2001) Shaping things to come. *People Management*. 27 December, pp30–31.

Pension Investment Research Consultants Ltd (2003) Directors' remuneration. PIRC evidence to the Trade and Industry Select Committee, June.

People Management (2001). Pay per view. *People Management*. 3 February, p40.

Pfeffer, J (1998a) Six dangerous myths about pay. *Harvard Business Review*. May–June, pp109–119.

Pfeffer, J (1998b) *The human equation: building profits by putting people first*. Harvard Business School Press.

Pfeffer, J (1999) Putting people first for organisational success. *The Academy of Management Executive*. Vol 13, no 2, pp37–48.

Poole, M and Jenkins, G (1998) Human Resource Management and the Theory of Rewards: Evidence from a national survey. *British Journal of Industrial Relations*. Vol 36, no 2, pp227–247, June.

Porter, L and Lawler, E (1968) *Managerial Attitudes and Performance.* Irwin.

Purcell, J (1999) Best practice and best fit: chimera or cul-de-sac? *Human Resource Management Journal.* Vol 9, no 3, pp26–41.

Purcell, J, Kinnie, N and Hutchinson, S (2003) Inside the black box 1: open minded. *People Management.* 15 May, pp30–33.

Richardson, R and Thompson, M (1999) *The impact of people management practices on business performance: a literature review.* Institute of Personnel and Development.

Schuler, R and Jackson, S (1987) Linking competitive strategies with human resource management practices. *Academy of Management Executive* 3.

Schuster, J and Zingheim, P (1992) *The new pay: linking employee and organisational performance.* Lexington.

Sisson, K and Storey, J (2000) *The realities of human resource management.* Open University Press.

Taylor, F (1911) *Principles of scientific management.* Harper.

Taylor, S, Redpath, C, Sweeney, C and Veitch, M (2002) Pay and employee retention: evidence from a qualitative survey. Paper presented at the Performance and Reward Conference, Manchester Metropolitan University, 9 April.

Thompson, M and Heron, P (2001) *Innovation and the psychological contract in the knowledge business.* Templeton Oxford Executive briefing paper.

Thorpe, R and Green, J (2002) Performance management in English schools: methodological concerns regarding the impact of performance-related pay. Paper presented at the Performance and Reward Conference, Manchester Metropolitan University, 9 April.

Trades Union Congress (2002) *Executive stress.* TUC.

Vroom, V (1964) *Work and motivation.* Wiley.

Walker, R (1999) *Motivating and rewarding managers.* Economist Intelligence Unit.

Wood, S (1996) High-commitment management and pay systems. *Journal of Management Studies.* Vol 33, no 1, January, pp53–77.

Work Foundation (2003) The psychological contract. *Managing Best Practice* 102.

Wright, P and McMahan, G (1992) Theoretical perspectives for strategic human resource management. *Journal of Management.* Vol 18, no 2, pp295–320.

Zingheim, P and Schuster, J (2000) Total rewards for new and old economy companies. *Compensation and Benefits Review.* Vol 32, no 6, November–December, pp20–23.

Useful website
e-reward.co.uk – Provides useful summaries of research and current issues in reward.

Pay determination

INTRODUCTION

Until the 1980s most of the textbooks that covered pay determination referred almost exclusively to the institutions associated with collective bargaining or to various forms of government or statutory controls on income. Quite separately other books aimed at personnel practitioners covered the topic of 'salary administration' (often focused almost exclusively on the pay and benefits of managers).

This chapter assesses this debate, addressing the various components of pay determination. It supports the following CIPD professional standards.

Operational indicators – Practitioners must be able to:

- contribute to local or national pay and benefit surveys
- advise senior management on whether to introduce job evaluation
- take part in the design and implementation of an appropriate scheme.

Knowledge indicators – Practitioners must understand and be able to explain:

- the factors affecting reward philosophies, strategies, policies, practices and levels of pay in organisations in the public, private and voluntary sectors, including pay determination through collective bargaining
- the concept of a market rate in local and national labour markets
- the objectives and limitations of job evaluation processes
- the significance of relevant legislation, including the national minimum wage.

DEVELOPMENT OF PAY DETERMINATION

Problems with government policies on income restraint in the 1960s and 1970s led to the 'return to free collective bargaining', which was supported by the Conservative governments of the 1980s and early 1990s. They turned to monetarist economic policies, entailing high levels of unemployment, combined with legislation reducing the power of trade unions, to more indirectly control pay growth. Pay determination continues to be influenced by national-level politics, but this may perhaps be seen as a rather more subtle process in the 21st century than hitherto.

EXTENT OF REGULATION

Until recent years reward was a lightly regulated area, with the notable exception of pensions and some other benefits. The development of European law and the implementation of

Long-term factors
Regulation – including laws on national minimum wage, equal pay, pensions and other benefits, contract law, corporate governance – eg Stock Exchange listing rules

Collective bargaining or individualised pay-setting institutions or processes

Use of job evaluation

Organisation's strategic reward orientation – for example, policies in relation to 'pay market' or regarding individual performance and pay

History and tradition in the sector/organisation

Short-term factors
Inflation and other general economic factors

Company performance/profit

Labour market trends – supply and demand for skills

Pay survey trends or comparability

Table 10   *Factors shaping pay determination at organisational level*

| | % of respondents by sector | | | |
	All*	Public	Private	Voluntary
Support business goals	83	71	85	80
Reward high performance	76	66	79	60
Recruit and retain high performers	71	49	75	55
Achieve/ maintain market competitiveness	60	34	64	55
Manage pay costs	55	63	54	65
Link pay to the market	50	23	53	55
Ensure internal equity	35	60	30	60
Source: CIPD (2003) Responses are a percentage of the total sample listing as an important goal – multiple responses provided. *Base = 323 respondents.				

Table 11   *Reported 'important' reward strategy goals*

minimum-standards employment law has extended the range of legislation affecting pay. The relevant law is broadly grouped into the following:

- national minimum wage (NMW) – see below
- equal pay – see Chapter 6
- hours of work and working time – see Chapter 1
- pensions and other benefits law and regulation – see Chapter 7.

National minimum wage

A national minimum wage was introduced in the UK for the first time in April 1999, setting a national minimum hourly rate of pay for adults and separate rates for young workers and trainees. The minimum rates are regarded as safety-net levels and there is no variation according to region, industrial sector or an individual's hours or pattern of work. The legal force for the national minimum wage is in the National Minimum Wage Act 1998.

Before its introduction the potential economic effects of a national minimum wage were widely debated, with some clear political differences (see, for example, Institute of Personnel Management 1991). Evidence based on econometric modelling and drawing on the experience of other countries with a national minimum wage attempted to estimate the scale of consequent potential job loss. The measure was a political pledge of the Labour Party, swiftly acted upon in government after Labour's success in the 1997 election. Once the fears of a devastation of employment opportunities proved unfounded, the Conservative Party dropped its opposition to the national minimum wage.

The Low Pay Commission was set up by the Government to make recommendations on the national minimum wage. The Commission considered a range of factors in making a recommendation, in line with its terms of reference.

The rates were set low and this factor partly accounts for the ease in the implementation of the national minimum wage.

Looking internationally, Metcalf (1999) shows that national minimum pay rates vary from country to country – between 30 per cent and just under 60 per cent of full-time median earnings. The initial rate of £3.60 decided on by the UK Government was worth about 44 per cent of median full-time earnings – so placing the UK in the middle of the international range, higher than the United States but lower than France. It also compared well with a notional rate based on uprating (now defunct) Wage Councils rates.

The NMW has been raised each year since its introduction, and from 1 October 2003 the adult rate was increased to £4.50 per hour, and the development rate and youth rate to £3.80 an hour. From October 2004 the youth rate is extended to cover 16- and 17-year-olds.

The impact of the NMW

In 2001 Incomes Data Services reported that low-paying companies (for example, in low-paid sectors such as clothing and textiles) and public-sector employers had increased their lowest rates to be more competitive than the minimum wage level, creating a 'lower mezzanine' or 'shadow floor', just above the level of the NMW . Some service-sector companies that employ large numbers of young staff decided to re-introduce age-related pay differentials, in response to the implementation of the NMW.

The Low Pay Commission (2001) concluded that the earlier fears that employers would adapt to the increased staff costs presented by the NMW by reducing the number of jobs were unfounded. Indeed, employment has expanded, even in traditionally low-paying sectors like retail and hospitality that were most affected by the NMW.

Dickens and Machin (1998) showed that while overall just under 8 per cent of the workforce was directly affected by the introduction of the NMW, it was beneficial for 11 per cent of women employees and 18 per cent of part-timers (the vast majority being women). The gender pay gap (see page 151) was marginally changed overall by the NMW. Between April 1999 and April 2000, the New Earnings Survey showed women's average part-time earnings increasing at a higher rate (8 per cent) than for full-time employees generally.

Regional differences in pay rates were also influenced by the introduction of the NMW. The *New Earnings Survey* 1999 showed that the biggest increases in median earnings over the previous year were in low-wage regions such as Wales and the North East of England.

There were particular concerns about young workers' employment opportunities being reduced as a result of the introduction of the NMW. Therefore a lower youth rate was set. Those aged 16 or 17 were originally excluded altogether but are covered from October 2004. Also excluded are voluntary workers who work for no pay other than expenses for charities or voluntary organisations, people on work experience programmes, armed forces personnel, prisoners, family members who help out on an informal basis and the genuinely self-employed.

Effect of the NMW on internal pay differentials

One of the key factors affecting the extent of any employment effects or job losses was the issue as to whether employers who raised their basic rates to the national minimum would restore internal pay differentials by applying similar percentage rises to other pay rates. The Bank of England and others were concerned this could fuel a wage–price spiral. There was little evidence of this applying in practice. As Metcalf (1999) comments, '*The low level of private sector unionisation (only around one-employee-in-five is a union member) coupled with decentralisation of collective bargaining, suggests that any reasonable NMW would be unlikely to have serious consequences for pay differentials and so would probably not fuel wage inflation.*'

NMW – some practical issues

Employers are obliged to keep records (to which the employee has access) and must provide the employee with a national minimum wage statement. Compliance is policed by the Inland Revenue, but the Low Pay Commission says that employers are effectively 'self-enforcing' the minimum rates.

The Low Pay Commission's 2003 report shows that the majority of beneficiaries of the national minimum wage are part-time women, especially within the hospitality, hairdressing, retail and social care sectors. Incentive payments and centrally collected tips may be included in the calculation of the minimum wage.

STUDENT REVIEW EXERCISE

■ Identify the reasons why the Low Pay Commission might have confidence in its view that the NMW has been successfully 'self-enforced'.

■ How might the self-enforcement view alter if you consider the situation of (a) a small hotel in the West Country, employing mainly seasonal staff with an average 30 per cent of earnings coming from tips; and (b) a car manufacturer based in the West Midlands, with historically strong collective bargaining?

■ Consider whether other law affecting pay – such as equal pay (see Chapter 6) – could also effectively be 'self-enforced'.

How far does collective bargaining still determine pay?

According to the CIPD (2003), negotiation between employers and trade unions plays a key role in determining salary levels for manual workers. Within the public sector, salary levels are largely determined by negotiation between employers and trade unions and by job evaluation. Market rates are less influential in the public than in the private sector, in which collective bargaining has less prominence.

Trade union influence in pay-setting in the UK has been in sharp decline since the early 1980s. Nevertheless, unions continue to 'modify the pay-setting behaviour of employers' according to a long-term analysis of pay settlements (Forth and Millward 2000), although this is 'largely in terms of process' rather than substance.

The process of pay-setting – and the nature of the manager's role – varies substantially between sectors, especially between the public and private sectors. In the public sector most employees have their pay set after multi-employer level bargaining, such as in the local government sector, or by some body external to the organisation – this latter process essentially describes the pay review body mechanisms. Under the pay review body system, independent committees appointed by the Government and comprising senior figures from industry, commerce, academia and the law meet to agree recommendations on the pay of major groups in the public sector – such as the armed forces, nurses, doctors, teachers, the judiciary and the senior Civil Service. These committees take evidence from both the Government and from employee representatives, but there is no collective bargaining.

The CIPD (2003) survey found that just over one-third of employers (36 per cent) use collective bargaining when establishing pay rates for manual staff. Practice differs by sector and by size of organisation. In the private sector, managers are most likely to be directly involved in setting the annual pay rise.

Assessing the influence of collective bargaining on pay – what does the pay-setting process cover?

It is important to distinguish the elements of pay and benefits that pay settlements cover. Some bargaining processes lead only to an agreed rise in the minimum basic rate of pay in the company – as, for example, in some engineering companies. Basic pay or salary may then be raised to maintain the same differential – but essentially this may be done outside the bargaining process, by management decision alone. Even in highly unionised environments collective bargaining may not cover the setting of policies in relation to benefits or performance pay systems, for example.

Pay decision-making level	Private-sector manufacturing	Private-sector services	Public sector
Collective bargaining exists	47	22	68
Multi-employer bargaining	5	5	42
Single-employer bargaining	19	14	21
Workplace-level bargaining	8	23	5
No collective bargaining	53	78	32
Decision-making external to organisation	–	–	22
Management at higher level	11	29	6
Management at workplace level	39	39	3
Level not known	2	6	–
Negotiation with individual	2	4	–
Base – percentages of employees working in establishments of more than 10 employees Drawn from Forth and Millward (2000) in an analysis based on the 1998 Workplace Employee Relations Survey			

Table 12   *Unionisation and pay determination*

From the legal perspective, the employment contract is seen differently under collective bargaining arrangements, because the employment contract contains, either expressly or by implication, the terms that are agreed by managers with union representatives. This is in addition to what is written in individual letters of appointment or other contractual documents. Many terms and conditions (both pay and benefits) are determined by management alone even when there is collective bargaining over some terms.

The trend to individualisation

A major report by Brown *et al* (1999) drew on a study of 32 firms, most of which had taken active steps to individualise employment contracts and reduce collective bargaining. For comparison purposes the study also looked at a few firms that had always used individual contracts and also at others that had retained collective bargaining.

What is individualisation?

Brown's study drew a distinction between *procedural individualisation* (or the removal of collective mechanisms for determining terms and conditions of employment) and *substantive individualisation* (the differentiation of individual employees' contracts).

In practice, the research revealed that employers' attempts at individualisation were predominantly concerned with procedural individualisation, through the derecognition of trade unions and withdrawal from collective agreements. However, this did not generally result in substantive individualisation because most terms and conditions remained common – certainly within the same occupational group in the respective organisation.

Why do the firms individualise contracts?

Brown *et al* (1999) showed that employers' motives in individualising was principally to save costs. Firms did so '*as part of a strategy to deal with deregulation, privatisation, intensification of competition in product markets or increased shareholder pressure*'. Employers took the opportunity for derecognition of unions and greater individualisation provided by legal changes in the 1980s that weakened the power of unions ('*combined with hostile economic conditions*'). In most cases the derecognition of unions was found to be neither a necessary consequence of the crisis in which firms found themselves nor a necessary precondition for survival.

What has individualisation entailed?

Brown *et al* (1999) found that firms that derecognised trade unions often adjusted their internal occupational pay rates differentially to reflect the levels of pay in the outside labour market for different occupations. But they were no better able to do this than those firms that retained unions. In most cases, there was a reduction in the number of grades used and this was directly linked to a broadening of job responsibilities. Union recognition had not substantially inhibited employers from devising grade structures comparable to those of their derecognised counterparts. For many firms, the advantage of breaking away from an existing structure of collective bargaining was to increase the dispersion of pay, both within grades and between hierarchical levels. A central objective of some employers in individualising was to steepen the gradient of pay across the organisation, to effectively reduce the relative pay of the less skilled in the organisation at the same time as increasing rewards at higher skill levels. The increase in pay dispersion in the UK is discussed below.

Individualisation and standardisation

While individualised pay tends to go hand in hand with linking pay rises to individual performance (see Chapter 5), there is also a trend towards greater standardisation of other terms and conditions. Brown *et al*'s study (1999) showed that employers who derecognised unions tended to gain substantial discretion to set individual pay, but paradoxically this led to increased standardisation of non-pay terms and conditions, in line with the trend to increased harmonisation of terms and conditions between managerial and non-managerial staff. Standardisation of non-pay terms and conditions was found to have increased rather than diminished at firms that took steps to individualise contracts. The trend towards harmonising non-pay terms and conditions is discussed further on page 96.

JOB EVALUATION

Most definitions of job evaluation refer to it as a systematic process or set of techniques used to assess the relative worth of jobs within an organisation. According to the CIPD (2003), job evaluation is cited as second only to the salary market as the most important influence on an organisation's pay levels. The use of job evaluation to develop pay structures is one of the techniques used in salary management, which in the UK was traditionally characteristic of pay-setting for managers and staff in (mainly large) organisations.

Job evaluation could also be viewed as a practical attempt to gain some agreement internally in organisations about the relative positioning of jobs in the pay and status order. As such the concepts of Adams's equity theory (see page 62) may be seen to have some bearing as

---

STUDENT REVIEW TASK

All for You utility company case study

The All for You utility company has been formed principally from a previously publicly owned water company, which merged in the 1990s with another utilities company. The company wants to encourage more organic types of business growth now, rather than the growth by acquisition in which it previously engaged. Top management wishes to reform its pay-setting process to give greater flexibility in being able to reward the entrepreneurial individuals in the company, now being encouraged to develop new business ideas. It is mindful of its experiences two years ago when a talented junior marketing manager who had tried to develop an idea for a new business venture within the company left to join a competitor, lured by greater encouragement and a better pay package/prospects – and subsequently turned his idea into a commercially successful enterprise. Some members of the Board are aware that their colleagues are bound by the traditions of the company they have grown up with – and there has been a consensus hitherto that the company should continue with essentially the same collective bargaining processes for pay-setting as it did when it was in the public sector.

Any change is going to be difficult, especially a major change to pay-setting.

■ As HR manager, you are asked initially to gather a focus group of managers, including some 'traditionalists' as well as 'entrepreneurial' types to assess the costs and benefits of moving away from the traditional form of collective bargaining to a new form of probably greater individualisation of pay determination.

■ Before the meeting you need to identify the cost and benefit headings, which might be relevant for discussion, not at this stage specific costs.

■ You are also asked to consider also how the concept of transaction costs may be useful in the case of your organisation considering individualising the terms and conditions of its employees. The transaction costs might include the time of HR or other managers and also of employees in setting up and monitoring any move to individualise pay or other terms and conditions.

---

theoretical underpinning for the rationalisation and systematisation of internal equity, through the mechanism of job evaluation. ACAS (1997) puts the case for it in the following way: 'In some large, stable organisations which do not, to any significant extent, have to compete in the labour market for rare skills, job evaluation can bring considerable benefits, and has a comfortable and reassuring feel about it. People can see their jobs being described and evaluated in a systematic way, are able to compare their assessments with those of other people and, normally, have the right of appeal if they are dissatisfied.'

Early developments of job evaluation

Job evaluation may be seen as stemming back to the scientific management era of the early 20th century – see Livy (1975). The ideas of FW Taylor placed emphasis on job analysis, breaking each job down into discrete tasks and measuring the time taken for each one. In another development, in the UK Civil Service increasing specialisation of jobs and a perceived need for an accountable method of deciding which jobs should be paid differently and at what level led to the use of job classification systems. Other large organisations also used various forms of whole job ranking or whole job comparison methods. These grew during the 1950s and 1960s and were principally used for staff and managerial groups.

This postwar period was also one of innovation in the art of job evaluation, with a number of very different methods being developed. By and large these were not analytical in nature – that is, they did not seek to split each job down into its constituent elements or factors, but rather considered the whole job.

In the 1960s Jacques (1964) advocated a method based on what he termed the 'time span of discretion'. In this method jobs are ranked according to the maximum period of time that individuals work on their own before they become accountable to a manager. This 'time span' was then used to gauge the levels of responsibility for each job.

J Gooch at Brunel University built on these ideas and developed a 'weight of responsibility' method, principally to evaluate research and development jobs or those for which it was difficult to assess the time span of discretion. The weight of responsibility concept combined the notion of time needed for managers to be aware of an individual employee's inadequate performance and the consequences of such inadequacy for the organisation.

Another innovator was Paterson (1972), who developed a method for the Southern Rhodesia Civil Service based on decision-making – the assumption being that a job's value to the organisation is related principally to the responsibility job holders have for making decisions on behalf of the organisation. Although none of these methods are now widely used, the concepts developed by these innovators have been incorporated into many schemes (see below).

One method that has stood the test of time is the consultancy-firm proprietary method – the Hay Guide Chart and Profile Method. The scheme was developed in the 1950s and retains a prominent role in industry and other sectors.

There is little recent academic research in this area, with the most notable that related to equal value and job evaluation (see below). As Arthurs (2003) says, '*Equity, frequently a source of interest and concern in previous decades, has been subject to little debate, except in the context of top people's pay.*' Some systematic studies were carried out under the centralised bodies' responsibility for conducting research during the Incomes Policy era of the late 1960s and 1970s. Robinson (1968) argued that American managers gained more control over potentially uncontrollable internal pay bills by using systems such as job evaluation, which injected some order into pay systems and hence prevented leapfrogging pay claims. The National Board for Prices and Incomes (1968) stated that an agreed framework such as that provided by job evaluation was: '*potentially important for dealing with one of the main reasons why growth in incomes tends to outstrip productivity – namely, the struggle engendered by what are regarded as inequitable, irrational and arbitrary pay structures*'.

Extent of use of job evaluation

While it might be argued that gaining control over pay was a clear motive for managers choosing to use job evaluation in the 1980s (Incomes Data Services 1987), it has been regulation that has ensured job evaluation has attained a primacy – albeit in spite of some profound concerns about its nature and efficacy.

As a broad generalisation, internal equity could be seen as having less significance for many organisations than perceptions about the salary market – suggesting that at least some of the nostrums of the 'new pay' school of thought (see page 3) have been taken to the heart of UK organisations.

Generally, larger employers are more likely to use job evaluation than smaller companies. The CIPD (2003) survey found that job evaluation was used by two in five respondents to set pay levels for non-manual non-management staff (39 per cent). For middle/first-line managers 44 per cent of organisations used job evaluation, while 41 per cent did so for senior managers.

Armstrong and Thompson (2003) report from their survey that 44 per cent of some 240 respondent organisations use formal job evaluation. Their data suggest it has become more widespread in the public and voluntary sectors, where it is used by 68 per cent of organisations, which compares with 39 per cent in the private sector. Some 74 per cent of the organisations that use job evaluation have only one scheme. Private-sector organisations are more likely to have several schemes – 29 per cent have more than one scheme. Two-thirds of respondents (67 per cent) who operate job evaluation use it for all employees.

Why use job evaluation?

Armstrong and Baron (1995) summarise the rationale that can be used to justify the time and expense that organisations must devote to job evaluation to make it work: '*Job evaluation can help to overcome difficulties in managing internal relativities and maintaining an equitable and competitive pay structure. It can address grading issues logically and systematically … It can help to produce order out of the chaos that exists in organisations which have allowed pay decisions to be made in an entirely ad hoc and subjective manner.*'

Such reasoning could be dismissed by the 'new pay' critics of job evaluation as 'old style' administrative reward management, rather than typical of a more strategic approach (see also Chapter 1) if it were not for the influence of equal pay for work of equal value.

The embedding of job evaluation into the equal pay laws has ensured its continued use in the UK. Armstrong and Thompson (2003) found that '*far from dying out, new job evaluation schemes are providing the foundation for major changes to pay structures in the NHS and local government designed to address equal pay and single-status issues*'. Many organisations without a formal job evaluation scheme had not considered the potential equal value implications of this policy.

Why do organisations not use job evaluation?

The proponents of the 'new pay' school – such as Zingheim and Schuster (2000) – argue that internal equity should no longer be a priority for employers and that market value should predominate. Lawler (1994) has been a vocal critic of job evaluation, suggesting that the notion of paying according to the status or requirements of a job is an outmoded idea in the context of a flexible, market-oriented approach to pay. He advocates a stronger focus on competencies and skills instead, claiming that individuals rather than jobs have value within organisations. The argument is that individuals should be paid for the skills they bring to the job, rather than for the responsibilities of the job itself.

Emerson (1991) argues that most job evaluation schemes have the effect of encouraging and rewarding non-adaptive employee behaviour. She proposes that modern organisations need systems that reward people for customer service, adaptability, profitability and market-related behaviour. More broadly, Moss Kanter (1987) suggests that in many organisations the rewards employees receive are differentiated primarily on the basis of status, not contribution, and that often the main way an individual can increase his or her pay is by being promoted. This system results in a great deal of time being spent by employees plotting how their present jobs might be upgraded or how otherwise they may get promotion, rather than striving to improve the contribution they are making to the business.

McNabb and Whitfield's (2001) study suggested from a comparison of two large quantitative data-sets – the Workplace Industrial Relations Survey and the Employer Manpower Skills Practices Survey – that job evaluation may be at odds with what are termed 'high-performance work practices'. Organisations with a full set of high-performance work practices were less likely to use analytical methods of job evaluation – although there were fewer 'contraindications' with non-analytical methods. Perhaps of greater concern is that when both analytical job evaluation and high-performance work practices were adopted, organisations had significantly worse financial performance than those that had one or other of these, but not both.

While the study gave statistical relationships, it did not reveal the processes at work at the organisational level. It is possible that the perceived inflexibility and top-down management style associated with using formal analytical job evaluation methods runs counter to the flexibility and employee-involvement approaches associated with high-commitment practices. This leads to something of a conundrum – if simpler, non-analytical methods of job evaluation might be better suited to an environment of high employee commitment, analytical methods must be used by organisations seeking to build a defence against equal value claims.

Traditional job evaluation certainly can seem to reward hierarchy as well as being a basis for codifying internal equity. If hierarchical values are implicit in the job evaluation scheme used, there would be a conflict with other priorities such as building employee commitment. Most UK organisations reporting problems with job evaluation to Armstrong and Thompson's (2003) survey said that job evaluation had not inhibited flexibility in their organisation, although 19 per cent said that it was over-bureaucratic and 14 per cent felt that it was too time-consuming. The most significant problem – reported by 34 per cent of organisations – was decaying over time and 'misuse'.

Job evaluation and equality

The introduction of the equal value law in 1984 held out a lifeline to job evaluation. Under the legislation, if a woman employee brings a claim for equal pay for a job of equal value, her employer can defend itself by giving evidence that the woman has a job that is given a lower value in the organisation's job evaluation scheme than that of the man with whom she is seeking equality of pay. The proviso is that the scheme used to evaluate the jobs is an analytical one and is not biased in favour of one gender. An analytical scheme is one that splits the jobs into factors, rather than comparing jobs on a 'whole job' basis. The reason for this emphasis on the analytical approach can be explored in the whole-job comparison exercise on page 51.

Research on equality and job evaluation

Discussion of the possible introduction of a law on comparable worth in the United States (similar but with crucial differences from the European concept of equal pay for work of equal value – see page 161) in the 1980s prompted research on the validity of different job evaluation methods. Writers from the feminist perspective questioned the value system

WHOLE-JOB COMPARISON EXERCISE

In groups consider four well-known jobs – nurse, police officer, primary school teacher and engineer. Compare the jobs in sets of two – for example, compare the nurse against the police officer, then against the teacher and finally against the engineer. If you consider the nurse is worth more then the police officer within society as a whole, put a 2 in the nurse row, if equal put a 1, if worth less put a 0. Discuss and agree a consensus score for each paired comparison within the group.

Compared with	Nurse	Police officer	Primary teacher	Engineer	TOTAL
Nurse					
Police officer					
Primary school teacher					
Engineer					

Total the scores in the final column.

The highest-ranked job is the one with the highest total score.

NB This ranking is obtained on a whole-job comparison basis, in a simplified version of the job evaluation method known as paired comparison, which was once widely used in the UK.

In groups, discuss how the 'evaluators' arrived at their individual decisions.

Did their view of the respective jobs include a picture of the typical person undertaking the job?

Was that person male or female?

Did the 'evaluators' use comparison within factors – eg the relative length of training needed or the responsibility level of each pair of jobs?

Discuss how easy the 'evaluators' found the process. Did discussion with others help?

underpinning job evaluation. Job evaluation schemes codify a set of organisational values – but if these are essentially male values that effectively undervalue women's role and contribution, then no schemes might be suitable for an 'objective' test of whether a job done by a man is of equal value to that done by a woman – particularly when there is such obvious gender segregation in occupations. A study by Madigan and Hoover (1986) that used six different job evaluation methods to assess the same public-service jobs found significant differences in the relative evaluations produced.

Arnault *et al* (2001) conducted an experimental study to assess the assumption – which seems central to the notion of equal value (or comparable worth) – that jobs possess an inherent worth independent of the labour market. The US-based researchers compared the values given by three commercial job evaluation methods to the same set of 27 jobs in an actual company. Statistical analysis of the experimental data indicated that the three evaluators differed in which factors they used to evaluate relative job worth.

Two further studies based on organisational case studies – coincidentally both of the operation of the Hay MSL method – led to different interpretations. From her feminist-perspective study of the State of Oregon, Acker (1989) argued that the method is riven with male values that tend to reinforce the status quo in the organisation, in which men predominate. She suggested, though, that all is not lost, that schemes such as Hay could be amended to reduce any bias and that *'job evaluation seems a more fair and open method of assigning relative value than market ... power'*. In contrast Quaid's (1993) study of a Canadian public-sector organisation criticised the move to *'purge sex bias from the weights and factors'* in job evaluation schemes, as this *'deflects attention away from the main issue ... (that) job evaluation cannot live up to its rational claims'*. Quaid adopted a social constructionist perspective to analyse the use and operation of job evaluation in the organisation she studied over a four-year period. Her analysis found that it is possible to interpret the growing acceptance of job evaluation and its terminology in the organisation as similar to the building of a myth, with its own rituals, symbols and language. She argued that the claims of job evaluation to be sufficiently 'objective' to judge equal value or comparable worth between jobs done by women and those done by men are spurious and *'job evaluation is nothing more than the expression of culturally sanctioned pay claims'* (Quaid 1993).

In the UK the Equal Opportunities Commission (1994) rather optimistically gave advice on *'freeing'* job evaluation schemes from sex bias. While it is perhaps rather more pragmatic to talk of reducing rather than eliminating bias, the guide is useful and the new generation of schemes, such as those in local government and the health service, have notably adopted some of its advice (see Table 13).

Factor selection – in the equality context

Following the *Bromley* v *Quick* legal case (see page 161), non-analytical job evaluation schemes diminished. Armstrong and Thompson (2003) report that 'not surprisingly' analytical schemes are substantially more widespread than non-analytical: 79 per cent of schemes are analytical and, of those, 71 per cent use point-factor rating. They also state that the average number of factors used to construct a job evaluation scheme is seven. The most frequently found factors are knowledge and skills, impact of job, communications and contacts.

'Knowledge and skills' or *'knowhow'* is clearly a most important factor present in most analytical job evaluation schemes. Arthurs (2003) says from his review of the literature that *'there is some consensus that the skills and knowledge dimension, present in nearly all methods, is an overriding predictor of job evaluation results'*. This gives weight to the argument that job evaluation mainly measures abilities or inputs that a person brings to the job. However, it also presents problems in the equal value context, as Table 13, drawn from the EOC guidance, indicates. Historically – at least – women have been much less likely to acquire 'paper' qualifications and have (for career break reasons) been unable to build up as much 'time-served' experience in organisations as men. This fact, together with the intense occupational segregation of jobs by gender, results in the EOC considering that most knowledge factors, particularly those reflecting the acquisition of qualifications or based on a

Factors	Favour men's jobs:		Neutral	Favour women's jobs:	
	Strongly	Weakly		Weakly	Strongly
Factors with a time dimension	Length of service Experience	Qualifications Age Education Knowledge Breadth of know-how Depth of know-how	Level of skill Training period		
Factors with a seniority dimension		Responsibility for cash or assets	Responsibility for confidential data or information Discretion Effect of decisions Supervisory responsibilities Accountability Decision-making Planning		
Factors with a relationship dimension			Safety of others Co-operation Creating new business Communication Co-ordination Personal appearance Expression	Human relations responsibility Contacts – internal or external Public relations Accuracy	Caring
Factors with a physical activity dimension	Heavy lifting Physical hazards Spatial ability Unpleasant working conditions	Technical expertise Responsibility for equipment Physical skills Physical effort Responsibility for product Responsibility for standards Operational knowledge Knowledge of machinery, tools, materials	Responsibility for materials Stamina Versatility Procedural know-how	Visual concentration Monotony Scanning	Dexterity Typing and keyboard skills
Factors with a mental activity dimension		Numerical calculation or ability Mathematical reasoning Problem-solving	Mental effort Initiative Originality Ingenuity Judgement Job complexity Planning Verbal skills	Concentration Memory Information ordering	
Factors with a sensory activity dimension		Differentiating sounds	Differentiating tastes Differentiating smells Tactile sensitivity Artistic or musical skills		
Adapted from Equal Opportunities Commission (1994)					

Table 13 *Job evaluation factors and gender*

53

time dimension, favour men (or more correctly they favour the jobs that men typically do). It is possible to reduce the bias in defining such factors, and the definition of the knowledge dimension in the NJC (local government) scheme, developed with equal value principles in mind and shown in Table 16, provides an example of an attempt to make this factor less gender-biased.

Of course it is also possible to build a job evaluation scheme that includes factors favouring the jobs that men mainly do – as long as these are balanced by factors favouring women. One factor that is said to favour women is the use of the contacts/human relations skills/interpersonal skills dimension. As Armstrong and Thompson's (2003) survey suggests, this dimension is now present in many schemes. However, the caring dimension, which strongly favours the jobs that women typically do, is rarely included – although it is evident in the jointly developed NJC local government scheme, within a 'responsibility for people' sub-factor.

It is not just the presence of a factor or dimension that is important in the equality context, but the relative weighting given to it. A high weighting given to a factor that favours men (and also theoretically women) might be seen as introducing sex bias into the scheme, which in turn would negate the value of the job evaluation process in providing a defence against an equal value claim.

Of course, from the practical perspective organisations that go to the time and expense of job evaluation want a scheme that works in that particular organisation and is defensive in the equal value context. These twin objectives may be achievable, but in any situation the process needs great care and testing. Simple solutions such as choosing all gender-neutral factors or ensuring there are women as well as men undertaking the evaluations are unlikely to provide either a viable scheme or ensure the resulting scheme is not biased.

Using the tried and tested: the influence of proprietary schemes

The alternative to organisations developing their own scheme, with all the perils that entails, is the use of a proprietary scheme. These schemes, typically run by management consultants, are more 'off-the-peg' than individually tailored. However, although most consultancy firms will have a preferred approach, most now say they will tailor the scheme to the needs of specific organisations.

One of the most popular (though not without its critics, and not the only proprietary method) is the Hay Guide Chart and Profile Method, developed in the 1950s and widely used for

---

Input factors – eg education, level of training, knowledge, communication skills, expertise, human relations/interpersonal skills, IT skills, thinking/reasoning skills

Process factors – Communication, job/role complexity, contacts, decisions, initiative, innovation, planning/organising, teamwork and leadership

Output factors – accountability, financial responsibility, impact/consequences of error, responsibility – for information, for money, for people, for staff, for resources; supervision received or supervisory responsibility

Demand factors – effort, mental effort, physical effort

Adapted from Armstrong and Baron (1995) and author's source material

---

Table 14   *Factors in use in local government and NHS job evaluation schemes*

management and other jobs in the UK and United States, as well as some other countries. It uses three main factors – know-how, problem-solving and accountability (an illustration from Quaid (1993) of the accountability chart is in Table 15, page 56). From the complex scheme, which requires training by the consultancy firm in order to use it, are produced job units (points). The scheme is used in 'blue-chip' companies and in the public sector.

Quaid (1993) points out the value perceived in the organisation she studied of adopting a system '*already being used by so many other well-known organisations*' and this is part of the consultants' 'sales pitch'. Paterson (1972) points to some technical problems with the scheme – for instance that '*accountability and problem-solving are indicative of practically the same entity*', adding that the use of geometric progression (rather than arithmetic) to give the points scores from one level to another in the charts is questionable because '*Dr Hay has nowhere expounded a theoretical basis for the use of the geometric progression*'. Overell (1997) reported more recent concerns – centring on the use of the method in the NHS and the question of equal value. These concerns focus on the difficult area of how responsibility for patient care is evaluated. The strong rebuttal from a Hay consultant (Cohen 1997) of the charges is indicative of commercial and other sensitivities in this field.

One highly specific benefit of using the Hay method is that the consultants collect pay data – related to points scores in a wide range of organisations across public and private sectors. This enables a comparison of market rates based on job weight and facilitates comparisons across sectors and functions. This is especially valuable for those jobs (usually managerial or senior-level posts) for which organisations will recruit nationally or internationally, rather than locally.

In summary, using a *proprietary* method can have the following benefits:

- expertise from the consultants in setting up and using job evaluation
- access to quality pay information
- the possibility of using the same scheme as well-known companies.

The advantages of a '*tailor-made*' scheme might be:

- control over the development of the scheme in-house to suit highly specific organisational environments
- possibly cost-effective, depending on which staff might be involved in developing a new scheme and how their time is accounted for
- opportunity for internal HR staff and managers to gain a detailed knowledge of the scheme – its drawbacks as well as its advantages.

Weighting of factors

Most job evaluation schemes weight some factors more highly than others, to reflect their relative importance. Some proprietary schemes have an in-built weighting, while for tailor-made schemes it is necessary to apply a weighting directly (unless unweighted factors are to be used). This is a potentially biased approach, since one of the traditional methods used to achieve weightings is a 'felt-fair' approach based on whole job comparisons (a process no longer considered valid in the equal value context).

Joint working parties or groups developing schemes can discuss and decide the weightings. Often the knowledge or skills factor is more highly weighted than others – to reflect the importance attached to skills in the organisation. However, if a very high weighting is attached to such a factor and it is designed primarily in terms of formal educational achievement, gender bias is possible. Decisions not to weight the factors selected can affect the workability of a scheme.

Job evaluation process

Because of what is at stake the process of evaluation can allow personal influence and power relationships within an organisation to come to the fore. One study (Smith *et al* 1989) found that when evaluators know the job title this significantly influences the results. Original concerns about the use of job evaluation in the equality context focused on ensuring that women as well as men were involved in the evaluation process. However, it is no longer suggested that improving the process of job evaluation alone can achieve a non-biased set of results.

Translating job evaluation scores into a pay structure

Organisations encounter problems both of principle and of practice in translating a set of job evaluation scores or a rank order of jobs into a viable pay structure. As Zingheim and Schuster (2000) highlight, there are perennial problems when jobs assessed as having the same value according to the job evaluation scheme differ markedly in their market value. Quaid (1993) and Arthurs (1994) illustrate from their respective case studies in using a proprietary system of job evaluation to assess relative job weight how the process of setting the pay structure entailed negotiation and compromises.

Guide chart used in 'Atlantis' case study – _Accountability factor_								
Magnitude*** (annual dollar value)	Minimal				Very small			
Impact**	Up to $10m				$10m–100m			
Freedom to act*	A	C	S	P	A	C	S	P
Restricted: These jobs are consistently subject to explicit, detailed instructions and/or constant personal or procedural supervision	5 6 7	7 8 9	9 10 12	12 14 16	7 8 9	9 10 12	12 14 16	16 19 22
Prescribed: These jobs are subject to direct and detailed instructions and/or close supervision	8 9 10	10 12 14	14 16 19	19 22 25	10 12 14	14 16 19	19 22 25	25 29 33
Controlled: These jobs are subject to instructions and established work routines and/or close supervision	12 14 16	16 19 22	22 25 29	29 33 38	16 19 22	22 25 29	29 33 38	38 43 50
∧∧∧∧∧∧∧∧∧∧∧∧∧∧∧∧∧∧∧∧∧∧∧∧∧∧∧∧ Drawn from Quaid (1993)								

Table 15 *Extract from Hay-developed job evaluation scheme used in a Canadian organisation*

KNOWLEDGE factor

This factor measures the level of knowledge required for the job. It covers all technical, specialist, procedural and organisational knowledge required for the job, including numeracy and literacy; knowledge of equipment and machinery; and knowledge of concepts, ideas, other cultures or languages, theories, techniques, policies, procedures and practices.

It takes into account the breadth, diversity and range of knowledge and the depth and complexity of the understanding required.

This factor does not take into account physical, mental and interpersonal/communications skills required, as these are covered by separate factors.

Level 1: The job requires knowledge of the procedures for a limited number of tasks and the operation of associated basic tools and equipment. The jobholder needs to be able to follow straightforward oral and written instructions and keep basic work records.

Level 2: The job requires knowledge of the procedures for a range of tasks and the operation of associated tools and equipment. The jobholder needs basic literacy and numeracy skills.

Level 3: The job requires knowledge of the procedures for a range of tasks, some of which, singly or in combination, are relatively complex, and of the operation of associated equipment and tools. Literacy and numeracy skills are required.

Level 4: The job requires predominantly practical and procedural knowledge across a technical or specialist area or an equivalent level of organisational, procedural and policy knowledge.

Level 5: The job requires theoretical plus practical and procedural knowledge in a specialist area or an equivalent level of organisational, procedural and policy knowledge.

Level 6: The job requires advanced theoretical, practical and procedural knowledge across a specialist area or an equivalent level of organisational, procedural and policy knowledge.

Level 7: The job requires advanced theoretical, practical and procedural knowledge across a specialist area plus detailed knowledge of the associated organisational policies, practices and procedures or an equivalent level of organisational, procedural and policy knowledge.

Level 8: The job requires advanced theoretical, practical and procedural knowledge across a specialist area plus detailed knowledge of the associated organisational policies, practices and procedures for that and other related specialist areas or an equivalent level of organisational, procedural and policy knowledge.

Table 16 *Extract from the Local Government NJC job evaluation scheme*

Student review exercise

Case study: Financial Specialist Co

You are asked to develop the basic outline for a job evaluation scheme for a given small company in the finance sector. You are provided with a set of job descriptions for the benchmark jobs for which you are asked to develop a scheme. In addition you should also note the following special circumstances in this company:

- The company HR manager has discovered some serious anomalies in the relative pay of people in different departments and is worried about the possibility of there being an equal pay case.

- Her boss is the finance director who is also deputy to the chief executive. The finance director seems to the HR manager to have created some of the unjustifiable anomalies by paying staff in her own department significantly more than staff in analogous roles in other departments. In addition the specialist insurance-linked staff in the departments that handle business with the company's clients have pay levels below those of what may be seen as comparable staff in the finance department. The HR manager is therefore concerned – from a business perspective – that staff who are providing the service that forms the main income stream of the company are being undervalued in comparison with a central support function (ie finance).

- To complicate matters – and aware that there may be potential legal problems – the chief executive has asked the HR manager without informing his deputy to 'quietly' develop 'something' (he means job evaluation) that will (i) help in maintaining consistency across the company and (ii) provide him with some basis on which to keep his deputy in check on the matter of her own staff's pay.

- The HR manager has to drop her initial idea that a job evaluation scheme would be best developed with the direct input of the staff covered by it, and opt instead to develop something to at least pilot stage that could be put to work quickly. She decides to rely on the generally good staff and management relationships and on the fact that there is a measure of trust in her as an 'honest broker', trusted to be fair and equitable.

- With colleagues from her own department she begins a series of working sessions to devise a job evaluation scheme that would suit the company. She has taken the view that the company needs a tailor-made scheme, because in many ways it is different from the organisations that tend to use the large-scale proprietary methods ('off-the-peg' schemes).

Using the information in the job description summary below:

- analytically consider the *content of the jobs* and their responsibilities
- identify which seem to be the *main factors* (with outline definitions) that could be used in a job evaluation scheme *designed specifically* for this company
- *consider your initial list of factors* for any potential gender bias
- develop a set of *level definitions* for at least one of your selected factors

- consider the relative value to this organisation of the different factors you have chosen, as a preparation for weighting.

As a context before framing your plans you should also consider:

- the extent to which this company might need to develop its own job evaluation scheme or might be best advised to buy in a proprietary scheme
- the key aspects of business success – key business 'drivers'
- any vulnerability to equal pay claims
- any salary market considerations.

Financial Specialist Co – summary of job roles/content
Note on qualifications
Where these were available, essential qualifications are given for each job role.
In general this company specifies few formal qualifications, although there is a blanket requirement that all staff must have the equivalent of 5 GCSEs.

Job roles and summary of job descriptions
Chief executive
Responsible to a board of stakeholders for the strategic direction and efficient running of the organisation and its future development.

Central Department
Finance director and deputy chief executive
Responsible to the chief executive for the financial management of the organisation.

Personal assistant to finance director and training administrator
PA duties to the finance director and a subsidiary role administering training courses – principally those with a cost for the organisation.

Admin Department
Human resources and admin manager
Responsible for human resources policies and practices, also for the line management of admin staff in the organisation, as well as for some statutory reporting duties. Essential qualification: Chartered Institute of Insurance qualification. Desirable qualification: CIPD-qualified or working towards the qualification.

Human resources assistant
Provides confidential administration and secretarial services primarily for the HR function. Tasks include monitoring sickness absence in the organisation and the organisation of recruitment and selection. Essential: must be IT-literate and have excellent communication skills.

Admin assistants (2)
Provide confidential admin and secretarial support to all areas of the organisation. Supervise office junior and organise rota for reception staff. Essential: must be IT-literate, have word-processing skills and have organisational skills.

Receptionists
Responsible for switchboard and for greeting personal visitors. Answer routine queries and other tasks such as booking meeting rooms. Essential: smart appearance, good telephone manner, must be IT-literate and have word processing skills.

Finance Department
Finance manager
Manages finance, client records and IT functions. (IT is outsourced.) Develops accounting systems, prepares forecasts, develops budgetary and cost control systems. Essential qualifications: ACCA-qualified or equivalent, inter-personal skills and product-related knowledge.

Management accountant
Responsible for preparing monthly accounts and annual budget, for liaising with professional advisers such as audit and for supervision of finance department staff. Essential: must be numerate and IT-literate. Preferable: has accounting background and product-related experience.

Senior finance assistant
Responsible for accounting activities in relation to expenses of the sales team. Essential: must be numerate and IT-literate, have accounting background and product-related experience.

Finance assistants
Responsible for maintaining ledger accounts and some reconciliation. Essential: must be numerate and IT-literate, have good communication skills. Preferable: accounting experience.

Marketing Department
Director of marketing and business development
Manages current marketing and sales activities, plans developments. A director of the company. Essential qualifications: graduate level, preferably with marketing qualification, senior management experience/experience in sales and PR, good communication skills.

National account managers
Manages field sales teams, obtains new business, achieves agreed sales targets. Essential: must be self-starter, have good communications skills and previous sales experience.

Business development manager
New post

Corporate communications specialist
Responsible for production of the organisation's newsletter for clients, maintaining house style, liaising with press and print providers as well as advertising agencies. Essential: must be graduate level, with communication skills and must be IT-literate.

Client development team leader
Responsible for planning work for development team, recruitment, training and motivating such staff, negotiations with key customers.
Essential: experience in sales/marketing and managing staff, commercial knowledge of the market.

Account managers
Field sales roles

Specialist Client Services Department
Client services manager
Liaises with clients and ensures that services for which they subscribe are provided. Manages department. Essential: must have knowledge of the product and market and detailed knowledge of professional service area, plus excellent communication skills and a Chartered Institute of Insurance qualification.

Client services supervisor
Deals with problems or complicated cases, supervises and trains client services assistants. Essential: must have knowledge of the product, market and professional service area. Should have excellent communication skills and be working towards Chartered Institute of Insurance qualification.

Client services administrator
Provides admin support for client services.

Client services assistants and senior assistants
The main focus of the job is the company's contacts with clients; responsible for dealing with client referrals promptly and accurately. Essential: must have knowledge of the product and professional service area, together with good communication skills.

MARKETISATION AND INTERNAL EQUITY

Zingheim and Schuster (2000) suggest that companies mainly now rely on market value, not internal (job-evaluated) value, as the basis for setting pay levels. Market forces are the key determinant when determining salary levels and pay ranges, according to the CIPD's 2003 survey, although the extent is dependent on employee group and sector. More than three-fifths of respondents determine pay levels in relation to the external market rate for non-manual non-management staff (62 per cent), middle/first-line managers (68 per cent) and senior managers (72 per cent). For manual staff, just under half of employees (47 per cent) use market rates. In the voluntary sector, market rates and the level of inflation appear as important factors in establishing salaries.

As Armstrong (1999) points out, '*classical (economic) theory is used as a justification for concentrating on external competitiveness at the expense of internal equity*'. This tendency is evident even in occupations in which there is no evident external 'market' – for example, in certain parts of the public sector.

It has been argued that the notion of supply and demand does not at a simplistic level fit the reality of pay. For example, the National Board for Prices and Incomes (1968) concluded that: 'Research has shown wide discrepancies in pay for similar jobs at different firms in the same locality ... it is not true that firms pay the same wages for specific occupations as are paid by other, competing, firms in their locality. It is difficult therefore to place any meaning on such phrases as "the going rate".' Pragmatically, most reward specialists certainly look to finding a range of market rates, rather than a singular rate, and it is sometimes difficult to interpret the rationale behind observed differences.

The emphasis on classical economic theory may itself not be the value-free process that is sometimes suggested – it can, for example, be viewed as a gendered tendency (Wajcman 2000). Hence, the move to emphasise the external market can be viewed as biased against women. Economists tend not to view the labour and salary markets in this way, but rather assume that markets operate perfectly – and when they do not, one source of imperfection can be put down to gender discrimination.

However, questions of equity can be broader than questions of discrimination. Adams's Equity theory (drawn from the psychological tradition) gives a different perspective on the internal and external equity versus market debate, suggesting that, motivationally, employee perceptions about fairness are not to be underestimated in achieving an effective pay system. Runciman (1966) used the concept of 'reference groups' to analyse perceptions about poverty, with individuals comparing themselves with those socially close to them. Similarly, Brown and Sisson (1975) suggest that people are particularly concerned about comparisons with the pay of those they consider to be socially close to them. A number of studies of pay satisfaction in the United States – summarised by Heneman and Judge (2000) – show that employees make comparisons within both the organisation or workplace, and outside it, in judging whether they are being treated equitably. But the process of pay setting is seen to be more important than the actual level of pay. Moreover, individuals' perceptions about how relatively fair their pay seems to be are, of course, affected by the extent of information they have on their own pay and that of relevant others. One of the interpretations of this research is that cleaners do not seek to compare their rewards with the rewards of the executives whose offices they clean. However, their perceptions about the relative processes used to set the two sets of pay are important.

Use of pay surveys to assess the salary market – quality issues

From a practical point of view, market pricing is a key activity for reward specialists in organisations. This process can range from informal contacts with other local HR managers – to find out directly comparable rates for locally recruited staff such as administrative or manual workers – to detailed salary club activities. With the growth in emphasis on the 'market', the number of sources offering pay data has grown. Incomes Data Services (2004) shows the extent of the statistically based pay surveys now available in the UK.

Data from such salary surveys are used to assess the 'market'. These market data are of sometimes questionable quality. For the reward practitioner, interpreting or using pay data is more an 'art than a science' (Gomez-Mejia and Balkin 1992). Taking a pragmatic view of using salary surveys, Incomes Data Services (1990) say that 'the best that can be hoped for ... is for a reasonable guide to the salary market. For this reason, most firms use a number of surveys to check the competitiveness of their salary policies.'

While there are some reasonable quality surveys – and the most expensive are not always the best – there are perennial problems with job/responsibility level matching, sampling, participation, data collection methods and timing.

Sampling
Few pay surveys are founded on structured samples. Most commercial surveys gain their participants from firms that are willing to contribute data in order that they can have access to aggregate statistical data on other organisations. Only the officially produced surveys – the New Earnings Survey (NES) and the Labour Force Survey (LFS) – aim to have large-scale representative surveys of the workforce. In the case of the NES, this is a 1 per cent structured sample of the workforce, with information gathered on the individuals based on National Insurance numbers but with the data collected from their employers, to ensure accuracy.

Specialist commercial surveys – for example, those based on a single industry – may indeed have samples representative of their sector. A survey that, for example, includes all the oil companies that operate in the UK would certainly be representative. However, the selection of participants in most commercial surveys can be, as Incomes Data Services (1990) comment, '*fairly haphazard and the resulting sample is more likely to be self-selecting, rather than truly random*'. Practising reward specialists must use the information they can get – on what both individuals and their employers often prefer to keep totally secret. When whole samples are not representative of the relevant population, particular questions arise about the nature of sub-samples. The more survey results are subdivided, the bigger is the likely 'sampling error'. Most reputable survey producers have thresholds below which they will not analyse data – and these need to be defined in the survey report. When sub-sample sizes are not given, questions to the survey producer are in order.

However, it is not just small samples that can be a problem. Another common problem occurs with sample clustering. For example, in a general survey, data from 200 companies on the pay of, say, 40 personnel officers may be seen to be more representative if the 40 are from most firms in the 200 sample, rather than 10 each from just four of the 200 participating organisations. To overcome the potential problems caused by the pay observations from a few very large companies overly influencing the data, some survey producers engage in various data-capping techniques. Reward specialists who are regular users of pay data will want to examine the participant list of any survey they are considering using for market-based comparisons.

Response rates
Equally important are the response rates to surveys. Only the official surveys are likely to have response rates of more than 80 per cent. Salary surveys based on voluntary participation are likely to have response rates well below 50 per cent. Response rates below 20 per cent may call into question the quality of the data provided.

Definitions of pay terms
The definitions used to compile pay data are also a quality issue. There are no official definitions of pay items. One survey might analyse data on basic (or base) pay and give a separate analysis of total cash earnings (which would usually include bonus pay and allowances as well as basic salary). Other surveys may be less specific about what heading or elements of pay and allowances are to be included by those providing data. The important aspect here is clarity of definition.

Job matching

Job matching is critical to data quality. Many reward specialists consider this to be the most important aspect of data quality. Some surveys use job title as a basis for analysis. Job title alone is an unreliable guide to job content and responsibilities. The New Earnings Survey (NES) uses the Standard Occupational Classification as a basis for analysing pay by occupation. However, while this gives a reasonably clear guide to the pay of cleaners or plumbers, for example, it simply does not give enough variation by level of responsibility for most managerial/professional or administrative jobs.

Levels of responsibility for managerial jobs may be defined as in the example in Table 17, adapted from managerial salary surveys. The job of a general manager is simply different in a very small firm from that in a large, potentially complex, organisation. All salary surveys that cover managerial jobs to any extent (aside from the NES) use corporate size as an analytical category. Another method of capturing varying levels of responsibility is to collect salary information in relation to the same job evaluation method. The Hay Group salary surveys are a good example, analysing pay levels by job units (points scores).

Another method of ensuring greater accuracy in job matching is the use of capsule job descriptions. This method is especially used in salary club surveys, and in some consultancy firms' surveys. Typically, the participants who are providing pay information are asked if they have such a job in their organisation – and to give pay details. If they do not have such a job they may be asked to estimate the level of pay a job of that sort would attract. Clearly, it is important to know how much of the information analysed is based on actual as distinct from estimated pay.

Statistical terms used in surveys

Median or mean?

Both mean averages and median are used in salary surveys to give an indication of the middle of the market.

The arithmetic mean (average) is the sum of the number of salary observations divided by the number of observations. So if there were just five salary observations for the same job and they were £18,000, £19,000, £20,000, £22,000 and £23,500, the mean would be (£102,500 divided by 5) or £20,500.

The median figure is the middle figure in the rank order – ie £20,000.

In pay surveys, the average will tend to be higher than the median, since the distribution of pay tends to be skewed to the higher end of the distribution of observations. While the inclusion of outliers in the distribution is reasonable to represent the range of pay for particular jobs, they are not representative of the middle of the market. Hence the median tends to be a preferred measure.

Quartiles and inter-quartile range

Because there is often a wide range of pay for any job, reward specialists tend to use the quartiles (and sometimes deciles) in the distribution, to give a more rounded picture of the range of pay rates.

- The upper quartile cuts off the top quarter (or top 25 per cent) of observations.
- The lower quartile cuts off the lowest quarter.

Job Level 1
The most senior full-time executive of the company, responsible for defining strategy in agreement with the stated policy of the Board/stakeholders. Makes suggestions regularly to the Board regarding the policy to be adopted. Responsible for the profit/loss and overall management of the organisation; reports to Board.

Job Level 2
Usually a director of the company, normally sits on the Board or Executive Committee of the organisation. Responsible for developing strategy and planning within a business unit or function. Reports to Level 1.

Job Level 3
The head of a major department, not a director. May be referred to as senior management. Responsible for developing planning and implementation of strategy within the department. Usually reports to Level 2.

Job Level 4
A senior manager of the organisation. Responsible for establishing new methods of implementing strategy within a given discipline. May report to Level 2 or Level 3.

Job Level 5
A middle manager of the organisation. Responsible for the achivement of defined objectives. Reports to Level 3 or Level 4.

Table 17   *Example of defined responsibility levels and pay: executive pay*

- The highest decile cuts off the top 10th.
- The lowest decile cuts off the lowest 10th.

The inter-quartile range looks at the range of pay from the lower quartile to the upper quartile.

SHAPING THE CURRENT REWARD BUDGET

When asked what current pressures are influencing the current reward spend, three factors are likely to feature most prominently:

- organisation performance
- salary/pay market pressures
- inflation.

In terms of the level of the pay settlement there is evidence from a number of sources that the most important factor has been inflation (see eg, Incomes Data Services 2003). From their study of long-term trends, Forth and Millward (2000) confirm that the level of pay increase – regardless of whether collective bargaining takes place or not – is a '*few whole or half percentage points*' around the prevailing inflation rate. The next most important factor – the '*going rate*' of increase in the same sector – has also been shown not to vary significantly between unionised and non-unionised workplaces.

How is inflation measured?

As inflation remains low, other factors are achieving greater significance. According to the CIPD's 2003 survey, organisations report that in the private sector the primary influences on the reward budget are the performance/profitability of the organisation (87 per cent) and salary market rates (61 per cent). Within the public sector the main drivers are the going rate of pay awards (53 per cent), the organisation's ability to pay (49 per cent) and union/staff pressure (48 per cent). In the voluntary sector, inflation has been the most important factor (56 per cent), followed by affordability (51 per cent) and market rate pressures (51 per cent). The inability to pass on increased costs by raising prices is also a key factor for the voluntary sector (23 per cent).

The Retail Prices Index (RPI) was for many years the UK's principal measure of consumer price inflation, and was widely used in budgeting for and negotiating over pay rises. This measure was replaced in December 2003 by the Consumer Prices Index (CPI). The CPI is now the main measure of inflation, as it is calculated on the same basis in each member state of the European Union for the purposes of European comparisons, as required by the Maastricht Treaty. For further details, see www.statistics.gov.uk/hicp. Detailed, latest-released figures can be found in the Consumer Price Indices Press Release and the Focus on Consumer Price Indices, which has detailed data tables. See www.nationalstatistics.gov.uk.

The CPI measures the average change in the prices of goods and services bought by households in the UK. General pay increases are often linked directly to the inflation rate. IDS (2003) discusses the vital significance that current inflation (and inflation projections) continue to have in setting the contours of negotiated annual pay increases.

STUDENT REVIEW QUESTIONS

1   Should the market or internal equity be the most important determinant of pay levels? Discuss this question by reference to a specific organisation or sector.

2   'Information on the job evaluation method used to evaluate their jobs should not be shared with employees.' Discuss this proposition, giving reasons for your position, referring both to theory and practice in your answer.

REFERENCES

Acker, J (1989) *Doing comparable worth: gender, class and pay equity*. Temple University Press.

Advisory, Conciliation and Arbitration Service (1997) *Motivating and rewarding employees*. ACAS.

Armstrong, M (1999) *Employee reward*. IPD.

Armstrong, M and Baron, A (1995) *The job evaluation handbook*. IPD.

Armstrong, M and Thompson, P (2003) *Job evaluation continues to flourish*. Article posted on website *www.e-reward.co.uk*, 7 February.

Arnault, E, Gordon, L, Joines, D, Douglas, G and Phillips, G (2001) An experimental study of job evaluation and comparable worth. *Industrial and Labor Relations Review* Vol. 54, no 4, July, p806.

Arthurs, A (1994) *Equal value in British banking: the Midland Bank case*, in Kahn, P and Meeham, E, *Equal value/comparable worth in the UK and the USA*. Macmillan Press.

Arthurs, A (2003) *Performance and equity: the surprising survival of job evaluation*. Paper presented at the Performance and Reward Conference, Manchester Metropolitan University, 9 April.

Brown, W and Sisson, K (1975) The use of comparisons in workplace wage determination. *British Journal of Industrial Relations*. Vol 13, no 1.

Brown, W, Deakin, S, Hudson, M, Pratten, C and Ryan, P (1999) *The individualisation of employment contracts in Britain*. Research paper for the Department of Trade and Industry, Centre for Business Research, Department of Applied Economics, University of Cambridge.

Chartered Institute of Personnel and Development (2003) *Reward Management Survey 2003: survey report*. January. CIPD.

Cohen, P (1997) Letter to the Editor, *People Management*. 20 November.

Dickens, R and Machin, S (1998) Minimum wage: maximum impact? *Centrepiece*. Vol 3, no 3, Autumn, pp10–13.

Emerson, S (1991) Job evaluation: a barrier to excellence? *Compensation and Benefits Review*. Jan–Feb, pp39–51.

Equal Opportunities Commission (1994) *Job evaluation schemes free of bias*. EOC.

Forth, J and Millward, N (2000) *The determinants of pay levels and fringe benefit provision in Britain*. Discussion Paper 171. National Institute of Economic and Social Research.

Gomez-Mejia, L and Balkin, D (1992) *Compensation, organizational strategy and firm performance*. Southwestern Publishing.

Heneman, H and Judge, T (2000) *Compensation attitudes*, in Rynes, S and Gerhart, B (eds) *Compensation in organizations: current research and practice*. Jossey-Bass.

Heneman, R, Ledfor, G and Gresham, M (2000) *The changing nature of work and its effects on compensation design and delivery*, in Rynes, S and Gerhart, B (eds) *Compensation in organizations: current research and practice*. Jossey-Bass.

Incomes Data Services (1983) *Job evaluation review*. IDS Top Pay Unit.

Incomes Data Services (1987) *Job evaluation review*. IDS Top Pay Unit.

Incomes Data Services (1990) *Using salary surveys*. IDS Top Pay Unit.

Incomes Data Services (2001) The impact of the NMW in 2001. *IDS Report* 844.

Incomes Data Services (2003) Pay prospects 2003/2004, *IDS Report* 890.

Incomes Data Services (2004) *Directory of salary surveys: 2004*.

Institute of Personnel Management (1991) *Minimum wage: an analysis of the issues*. IPM.

Jacques, E (1964) *Time span handbook*. Heinemann.

Lawler, E (1994) From job-based to competency-based organizations. *Journal of Organizational Behavior*. Vol 15, pp 3–15.

Livy, B (1975) *Job evaluation: a critical review*. Allen and Unwin.

Low Pay Commission (2001) *The national minimum wage: making a difference*. 3rd Report of the Low Pay Commission. March.

Low Pay Commission (2003) *The National Minimum Wage*. 4th Report of the Low Pay Commission.

Low Pay Unit (2000) *The case for a decent minimum wage*. Low Pay Unit. October.

Madigan, R and Hoover, D (1986) Effects of alternative job evaluation methods on decisions involving pay equity. *Academy of Management Journal*. Vol 29, no 1, pp84–100.

McNabb, R and Whitfield, K (2001) Job evaluation and high performance work practices: compatible or conflictual? *Journal of Management Studies*. Vol 38, no 2, March, pp 293–312.

Metcalf, D (1999) *The British national minimum wage*. Centre for Economic Performance, London School of Economics. March.

Moss Kanter, R (1987) The attack on pay. *Harvard Business Review*, March–April, pp60–67.

National Board for Prices and Incomes (1968) *Job evaluation*. NPBI Report 83.

Overell, S (1997) NHS seeks cure for equal value malaise. *People Management*. 23 October.

Paterson, T (1972) *Job evaluation: volume 1: a new method*. Business Books.

Quaid, M (1993) *Job evaluation: the myth of equitable assessment*. University of Toronto Press.

Robinson, D (1968) *Wage drift, fringe benefits and manpower distribution*. OECD.

Runciman, W G (1966) *Relative deprivation and social justice: a study of attitudes to social inequality in twentieth-century England*. Routledge and Kegan Paul.

Smith, B, Hornsby, J, Benson, P and Wesolowski, M (1989) What is in a name: the impact of job titles on job evaluation results. *Journal of Business and Psychology*, Vol 3, pp 341–351.

Soskice, D (1990) Wage determination: the changing role of institutions in advanced industrial economies. *Oxford Review of Economic Policy*. Vol 6, no 4.

Wajcman, J (2000) Feminism facing industrial relations in Britain. *British Journal of Industrial Relations*. Vol 38, no 2, June, pp13–201.

Zingheim, P and Schuster, J (2000) *Pay people right!* Jossey-Bass.

Websites
Government-sponsored websites:
lpc.gov.uk – research and recommendations from the Low Pay Commission
nationalstatistics.gov.uk – free access to the *New Earnings Survey*, the Index of Average Earnings and the Labour Force Survey

Pay structures

CHAPTER 3

INTRODUCTION

Pay structures have become an increasingly complex area of reward policy as the number and flexibility of pay options has grown. At a time when manual workers were the largest occupational group in the economy a simplified approach to pay was evident in which many jobs had a single 'spot rate' for the job, and this was uprated typically by collective bargaining (or during the Incomes Policy eras of the 1960s and 1970s in line with statutory norms). The greater flexibility of pay evident since the early 1980s has been characterised by increasing complexity and by the harmonisation of manual and non-manual pay arrangements, with an increasing use of salary-based systems previously only used for staff and managerial pay.

This chapter aims to:

- define and set out the trends in pay structures
- identify different pay structure options, their advantages and disadvantages
- explore pay structure choices, using examples, in different sectors
- assess equality issues in relation to pay structures
- discuss the issues concerning the process of pay restructuring.

The chapter can contribute towards the following CIPD professional standards. *Operational indicators*. Practitioners must be able to:

- advise senior management on the design or modification of a pay structure and methods of introducing it
- advise on the management of change when introducing or modifying elements of the reward system.

Knowledge indicators. Practitioners must understand and be able to explain:

- the concepts of reward structures
- the criteria for an effective pay structure.

Pay structures may be defined as the pay levels, ranges, scales or grades for jobs or roles that are treated similarly. As discussed in Chapter 1, the very nature of jobs and of organisations has been under review; it is perhaps not surprising, therefore, that the structure of pay at the organisational level should also have been subject to change. Many organisations have sought in recent years to make pay structures more flexible (Industrial Society 1997) by, for example, introducing performance-based pay or progression within basic pay structures or, more recently, by adopting broader salary bands. The process of setting broader bands might still entail the use of job evaluation techniques, while these systems tend to be flexible enough to permit progression on the basis of individual performance assessment or in relation to competencies/skill acquisition. Many organisations ventured into new pay structures saying that the old system was too 'bureaucratic' or 'inflexible' and many wanted to open up pay structures to the possibilities of individual performance pay (Industrial Society 1997).

Academic research evidence in this area tends to be limited to that from the industrial relations and performance pay perspective (see Chapter 5). It had long been noted that collective bargaining tended to compress pay structures. The widening out of pay differentials – particularly to facilitate the growth of higher rates of pay – was a notable motive for reducing the influence of collective bargaining at the level of the firm (Brown *et al* 1998). Such changes put considerable pressure on the existing pay structures, leading to some experimentation.

JOB EVALUATION, MARKET RATES AND PAY STRUCTURES

Whatever care is taken to be as systematic as possible with job evaluations, the overall effect of a new or revised set of pay arrangements implemented following these evaluations is crucially changed by the process of setting the pay structures. This process is often secretive and entails use of judgement and perhaps negotiation. As Arthurs (1994) and Quaid (1993) describe in their case histories, a good deal of debate, negotiation and detailed work goes into the decision about the type of structure and its application. Arthurs's (1994) account of the case of the Midland Bank – seeking to use job evaluation to provide for equal pay for work of equal value – shows that at the end of an evaluation exercise in which the influence of consultants had been prominent, negotiations between union and management took over to agree 'the number of grades and the location of the break points'.

Little research supports the view that the process of pay structure creation can be reduced to a purely mathematical exercise, in spite of the impression created in some salary administration texts. The typical methodology entails plotting job evaluation scores against salary (current salaries and market rate salary data) on a graph and then using lines of best fit and pay modelling techniques to help in deciding the optimum structure. Computerised paybill modelling can (see also Figure 7) help to estimate the costs of transition to a new structure. Of course, the overall costs of a change of structure may be considerably higher than the immediate transition costs. Estimates of pay progression rates are also needed to establish the costs over a medium term.

Why not structure-less?

Given the inevitable problems in setting pay structures, why do organisations not dispense with them altogether? In the United States some companies have experimented with (almost) structure-less environments. Arguing the case for this at the 1996 IPD Annual Conference at Harrogate, Dan Gilbert, Staff Consultant, Compensation with US corporation General Electric, said 'You can't get creativity with structure', giving a clear exposition of some of the benefits of greater flexibility.

Types of pay structure

Types of pay structure include spot rates, individual job-range structures, graded pay structures, pay spines, broad-banded pay structures and job family structures.

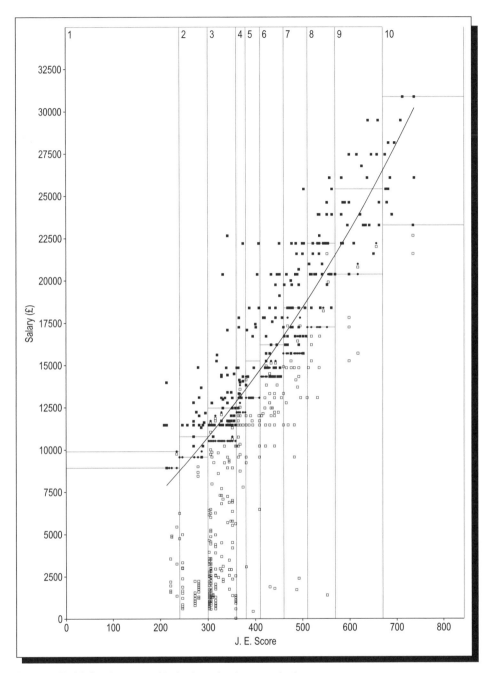

Figure 7 *Model of scattergram used to develop and cost new pay structure*

Spot rates or rate for the job

The CIPD's 2003 survey shows individualised salary rates, individual ranges or spot rates are the most popular pay arrangements for senior managers (53 per cent), middle/first-line managers (36 per cent) and manual staff (27 per cent). Manual workers traditionally worked for a single 'spot rate' for the job, with no progression of their basic pay other than via a general increase in rates. They typically also received bonus payments, but these were not routinely consolidated into basic pay, which would have made the value of them count for the calculation of benefits such as pensions or sick pay (Chapter 7).

As manual workers' jobs – certainly in manufacturing industry – decline in number so the preponderance of use of spot rates is also in decline.

More recently, though, some employers, questioning the efficacy of individual performance pay, have begun to look again at the potential of spot rates. Some of the advantages of spot rates are that the structure is simple to understand and transparent. One disadvantage is the pressure to get the rates positioned appropriately in relation to the market, where a range of market rates for most jobs is evident.

One company example of the use of spot rates is Boots the Chemist, which wanted to change the pay structure applying to 40,000 staff in the retailing business, to move away from a performance-based scale to a more transparent spot-rate structure. The company set different spot rates for each of three 'job families' – customer-facing staff, operations support staff and technicians (photographic and medical roles) – within four geographical zones. A job evaluation exercise placed jobs in each family in one of three groups (see Table 18) on the basis of the job evaluated score for 'know-how' . Each of these job-evaluated groups with the relevant job family has an entry-level spot rate and an established rate.

	Job example	Zone 1 £ph	Zone 2 £ph	Zone 3 £ph	Zone 4 £ph
Group 1 know-how points 87	Sales assistant	4.62 (4.39)	5.09 (4.83)	5.39 (5.12)	6.20 (5.89)
Group 2 know-how points 100	Baby consultant	4.89 (4.64)	5.38 (5.11)	5.70 (5.42)	6.56 (6.23)
Group 3 know-how points 115	Beauty consultant	5.29 (5.02)	5.82 (5.53)	6.17 (5.86)	7.09 (6.74)

Note: the figures shown in brackets are entry rates which apply for the first six months of employment. Staff aged under 18 are paid 80 per cent of the above rates.

Adapted from Incomes Data Services (2002, pp16–17)

Table 18 *Job family spot rate regionally based pay structure at Boots the Chemist*

Individual job range structures or pay maturity curves

At their most basic, individual job range structures are merely a variation on the spot rate theme, except that they define a separate pay range for each job rather than a single rate. The CIPD's (2003) survey shows that smaller employers (with fewer than 250 staff) tend to use individual pay rates and ranges most frequently.

Further variations on the theme of individual pay structures include a very small number of schemes that convert job evaluation points to pounds by the application of a formula. Pay (maturity or progression) curves provide different pay progression tracks, along which individuals can move according to their levels of competence and performance. Such schemes may be used in environments in which a highly individualised approach is required – for example, research scientists with unique skills in a competitive R&D context.

Graded pay structures

Traditionally, UK organisations may have liked the sense of order and social certainty that hierarchical graded structures provide. For example, in the UK Civil Service people may still refer to themselves by grade. Organisations whose culture emphasises hierarchy and status are more likely to have used graded structures, but the CIPD's 2003 survey shows that 'traditional graded' structures have become much less common within the private sector, with just 6 per cent using them for senior managers, 10 per cent for middle/first-line managers, 17 per cent for non-manual non–management and 26 per cent for manual staff.

Graded structures have a sense of order that can be appealing, with grades into which jobs of broadly equivalent value are slotted. In practice, many graded structures tend to have a narrower span of pay than more flexible ranges, with the maximum pay for each grade perhaps 50 per cent above the minimum.

The illustrative example of ICI staff's structure shows that some flexibility can be introduced while retaining a graded system (see Table 19). Grade minimum and maximum boundaries may be set by a range of job evaluation points, or there could be simpler, general grade definitions or (risky in terms of equal-value principles), even simpler, by managers slotting jobs into grades.

Grades provide scope for pay progression on the basis of service or performance, but the typically short length of grades gives rise to the potential for a large proportion of employees within each grade being 'stuck' at the top of the scale, with no further opportunity for pay progression. Grades may overlap with adjacent grades by as much as 50 per cent.

Graded structures have advantages because they:

- seem orderly
- allow employers to control costs
- are transparent.

However, the downside is that such structures:

- are often perceived as overly emphasising hierarchical relationships
- may provide little scope to cope with special salary market pressures
- when too narrow can encourage a plethora of 'upgrading claims'
- can lead to 'top of scale' problems.

The need that many organisations saw for more flexibility often found expression in broad-banding (see page 75). This need can also be met by the use of the sort of approach adopted by ICI – see Table 19 – which uses control or reference points.

Reference points

Movement through the salary ranges is performance-related. Each salary range is centred on the reference salary (100 per cent), with the minimum salary at 80 per cent and the maximum at 130 per cent. Progression to the reference point salary generally takes four to five years and is dependent upon fully satisfactory performance. Progress beyond the reference salary is dependent on performance being exceptional or outstanding. Each employee has an annual individual salary review, potentially yielding merit-based increases on top of the general increase. (Staff are also eligible for individual and group bonuses to reward a special achievement in a discrete task or where short-term performance is very good but does not justify a salary increase).

Pay spines

Pay spines, which consist of a series of incremental points stretching from the highest- to the lowest-paid job, are popular within the public sector and, to a lesser extent, in the voluntary sector. Just over half of employers in the CIPD's 2003 survey use this system to manage middle/front-line managers' (51 per cent) and white-collar staff (55 per cent) salaries, compared with around two-fifths who do so for manual workers (43 per cent) and senior managers (39 per cent). A prominent example of a pay spine is that used in the local government sector – see Table 20. This national spine is set annually following national pay

Grade	Job examples	Minimum*	Reference point*	Maximum*
25	Mailroom clerk	9,779	12,249	15,924
26	Word processor operator	10,778	13,472	17,514
27	Junior secretary, laboratory assistant	11,966	14,958	19,445
28	Secretary, research assistant	13,282	16,602	21,583
30	Scientist, senior secretary, mechanical engineering draughtsman, warehouse distribution supervisor	16,660	20,825	27,073
31	Research chemist, single-craft maintenance supervisor	18,742	23,427	30,455
32	Senior engineering designer, senior scientist	21,085	26,356	34,263
Adapted from IDS (2000) *Salary levels as at 1 June 2000				

Table 19 *Example of a graded pay structure – ICI staff*

negotiations, but has the facility for each local council to set the actual ranges of pay for specific jobs on the spine, according to local job evaluation decisions and market pay rates. Each job pay range may span four or five incremental points.

A pay spine structure is also being used in the harmonised pay arrangements for the NHS under the Agenda for Change agreement.

Broad-banded pay structures
When flexibility is required, broad-banded structures are an option. In such systems the range of pay in a band is significantly wider than in a conventional graded structure. The width of the band may be 100 per cent or even more, and there may be only four or five bands in the structure. The CIPD's (2003) survey found that broad-banded pay structures are the most popular pay structures applied to white-collar staff (29 per cent) and the second most common approach to both senior (25 per cent) and middle/line managers (32 per cent). These structures have been replacing traditional narrow-graded pay systems, reducing the number of grades and making the pay ranges wider. The pay range minimum and maximum

SPINAL COLUMN POINTS				
Sp			Sp	31	22,689
	4	10,278		32	23,358
	5	10,521		33	24,048
	6	10,668		34	24,726
	7	11,013		35	25,245
	8	11,361		36	25,911
	9	11,706		37	26,640
	10	11,949		38	27,420
	11	12,720		39	28,320
	12	12,987		40	29,067
	13	13,335		41	29,835
	14	13,581		42	30,594
	15	13,863		43	31,356
	16	14,196		44	32,127
	17	14,532		45	32,847
	18	14,817		46	33,642
	19	15,372		47	34,413
	20	15,933		48	35,181
	21	16,515		49	35,934
	22	16,944		50	36,870
	23	17,442		51	37,833
	24	18,012		52	38,784
	25	18,582		53	39,711
	26	19,185		54	40,644
	27	19,824		55	41,595
	28	20,469		56	42,558
	29	21,282		57	43,542
	30	21,993		58	44,559

Table 20 *Pay spine – local government sector, 2003*

levels are typically set in relation to salary market assessments. Jobs may be assigned to the ranges after job evaluation, or jobs may be placed in the bands purely by reference to market rates or by a combination of job evaluation and market rate analysis.

Some of the rationale of the move to broad bands relates to managers' wish to reduce the in-built incentive in narrow graded structures for individuals to seek to get their jobs upgraded, especially when they have been in a grade for a few years and are stuck at the top of the grade. Broad bands in effect can integrate an element of career development, which was hitherto only available if individuals achieved promotion to a higher grade.

Broad bands include a broader spectrum of jobs within a small number of grades or bands. The use of broad-banding therefore will encompass jobs that might previously have been in different bands or grades. Such a structure can facilitate lateral career moves within the organisation when promotion opportunities have become reduced, typically as a result of de-layering and the flattening of organisation structures.

The IPD's (1997) guide to broad-banding, based on case studies of well-known organisations, sought to identify the organisational conditions in which broad-banding can be implemented successfully. These are when:

- there is a large proportion of `knowledge workers' in the organisation
- de-layering has taken place, or is about to take place
- there is a lack of status-consciousness in the organisation
- greater flexibility in paying for the person, not the job, is needed
- managers and employees are able to live with a great deal of flexibility.

Among the pioneers of broad-banding were IBM and Reckitt & Colman. Both developed flexible approaches initially for executives, and implemented them internationally.

Incomes Data Services research (2002c and 2002d) suggests that the take-up of broad-banding has been more general than restricted to those organisational contexts described above. IDS says that the pressures in local labour markets mean a growing number of organisations are turning to pay systems based on broad bands that offer them more market flexibility. An earlier survey by Industrial Relations Services (1996) found that 26 per cent of the 270 organisations studied had introduced broad-banding and a further 10 per cent were planning to do so.

The IPD's (1997) research showed that organisations were most likely to introduce broad-banding when they were:

- undergoing 'swift and pervasive change'
- developing new pay strategies
- seeking to integrate their reward practices with other human resource processes
- aware of the need to develop levels of competence and define career paths in de-layered structures
- 'disenchanted with the inflexibility of their current system'
- devolving pay decision-making to line managers.

The IPD also pointed to the following problem areas in broad-banding:

- Broad-banding may appear to restrict promotion opportunities.
- Unions or employees may resist the change.
- Previously higher-graded staff may feel devalued.
- There may be concern about lack of precision and the 'career signposts' that more defined structures give.
- Broad-banding may be seen as subjective.
- Time and training resources have to be committed if the development is to succeed.
- Broad-banding can inflate employees' pay expectations.
- Broad-banding may make it more difficult to control pay costs.
- Traditional status considerations may be undermined.
- Broad-banding may lead to difficulties in justifying equal pay for work of equal value.

Training implications for managers
It is likely that when any flexible pay system such as broad-banding is introduced line managers will require training in the principles and practice of managing reward. Not only will they have to budget and plan, but they may also need to understand and use pay data, as well as assess individual employees' performance and/or competencies.

'Job family' structures
A 'job family' structure consists of separate pay structures for occupational groupings or 'job families'. Traditionally, organisations may have developed separate structures for occupations for which there was strong salary market competition – for instance, IT staff or accountants.

Zingheim and Schuster (2000) argue for greater use of job-evaluated systems based on job families. One of their perceived advantages is that career progression on the basis of increases in skill or competence can be planned and individuals 'can be made aware of the development opportunities available to them in their job family'.

Job family structures are used because it is felt that some occupations need distinctive treatment, in the light of market conditions and skill or competence progression. Companies with research and development divisions or departments may also prefer separate structures for specialised, high-knowledge content work, in which the level of pay can be differentiated by the level of responsibility, skill or competence. The example of Boots the Chemist on page 72 shows that job family approaches are also being used more generally.

Pharmaceutical firm Glaxo (Carrington 1989) moved away from traditional job evaluation to a system in which jobs are grouped by family – for example, finance, personnel and buying, within each of which a hierarchy is established based on proficiency (skill) levels. A pay curve for each family is established by reference to market rates.

Overall, however, as the IPD (2000) survey shows, job families are only used in a minority of organisations – 16 per cent of companies in the IPD's sample. The objectives of companies in going down the job family route were found to be related principally to providing career paths, achieving more flexibility and linking to the salary market.

Critically, job family systems can be seen as divisive in organisations that want to promote the working together of employee groups – since in some ways moves to job families run counter to the trends to harmonise pay and conditions arrangements for different groups. Another potential disadvantage is that when different job families are predominately populated by either men or women, and pay levels are different for jobs that could be seen as of 'equal value', then employers can be more vulnerable to equal pay claims than if there is a single structure.

Pay structures and pay progression

There is little point in organisations having elaborate pay structures unless they are offering employees some progression opportunities for their pay *within* the pay structure. As the CIPD (2003) and IDS (2003) surveys show, most organisations uprate the pay structures annually in line with inflation or with an agreed negotiated percentage rise. It is usual for those organisations that pay a general or 'economic' pay rise also to uprate the pay structure annually by similar percentages. A structured pay progression is in addition to this general increase, although in response to the twin influences of low inflation and greater emphasis on performance-based progression, many organisations now integrate these two elements.

Replacing traditional 'across-the-board' increases, performance-related pay became popular for most managers, as well as for non-manual staff in industry, the service sector and increasingly in the public services.

In the traditional graded structure, additional to this general increase each year would be a service increment. Some public-sector organisations continue to use service increments, although they have now largely given way to performance payments. They are also under challenge from the equal pay standpoint. However, it was at a time of consistently low inflation that service increments – typically worth 3 or 4 per cent of salary, when inflation was running at 2 to 3 per cent per annum – seemed to many organisations to have outlived their value as 'incremental' increases in pay to reflect a steady increase in skills brought about by experience in the job.

Competency-based progression grew in popularity during the 1990s, partly as a response to the inadequacies of performance pay. A number of organisations began to use this form of pay progression. For example, the Volkswagen Group developed a competency-based system that was geared to encourage lateral career moves across job families.

Bergel (1994) suggests that three 'pay delivery mechanisms' work well in a broader-banded environment: career development pay, skill-based pay and individual performance or merit pay. He argues that each offers the opportunity to use a system of rewards to support the achievement of strategic objectives, through rewarding skill acquisition, lateral career development, continuous learning and team flexibility.

STUDENT REVIEW EXERCISE

Consider the illustrated examples of pay structures at Virgin Trains (Table 23), ICI (Table 19) and National Grid (Table 22). Identify the relative strengths and drawbacks of each structure.

Separate skill-related pay structure – example from Virgin Trains

Pay for drivers employed by Virgin Trains was restructured in the wake of the Hatfield rail crash. It was agreed that the basic rate for mainline drivers with all routes and traction knowledge would be increased to £27,006 a year. The new pay structure was linked to skills and regionally based.

	ENTRY Zone	TARGET	ADVANCING	ADVANCED
BAND A Min £8,500	Max £9,500 Average annual increases of 2%–4%	Max £11,000 Average annual increases of 2%–4%, performance-linked	Normal band max £14,000 Average annual increases of 2%–4%, performance-linked	£16,800 Average annual increases of 2%–4%, performance-linked

Market premium zone: The overall maximum of the band is also extended to £18,000 (exceptional cases only) in line with an assessment of market rates.

	ENTRY Zone	TARGET	ADVANCING	ADVANCED
BAND B Min £14,000	Max £16,000 Annual increases of average 2%–4%	Max £18,000 Average annual increases of 2%–4%, performance-linked	Normal band max £20,000 Average annual increases of 2%–4%, performance-linked	£22,000 Average annual increases of 2%–4%, performance-linked

Market premium zone: The overall maximum of the band is also extended to £25,000 (exceptional cases only) in line with an assessment of market rates.

	ENTRY Zone	TARGET	ADVANCING	ADVANCED
BAND C Min £16,000	Max £19,000 Average annual increases of 2%–4%	Max £22,000 Average annual increases of 2%–4%, performance-linked	Normal max £24,000 Average annual increases of 2%–4%, performance-linked	£27,000 Average annual increases of 2%–4%, performance-linked

Market premium zone: The overall maximum of the band is also extended to £30,000 (exceptional cases only) in line with an assessment of market rates.

	ENTRY Zone	TARGET	ADVANCING	ADVANCED
BAND D Min £22,000	Max £25,000 Annual increases of average 2%–4%	Max £28,000 Average annual increases of 2%–4%, performance-linked	Normal max £32,000 Average annual increases of 2%–4%, performance-linked	£35,000 Average annual increases of 2%–4%, performance-linked

Market premium zone: The overall maximum of the band is also extended to £40,000 (exceptional cases only) in line with an assessment of market rates.

	ENTRY Zone	TARGET	ADVANCING	ADVANCED
BAND E Min £30,000	Max £35,000 Annual increases of average 2%–4%	Max £40,000 Average annual increases of 2%–4%, performance-linked	Normal max £45,000 Average annual increases of 2%–4%, performance-linked	£55,000 Average annual increases of 2%–4%, performance-linked

Market premium zone: The overall maximum of the band is also extended to £60,000 (exceptional cases only) in line with an assessment of market rates.

Entry zone is the normal 'target zone', the advancing zone becomes the target zone and so on. Pay progression payments are based on annual individual performance assessment, with the competencies in the role; sales staff are eligible for lump sum/non-cash sales incentive payments from an annual budget of about 1.5 per cent of the salaries of sales staff. These payments are linked to the achievement of specific sales targets, agreed in advance by the sales and marketing manager with the staff concerned.

Table 21 _Illustrative model of structure with competency-based pay progression, with provision for the treatment of market-rate premiums_

NATIONAL GRID PAY STRUCTURE

National Grid owns and operates the high-voltage electricity transmission network in England and Wales, carrying electricity from about 90 generating sites to the regional electricity companies. The network is made up of overhead transmission lines, pylons, underground cable and substations. Staff are primarily engaged in the control and maintenance of this system and include such skills as fitters, HV electricians, technicians, power engineers, software/IT engineers and telecom engineers.

New pay structure
The number of job groups was reduced from eight to five. The new ranges effective from 1 July 2000 incorporated the first-year basic pay increase of 4.05 per cent but the maximums and minimums of the new ranges are increased by more, in order to 'provide additional headroom and reduce overlap'.

'Reference points'
In between the highest and lowest rates on each pay band the new pay structure also includes 'reference points' that broadly correspond to the median salary for the comparative market sector. The company has said that this will enable staff in all ranges to progress to the market average salary through its performance-management arrangement. The market average had been determined with reference to the 'process industries' sector, which includes both energy sector comparators and continuous process companies whose technology is thought to 'broadly resemble' that of National Grid.

Progression up to and beyond each of the reference points will be achieved at differential rates, according to individual performance. The company foresaw two main benefits from this kind of arrangement: one is that employees who perform well are able to progress beyond the reference point; the other is that it removes the current barriers on incentives for staff currently at the top of their grades.

Minimum reference salary

Old structure				New structure			
Job group	Min	Max	Range	Min	Ref point 1	Ref point 2	Max
1	9,747	16,163	A 10,142		16,858	19,459	21,988
2	13,277	18,602					
3	15,716	21,410	B 19,459			22,373	25,286
4	18,602	26,807	C 20,603	23,725	30,697	34,839	
5	20,815	31,730					
6	28,354	37,555	D	30,780		35,380	39,979
7	37,013	46,004	E	37,525		42,404	47,916
8	41,926	50,952	E+	(No longer used)		53,016	

Adapted from IDS (2001)

Table 22 *Example pay structure – National Grid*

	Pay level*
Trainee rate	13,500
Driver competent rate	18,000
Experienced	21,150
Qualified driver, London	£pa
After 1 year	25,650
pp	2,086.80 (£40pw)
After 2 years	27,006
pp	3,130.20 (£60pw)
Qualified driver (rest of UK)	£pa
After 1 year	24,300
pp	1,043.40 (£20pw)
After 2 years	25,650
pp	2,086.80 (£40pw)
After 3 years	27,006
pp	3,130.20 (£60pw)

Pay rates effective as of May 2000

Source: IDS (2001)

Table 23   Example pay structure – Virgin Trains drivers

Percentage salary increase in the following ranges:

Competency assessment:	Individual performance against set targets:			
	Unsatisfactory	Satisfactory	More than satisfactory	Outstanding
Rarely displays competence	Nil	Deferred	Deferred	up to 3%
Inconsistently displays competence	Nil	up to 2%	up to 2%	up to 5%
Consistently displays competence	Deferred	3%	up to 5%	up to 10%
Exceeds competence requirements	Deferred	up to 5%	up to 10%	up to 15%

Table 24   *Illustrative example of pay rise matrix, using performance and competences*

Pay structure trends and gender

Research conducted in 1990–91 by Industrial Relations Services with the Equal Opportunities Commission looked at the nature of pay structures and the implications for gender differences. Among the survey's key findings were:

■ Organisations tended to group employees in separate structures for pay purposes. The average number of structures per organisation in the survey of private-sector firms was 3.6, with just 8 per cent grouping all their employees together in one structure. The rationale behind these groupings varied from organisation to organisation, reflecting a wide range of factors.

- There was very little standardisation in the coverage of pay structures that may follow occupational groupings but may be differentiated on other grounds. Whatever the coverage of pay structures, they tended nevertheless to be highly segregated and clearly dominated by either men or by women.

- Most pay structures studied were based on a grading system, averaging seven grades in length, with pay structures covering more men than women employees being longer (with greater pay progression potential) than those where women predominated.

- Very little attention had been paid by employers to assessing whether or not their pay structures provide equal pay for work of equal value. The research results suggested that many personnel managers did not appreciate the potentially wider ramifications of adopting different pay schemes for women and men when they work in different occupations.

The increasing flexibility of pay structures and the adoption of broader salary bands present problems for organisations seeking to reduce bias in their pay. The process of setting broad bands might still entail the use of job evaluation, but if these systems are used too flexibly their value as an equal-value yardstick may be diminished.

Pay structures that permit progression on the basis either of individual performance assessment or in relation to competencies/skill acquisition are quite simply not going to have anything like the easily recognisable or transparent pay rate or narrow range for the job evident in a traditional graded structure.

Revising pay structures

Before beginning to work up changes to pay structures it is vital to examine critically the reasons changes are needed. Revising a pay structure when it is the organisation's structure or career development process that needs change will clearly not solve the problem!

Some organisations seeking to revise pay structures the better to deliver greater pay equality have turned away from broad bands to narrower pay ranges. Such initiatives tend to be led by the public sector, under government direction to attempt to end the endemic equal pay problems in public services. ACAS staff (see Table 25) and the National Assembly for Wales staff are illustrative of this move.

Employee involvement in the change process

Pay structures certainly have a limited time span and tend to deteriorate over quite a short period of time (perhaps over as little as five years). Survey evidence (for example, Industrial Society 1997) tends to show that in recent years the life span of pay systems or structures has been limited. How is redevelopment of pay structures then achieved? A number of studies show that line managers are crucial in the development of effective systems and a partnership approach with employees is needed to make any aspect of pay work effectively.

In spite of the known importance of employee 'buy-in' to any new pay system, it appears in practice that restructuring of pay is largely the responsibility of the personnel department and the board. In other words it is largely a top-down, HR-driven approach.

ACAS pay structure at 1 April 2002

Grade	Job examples		Entry £pa	Step 1 £pa	Step 2 £pa	Step 3 £pa	Step 4 £pa	Step 5 £pa	Step 6 £pa
12	Administrative assistant	National	11,220	11,425	11,631	11,837	12,043	–	–
		London	15,122	15,327	15,533	15,739	15,845	–	–
11	Administrative officer	National	13,006	13,370	13,713	14,077	14,441	14,784	15,149
		London	16,908	17,272	17,615	17,979	18,343	18,686	19,051
10	Helpline staff, office supervisor	National	16,361	17,001	17,604	18,245	18,885	19,488	20,129
		London	20,263	20,903	21,506	22,147	22,787	23,390	24,031
9	Conciliator, office manager	National	21,739	22,519	23,254	24,034	24,814	25,549	26,330
		London	25,641	26,421	27,156	27,936	28,716	29,451	30,232
8	Senior adviser/conciliator, conciliation manager, resource manager	National	28,436	29,236	29,990	30,791	31,592	32,346	33,147
		London	32,338	33,138	33,892	34,693	35,494	36,248	37,049
7	Assistant director	National	35,799	37,276	38,666	40,144	41,621	43,011	44,489
		London	39,701	41,178	42,568	44,046	45,523	46,913	48,391
6	Regional director	National	48,048	49,158	50,204	51,213	52,426	53,472	54,583
		London	51,950	53,060	54,106	55,217	56,328	57,374	58,485

Adapted from IDS (2002)

Table 25 *Pay structure for ACAS Staff, implemented equal value case*

FIRE SERVICE PAY STRUCTURE – WHAT WENT WRONG?

The fire service pay formula was introduced after the first national firefighters' strike in 1977. The formula was agreed by the Government with the Fire Brigades Union as a way of avoiding strikes in this essential public service. It linked the earnings of a qualified firefighter in his or her fifth year to the upper quartile of male manual workers' earnings, as indicated by the annual *New Earnings Survey*. The formula remained unchanged for a quarter of a century, but became outdated because of shifts in the occupational structure of the workforce and the strong growth of senior levels of pay from the late 1970s onwards, which meant that the relative pay of manual workers fell in the national earnings distribution in relation to the earnings of non-manual employees. According to *IDS Report* 867, October 2002, in 1979 – just after the formula was agreed – the upper quartile of male manual workers' earnings was worth 92 per cent of the upper quartile for all male workers. By 2001 this proportion had declined to 76 per cent.

STUDENT REVIEW EXERCISE

1   Consider the value and transaction costs of HR efforts in developing new pay systems with and without involving the staff that will be affected.

2   Assess the case for and against changing the current pay structure(s) in your organisation (or an organisation you know well), analysing the organisation's use of job evaluation, its market pay rate position, pay progression arrangements in relation to service, performance/skill and/or competency development.

3   Evaluate the respective responsibilities of line managers and personnel staff, and pay budgeting and pay control processes.

4   What case is there for change, to fit with organisational priorities? What are the arguments against?

Service increments and contractual issues

When staff are no longer eligible for increments based solely on service, attention to the contractual position is needed. Almost all staff who have been receiving increments will have a contractual right to them. These entitlements can be changed within the law on contractual change, provided that staff agree to the change. In the absence of a collective or individual agreement, increments may need to be phased out over a period of time. Once a change is decided, most organisations will begin changing the contractual terms for new starters to exclude the right to increments.

Case study – Academic Services Ltd

Academic Services Ltd, a corporate offshoot of a university, devised a four-year programme to build a new reward structure that would better suit its business objectives over the next few years. The principal business challenges faced by the organisation were identified by the senior managers as:

- increasing technological sophistication in its business

- meeting the impact of changes in the wider sphere of higher education that were likely to require Academic Services Ltd to be more flexible and innovative

- facing increasing competitive pressures from other parts of its business sector

- taking advantage of market opportunities.

Meeting these challenges would require significant change for its 130 staff. Some essential key developments, as summarised by senior staff, were as follows:

- staff would need increasingly to focus on the needs of customers

- levels of professionalism required would increase ever higher

- staff would need to be more proactive in using their expertise

- the organisation would need a structure that was more integrated, rather than departmental

- the organisation would need to be more performance-oriented and to build a 'performance culture' based on continuous improvement

- the organisation would need a culture that nurtured creativity and innovation and in which flexibility was the key concept.

Management proposed building a new reward strategy and pay structure that would fit with the business strategy and key organisational structure/cultural demands.

The change process
Various consultants were contacted, and senior management decided to opt for a broadly competency-based pay structure that would fit with the development of an integrated human resources strategy – feeding into parallel programmes aimed at effecting cultural change, staff development of skills/competencies, managing performance, employee recruitment and selection.

A working party representing a broad cross-section of the organisation was set up to devise a tailor-made job evaluation scheme as a basic building block for the new pay structure. With a consultant as facilitator, the working party discussed and drafted the key factor headings and then defined levels under each heading, to be used in evaluating all jobs. These were then tested and agreed by senior management, who also directly decided the weightings to be given to each factor.

As information essential to the setting of new pay ranges, an analysis of market-pay rates was undertaken by the HR manager and proposals for the new pay ranges were put forward to senior management. The HR manager used salary market information and looked at the 'natural break points' in the rank order of job evaluation points against jobs, and crafted what she believed would be a workable structure, within an additional cost of 4 per cent of the pay bill.

The original plan had been to have a broad-banded pay structure, allowing progression within the bands on the basis of skills/competencies and pay for performance against objectives, rather than the service increments paid at present.

Currently the value of the increments – in the region of 3 per cent – was seen to be high in an era of low inflation. However, intervention by some senior managers resulted in amendments of the HR manager's plan for the company (with 190 staff) – increasing the proposed number of new bands from four to five.

As the HR manager was beginning the process of communication with staff and briefing of line managers on the new reward structure and the plans for the future, two of the most senior managers in the company asked to see her.

- They told her that they – and also, they believed, the staff – favoured a reward structure that was more open and transparent than the broader bands she was proposing, in which there would be 'no rational explanation' as to whereabouts in the bands staff would be placed.
- They intimated that they preferred the certainty and rationality of the current incremental system, where 'people knew where they stood' and managers did not have to make ' the judgement of Solomon' on individual staff pay levels.
- They said that they wanted to have a reward structure that met the new business environment in which they found themselves, but felt broad bands – even if there were five not four – represented a 'flexibility too far'. They anticipated that when, after the new pay bands had been announced and each employee had been told in which band their job was placed, there would be many complaints from staff. This, they said, was 'not on' in a small company that required some very close working relationships.
- They said that their academic colleagues in the University's legal department had also told them that transparency was a requirement under equal pay legislation, and they believed the proposed new system would be difficult to justify on these grounds.

Your task
You as HR manager must answer the points the senior managers made, and put forward any revisions to your planned approach – either in the design of the proposed system or the way it is operated and managed.

Put forward arguments both for and against a broader-banded pay structure in this organisation and for a narrower-banded system, taking into account the abilities of line managers to handle broad bands in such a way that they are fair to all in such a close-knit small organisation.

STUDENT REVIEW QUESTIONS

1 'Broad salary banding could prove a costly mistake for some organisations.' Discuss this proposition, quoting examples and research evidence.

2 Many organisations need to control pay growth costs and yet have pay structures that allow employees to significantly progress their pay. Summarise the control measures that might be used.

REFERENCES

Arthurs, A (1994) *Equal value in British banking: the Midland Bank case*, in Kahn, P and Meeham, E, *Equal value/comparable worth in the UK and the USA*. Macmillan Press.

Bergel, G (1994) Choosing the right pay delivery system to fit banding. *Compensation and Benefits Review*, Vol. 26, no. 4, July–August, pp34–38.

Brown, W, Deakin, S, Hudson, M, Pratten, C and Ryan, P (1999) *The individualisation of employment contracts in Britain*. Research paper for the Department of Trade and Industry, Centre for Business Research, Department of Applied Economics, University of Cambridge.

Carrington, L (1989) Not written on tablets of stone. *Personnel Today*, 26 September, pp27–28.

Chartered Institute of Personnel and Development (2003) *Reward Management Survey: survey report*. January. CIPD.

Incomes Data Services (2001a) *IDS Report 826*. February.

Incomes Data Services (2001b) *IDS Report 827*.

Incomes Data Services (2002a) *IDS Report 817*. September.

Incomes Data Services (2002b) *IDS Report 852*.

Incomes Data Services (2002c) Clerical & secretarial pay. *IDS Study* 737. October.

Incomes Data Services (2002d) Computer staff pay. *IDS Study* 739. November.

Incomes Data Services (2003) Pay prospects 2003/2004. *IDS Report 890*.

Industrial Relations Services (1996) *Pay in the 1990s* IRS Management Review. October.

Industrial Relations Services/Equal Opportunities Commission (1991) *Pay and gender in Britain*. IRS.

Industrial Society (1997) Managing Best Practice 39. September.

Institute of Personnel and Development (1997) *IPD guide on broad-banding*. IPD.

Institute of Personnel and Development (2000) *Survey of broad-banded and job family pay structure*. IPD.

Quaid, M (1993) *Job evaluation: the myth of equitable assessment*. University of Toronto Press.

Zingheim, P and Schuster, J (2000) Total rewards for new and old economy companies. *Compensation and Benefits Review*. Vol 32, no 6, November–December, pp20–23.

Reward in specific contexts

INTRODUCTION

Variety and diversity characterise the developing challenges of reward, with different patterns evident in different countries, in different sectors of the economy and for different occupational groups.

This chapter:

- briefly examines the international dimension and summarises the regionalisation/location-based pay debates
- refers to the occupational context and examines trends and developments in bringing terms and conditions together for different groups in a process of harmonisation and single status
- examines reward in specific sectors and occupational contexts – executive pay, public and private sector contrasts and reward in the voluntary sector.

The material in this chapter can contribute to the development of the following CIPD professional standards in reward.

Operational indicators – Practitioners should be able to:

- provide accurate and timely advice to line management, colleagues and employees on all aspects of employee reward policy and practice and the composition of an individual's reward package.

Knowledge indicators – Practitioners must understand and be able to explain:

- The factors affecting reward philosophies, strategies, policies, practices and levels of pay in organisations in the public, private and voluntary sectors, including pay determination through collective bargaining.

THE INTERNATIONAL DIMENSION

Increasing emphasis on the global dimension in reward stems from a business context in which there is much debate about globalisation, with technology allowing ever-swifter communications across continents. Greater potential for multinational corporations to switch business operations readily between different overseas locations leads to questions about relative pay costs as well as productivity. In addition greater potential mobility of people between countries also raises questions about reward strategies and comparative reward practices as well as relative levels of pay. Bradley *et al* (1999) observe that a high degree of pragmatism is evident in international reward practice, as local fiscal, institutional and/or market pressures override more strategic business intent. Much of the literature on international reward is also concerned with managing the expatriate package, rather than with strategic reward.

To begin to analyse reward more clearly from the perspective of international companies, Perkins and Hendry (1999) draw on the work of Bartlett and Ghoshal to identify what might conceptually be expected of multinational companies that are divided into the following categories on the basis of their structure: decentralised federations, co-ordinated federations, centralised hubs and the trans-national 'solution'. Table 26 (page 90) summarises Perkins and Hendry's ideas about the approaches to reward that might be appropriate within the various identified structures.

Comparative data

One of the key challenges for reward specialists working in the international arena is to overcome the difficulty in gaining information about market pay rates. An essential component is comparison. The field is under-researched by academics, there is insufficient high-quality data and there are significant institutional and cultural differences, which make formidable barriers to the making of judgements.

At the European level (via Eurostat) there are moves to increase the uniformity of pay data and inflation measures across the EU have already been harmonised. However, comparisons are fraught with difficulty because there is much more than cash-based pay to consider. As Incomes Data Services (2002a) comments, the 'social wage' is also important – employees in countries with well-developed welfare systems may accept more moderate pay in return for a sustained high level of social provision, supported by high rates of taxation and/or social charges. The variable involvement of the state in providing or setting standards for aspects of reward is a significant variable. In some countries (for example Scandinavian countries) employee benefits are principally provided by the state, whereas in the United States there is comparatively little state provision.

There has been much speculation about the development of a European-wide approach to pay as a result of the implementation of the Euro. This remains a dream for some in the European trade union movement, but for many reward specialists the tasks of managing reward rely on some perennial problems such as establishing market rates and working with variable systems of pay determination.

Institutional structures

The nature of pay determination varies considerably from country to country. Collective bargaining is variously influential in setting pay systems and structures – although, generalising broadly, it can be seen that the role of collective bargaining is declining in many countries. With increased pay system flexibility, the methods of pay determination may be less open and clearly obvious than under centralised collective bargaining systems. Flexibility in pay-setting arrangements tends to be encouraged at the political level in Europe with a view to promoting labour market flexibility, which in turn is seen as an element in creating jobs and reducing unemployment levels. For instance, the European Union's annual Broad Economic Policy Guidelines in 2002 sought to 'encourage wage formation processes that better take into account productivity and local labour market conditions'.

	Decentralised federation	Co-ordinated federation	Centralised hub	Synthesised (transnational)
Operational focus	Local identification/ exploitation of discrete opportunities	Adaptation and deployment of parent company core competences	Implementation of corporate strategies	Diverse but interdependent perspectives and capability and exploitation
Resourcing	Local self-sufficiency	Core capability sourced centrally – application dispersed	Centralised and globally scaled	Multiple and flexible co-ordination
Knowledge management	Locally emergent/ retained learning	Centralised innovation and core learning transferred to overseas units	Centrally developed/ retained learning	Shared corporate vision and individual commitment
Reward structures and processes	Minimal consistency of approach: benchmarking to local labour markets; performance rewards – based on value created in discrete markets, a share of which returned to core investor at the discretion of 'local barons'	Blueprint reward structure and systems, transfused by roving parent company agents at top levels. Disconnection between parent and local reward practice and performance objectives and recognition, other than for piecemeal 'initiatives'	Discrepancies of treatment between expatriate 'headquarters' employees and locals, both in levels and delivery of reward. Emphasis on maximising return to centre from operational 'franchises'	Respect for diverse traditions and local market regulation, but common framework for reward and performance emphasis on shared value creation and integrative dispersion among stakeholders
Taken from Perkins and Hendry (1999); developed with acknowledgement to Ghoshal and Bartlett (1998)				

Table 26 *Multinational companies: structure and approaches to reward*

The discussion on pay equality within the EU (see Chapter 6) indicates that asking key questions about why pay between men and women seems to vary significantly also begs many – difficult to answer – questions about the nature and causes of cross-national reward system differences.

Cultural contexts

Understanding different national culture contexts is another key factor for developing international reward perspectives. Milkovich and Bloom (1998) argue that for multinational corporations strategic flexibility rather than national culture should be at the fore in managing reward systems internationally.

However, Gomez-Mejia and Welbourne (1992) show how understanding cultural differences can play a role in developing systems. They use the framework developed by Hofstede (1980) to aid a cultural analysis of links between national culture and reward policies/practices. Using Hofstede's four dimensions of national culture, they seek to define how that might translate into reward policies (see Table 27).

STUDENT REVIEW EXERCISE

Consider the relative importance of national culture and company or organisation culture in setting and managing reward systems. Either reflect on your experience working in a multinational organisation or consider the example of Microsoft, first reading the profile on Microsoft by Persaud J. Keep the faithful, *People Management*, 12 June 2003. What evidence is there of the comparative influence of national and corporate culture in Microsoft's approach to HR and reward?

Principles of expatriate salary administration

CIPD (2003) summarises the literature on the administration of ex-patriate reward, identifying two principal methods:

1. **The balance sheet method** Employers offer a reward package in which employees maintain their home living standards abroad on a day-to-day expenditure basis, taking into account differences in taxation and cost of living. Incentives can be added to make the package more attractive. The concept of 'disposable income' (pay left after deductions for tax etc) is important in this method since this is the part of the salary that reflects the cost of living differences and assumes that the employee will maintain their home level of consumption in the host country.

2. **The host country method** Expatriates receive the same terms and pay as host-country nationals performing comparable jobs. This may mean they contribute to the local social security system, pension plan and pay local taxes. Certain additional benefits may be paid – for instance, free housing, school fees paid, a 'settling in' allowance and a foreign service premium paid.

Expat reward and social issues

Some companies find that regardless of the generosity of the reward package there is scope for overseas assignments to be viewed negatively by employees. In an era in which Western countries have increasing numbers of dual-career families, the extent to which relatively small additional allowances can make up for a spouse's career interruption is debatable. If children are older, then their schooling and social networks can be disrupted by a move overseas. The

Power Distance, Organisational Characteristics, and Reward Strategies

	Dominant Values	Corporate Features	Reward Strategies	Sample Countries
HIGH	■ top-down communications ■ class divisions as natural ■ status important ■ authoritarian ■ dependence on superiors ■ power symbols ■ white-collar jobs valued more than blue-collar jobs	■ centralisation and 'tall' organisation structures ■ traditional command and control	■ hierarchical reward system ■ differences in pay and benefits reflect job and status differences; large differential between upper and lower echelons ■ visible rewards that reflect power	■ Malaysia ■ Philippines ■ Mexico ■ Arab nations ■ Venezuela ■ Spain
LOW	■ egalitarian ■ joint decision-making ■ high value on participation ■ inner directed with low dependence on superiors ■ disdain for power symbols ■ hard work valued even if manual in nature	■ flatter organisational structures ■ decentralised control ■ greater reliance on matrix-type networks ■ great degree of employee involvement	■ egalitarian reward systems ■ small differences in pay and benefits beween higher- and lower-level jobs ■ participatory pay strategies such as gainsharing more prevalent	■ Netherlands ■ Australia ■ Switzerland ■ Sweden

POWER DISTANCE

Individualism, Organisational Characteristics, and Reward Strategies

	Dominant Values	Corporate Features	Reward Strategies	Sample Countries
HIGH	■ personal accomplishment ■ individual-centred ■ independence ■ individual attributions ■ internal locus of control ■ belief in creating one's own destiny ■ utilitarian relationships	■ organisations not compelled to care for employees' total well-being ■ employees look after their individual interests ■ explicit systems of control necessary to ensure compliance and prevent wide deviation from organisational norms	■ performance-based pay ■ individual achievement rewarded ■ external market emphasised ■ extrinsic rewards are important indicators of personal success ■ attempts made to isolate individual contributions (ie, who did what) ■ emphasis on short-term objectives	■ United States ■ Great Britain ■ Canada ■ New Zealand
LOW	■ team accomplishment ■ sacrifice for others ■ dependence on social unit ■ group attributions ■ external locus of control ■ belief in the hand of fate ■ moral relationships	■ organisations committed to a high level of involvement in employees' personal lives ■ loyalty to the firm is critical ■ normative, rather than formal, systems of control to ensure compliance	■ group-based performance is important criterion ■ seniority-based pay utilised ■ intrinsic rewards essential ■ internal equity is key guiding pay policy ■ personal need (eg, number of children) affects pay received	■ Singapore ■ South Korea ■ Indonesia ■ Japan ■ Taiwan

INDIVIDUALISM

Table 27 *National culture analysis and reward*

Uncertainty Avoidance, Organisational Characteristics, and Reward Strategies

UNCERTAINTY AVOIDANCE	*Dominant Values*	*Corporate Features*	*Reward Strategies*	*Sample Countries*
HIGH	■ fear of random events and the unknown ■ high value placed on stability and routine ■ low tolerance of ambiguity ■ low risk approach ■ comfort in security, lack of tension, and lack of contradictions	■ mechanistic structures ■ written rules and policies guide the firm ■ organisations strive to be predictable ■ management avoids making risky decisions ■ careful delineation of responsibilities and work flows	■ bureaucratic pay policies ■ reward systems tend to be centralised ■ fixed pay more important than variable pay ■ little discretion given to supervisor in dispensing pay	■ Greece ■ Portugal ■ Yugoslavia ■ Italy
LOW	■ unexpected viewed as challenging and exciting ■ stability and routine seen as boring ■ ambiguity seen as providing opportunities ■ high risk propensity ■ tensions and contradictions span innovation, discovery, and mastery of change	■ organic structure ■ less-structured activities ■ fewer written rules to cope with changing environmental forces ■ managers are more adaptable and tend to make riskier decisions	■ variable pay a key component in reward ■ external market emphasised ■ decentralised pay decision-making ■ much discretion given to supervisors and business units in pay allocation	■ Singapore ■ Denmark ■ Sweden ■ Hong Kong

Masculinity/Femininity, Organisational Characteristics, and Reward Strategies

MASCULINITY	*Dominant Values*	*Corporate Features*	*Reward Strategies*	*Sample Countries*
HIGH	■ material possessions important ■ men given higher power and status ■ rigidity of gender stereotypes ■ gender inequities in pay accepted	■ some occupations labelled as 'male' while others are 'female' ■ fewer women in higher-level positions	■ differential pay policies that allow for inequities by gender ■ tradition an acceptable basis for pay decisions ■ 'male' traits rewarded in promotions and other personnel decisions ■ 'paternalistic' benefits for women in the form of paid maternity leave, childcare, flexible hours etc	■ Austria ■ Mexico ■ Germany ■ United States
LOW	■ quality of life valued more than material gain ■ men not believed to be inherently superior ■ minimal gender stereotyping ■ strong belief in equal pay for jobs of equal value, regardless of gender composition	■ more flexibility in career choice for men and women ■ more women in higher-level jobs	■ jobs-evaluated system ■ focus on work content rather than tradition to assess value of different jobs ■ well-developed 'equity goals' for pay determination ■ 'masculine' traits carry no special value for promotions and other personnel decisions	■ Netherlands ■ Norway ■ Sweden ■ Finland ■ Denmark

Adapted from Gomez-Mejia and Welbourne (1992), with acknowledgement

Table 27 *continued*

ageing of the population in Western countries also means that familes may have older dependants whose welfare must be considered. Within the organisation, worries about missing out on career advancement opportunities while on overseas assignment can be a further consideration for employees – as well as feeling that they are 'out of the loop' for sharing information and making decisions. Some companies offer cultural sensitivity training and familiarisation with the potential problems of working in an unfamiliar climate and culture.

REGIONALISING PAY

Within the UK, overall average pay by region conceals substantial variation – especially, it is argued by Oswald (2002), in the private sector. Oswald attributes this to variations in the local cost of living. Responding to this in different parts of the country is particularly difficult for the public sector, which he says 'does not allow enough spatial variation in its wage rates'. Therefore, he argues, the public sector cannot compete properly for staff in high-wage parts of the country, notably in London. He suggests the right approach for the public sector is to match the pay differentials found area by area in the private sector, rather than looking at relative living costs to set flat-rate London allowances. This would mean matching the *percentage* differentials between the different regions (see Table 28). Therefore, it is suggested, if private-sector employees earn 29 per cent more in an expensive region like Surrey than in a cheap one like Humberside, then so should those in the public sector.

Region	Pay relativity
Central & Inner London	53.9%
Outer London	23.6%
Rest of South East	13.2%
West Midlands	5.0%
Greater Manchester	4.5%
West Yorkshire	4.3%
East Anglia	3.5%
Rest of North East	2.2%
East Midlands	1.8%
South West	0.9%
Tyne and Wear	0%
Rest of North West	−0.1%
Rest of West Midlands	−0.8%
Merseyside	−1.4%
Rest of Yorkshire and Humberside	−2.7%
South Yorkshire	−3.6%

Notes: Based on a 'standardised worker' and private-sector employees. All figures for Tyne and Wear are used as the base. Data drawn from the Labour Force Survey for 1996–2001. All estimates are relative to Tyne and Wear wage levels

Adapted from work by David Blanchflower, Andrew Oswald and NERA, as quoted in London Assembly (2002)

Table 28 *Estimated regional pay relativities*

Location-based pay and allowances

'London weighting' or 'London allowances' continue to be paid by most large organisations with nationwide operations. They are typically paid as flat-rate allowances – or in tiers of allowances for different areas – in recognition of the fact that the costs of living and working in the capital and other high-cost areas are above those elsewhere. The concept of a London weighting or allowance as developed in both public and private sectors was influenced by the Pay Board report in 1974. The Pay Board (1974) recommended that an allowance should be an across-the-board, flat-rate payment. The board reviewed evidence of labour shortages in London for a variety of occupations such as architects, firefighters and public health inspectors. In recommending a flat rate it reasoned that 'special payments' given to such groups would distort internal pay relativities, which had been agreed as part of the collective bargaining process. Hence, it favoured the flat-rate allowance.

Flat-rate payments, of course, apply equally to those in well-paid jobs and those in low-paid employment. Assessing the effects of this, the Low Pay Unit's (2000) analysis revealed the following.

- Although average annual earnings in London were over £29,000 (2000 data), 53 per cent of London workers earned less than £24,000 and 32 per cent earned less than £18,000.
- Household expenditure on housing costs was greater for people living in London than for any other region.
- House prices were 79 per cent above the national average at the end of 2000.
- 56 per cent of families and people living alone in Greater London were unable to get on the housing ladder.
- London Weighting made up a greater proportion of average female earnings in London than male earnings.

Research for the London Assembly (2002) by IDS showed that during the 1990s London allowances were largely frozen or only rose in line with inflation. However, in the few years preceding 2002 there was also a growing gap between pay for workers within the London public sector – for example, London weighting for junior levels in HM Customs and Excise was £615, while for certain police ranks it was more than £6,000.

The London Assembly's report (2002) also suggested that employers in the public sector might move away from flat-rate allowances. In education and health services employers have turned to this method of payment – to attempt to deal with critical recruitment and retention issues in central London. For example, the School Teachers' Review Body (STRB) has recommended the creation of a separate pay scale for inner London to help attract teachers to inner London and encourage them to stay. This introduced a £5,943 differential over all teachers outside London.

As IDS (2002b) points out, large central London allowances, though, can produce other problems for those employing staff in outer London and near London. For example, the decision to pay a combined London allowance of £6,000 across the whole of the Metropolitan Police area in July 2000 led to police forces in the rest of the South East losing staff to the Met. Subsequently, from April 2001, a system of 'two-tier' allowances was introduced for the police in the forces in the counties around London. This allowance was set at £2,000 in

Essex, Hertfordshire, Kent, Surrey and the Thames Valley and £1,000 in Bedfordshire, Hampshire and Sussex. These levels of allowance, however, still resulted in forces losing staff to the Metropolitan Police, as the £4,000 differential between the Met allowance and the next tier outside London was too large.

OCCUPATIONAL PAY DIFFERENCES AND THE TREND TO HARMONISE

Traditionally, reward packages have been very different for different occupational groups. It can be argued that the commitment of all employees is not encouraged if some are treated differently from others. Differences other than in pay tend to be divisive and difficult to justify, especially when there are different sets of benefits, according to status, in provisions such as:

- pension schemes
- sick pay schemes
- holidays
- hours of work
- insured health benefits.

Harmonisation of the elements that make up the reward package is a perennially difficult aspect of reward to manage. Cost is, of course, always an issue and could slow progress towards harmonisation. The resistance of some groups may need to be overcome. A staged approach, involving negotiation, is typically used in large organisations – for example in the public sector.

There tend to be two main spurs to moves to harmonise terms:

- *manual and non-manual* groups being brought together to create '*single-status*' conditions in previously differently treated groups, within the same organisation
- organisational harmonisation of terms and conditions following *merger*, bringing together the often distinctly different arrangements used in the pre-merger organisations.

Single-status developments

Traditionally in the UK there were substantial differences in the terms and conditions applying to manual workers and those for non-manual workers. While a series of developments have resulted in the bringing together of blue-collar and white-collar terms in many organisations, it can be argued (as does Russell 1998) that the significant divide is now either between those who have relatively secure full-time 'core' jobs and those who are in 'peripheral' work. Sisson and Storey (2000) suggest that the key divide is now between managerial and professional groups on the one hand and the rest of the workforce on the other. Indeed, Cully *et al* (1998) show from the 1998 Workplace Employee Relations survey that just 41 per cent of workplaces report they have 'single-status' conditions between managers and non-managerial employees. Even when there have been moves to harmonise terms and conditions, these may not have been completed successfully (Price and Price 1994).

Harmonisation and high-performance work systems

Harmonisation or single status has been associated with the development of what have been termed high-performance work systems. Many organisations had complex arrays of allowances, varying for different employee categories that became difficult to manage. It also discouraged the development of teamwork when staff working together as a team had different allowances, overtime entitlements and bonuses. It was the pursuit of more harmonious industrial relations and the drive to modernise working practices for greater employee flexibility that influenced the development of harmonisation in the 1980s and 1990s. An Industrial Relations Services (1993) survey reviewing single-status developments found that employers cited two principal motives – related to fairness/removal of unjustifiable differentials and easing the introduction of new working practices. In practice the most common advantages of the introduction of harmonisation were reported by the companies as improved industrial relations, with a weakening of the adversarial 'them and us' approach, and greater flexibility on the part of the workforce. The most significant disadvantages quoted related to the increased cost of the new terms and the creation of 'unrealistic' expectations among employees of further improvements in terms and conditions.

The harmonisation of contractual working hours has had the effect of containing paid overtime levels for manual workers, and there are – as Incomes Data Services (2002a) shows – continuing moves in a number of sectors to harmonise the basic working week. Significant differences still remain, with 40 per cent of manual workers on a basic week of 39 hours – 35 hours remaining popular as a non-harmonising basic week for non-manuals. From the practical point of view, harmonising basic hours can be one of the most problematic for organisations to handle. The NHS is moving down this route, and this is taking time and money. Of course, it could be argued that with so many employees 'voluntarily' choosing to work more than their nominated hours, the contractual hours issue assumes less significance.

Organisational harmonisation

Harmonisation of pay and conditions as a result of business transfer or restructuring can prove tricky. The Transfer of Undertakings (Protection of Employment) Regulations (TUPE) significantly affect employer practice, as is illustrated in the example of AXA Sun Life (see page 98).

Under the Transfer of Undertakings (Protection of Employment) Regulations 1981 (SI 1794), as amended implementing the EU Acquired Rights, the following conditions apply.

- Employees employed by the previous employer when the undertaking changes hands automatically become employees of the new employer on the same terms and conditions. It is as if their contracts of employment had originally been made with the new employer.

- Certain occupational pension rights are not protected, although there is an agreement that in the public sector public services staff transferred under contracting-out or public/private-sector partnership arrangements are entitled to pension rights that are equal to those provided by the public-sector employer.

- Representatives of affected employees have a right to be informed about the transfer. They must also be consulted about any measures which the old or new employer envisages taking concerning affected employees.

The Regulations apply when an undertaking or part of an undertaking is transferred from one employer to another. They apply to the transfer of a large business with many thousands of employees or of a very small one. The Regulations apply equally to public- or private-sector undertakings.

Company example of post-merger harmonisation: AXA Sun Life

When Sun Life Assurance merged with AXA Equity and Law in 1997, the new company, then employing about 5,000 staff, set about harmonising the different terms and conditions. A specialist HR team was set up to work on the project, and were set some tough guidelines:

- costs of harmonisation had to be cost-neutral
- TUPE constraints meant that new terms could not represent any overall detriment to the employee
- the parent company wished the new terms to support their objective to build a 'performance culture'.

The HR team decided that it would not try to harmonise in one go, but rather created 'clusters' of terms and conditions, setting up working parties in each cluster. HR also established weekly meetings with union representatives and before any changes were implemented a joint consultation paper was issued to staff. After feedback from staff, formal joint negotiations took place.

The pay and grading structure was revised to merge the different approaches and philosophies in the two previous companies – one had had a structure based on a larger number of narrower grades, while the other had de-layered the organisation and used fewer, broader bands. One paid a 'cost of living' general salary increase each year plus individual performance pay, while the other only uprated salary ranges in line with salary market assessments, but had a range of both individual and group performance payments available.

The new structure looked more like the broader bands previously used by one company and progression was performance based. Staff transferred to the new structure on the basis of their current salary – with red-circling of staff moved to a lower grade. This task was eased as both companies had been using the same job evaluation method (Hay).

In terms of bonus and profit-sharing potential, a new scheme reflected the higher bonus potential previously available in one company.

Overtime pay generated concern from the union, and while it was decided to harmonise to the lower levels of paid overtime previously implemented in one of the companies, there were transitional arrangements agreed and a deferred implementation date.

The two companies had different holiday entitlements and flexitime arrangements. One company had more flexitime working than the other, and a variety of different working patterns. The merged terms gave a higher basic holiday entitlement, but did not allow so many 'flexi days' to be accrued under the flexitime scheme.

Changed arrangements to both private medical insurance and maternity leave/pay were made to merge the terms previously existing – in certain instances compensating for a reduction in one term by an increase in another.

There were problems in merging the pension schemes, which were not dealt with straightaway. (Adapted from: Case study: AXA Sun Life: post-merger harmonisation of terms and conditions, *IDS Report* 784, May 1999.)

Case study – Corporate Publishing Ltd

Corporate Publishing Ltd (CPL) is a successful publisher and, in common with other family-owned firms in the sector, it has strong product lines and a stable organisational structure. The Board of Directors is seeking to build a working alliance with other firms in the sector to stave off an unwelcome potential takeover from the ruthless US–European-owned Deadly Knight Publishing Inc.

Changes in family circumstances (a divorce and re-marriage) of the principal owner of the firm (and a consequent reassigning of company shares) have led the previously 'not for sale' company to become more vulnerable than before to a takeover.

CPL is regarded highly by its customers for its innovative developments in electronic publishing, in which it had developed market-leading skills. However, to achieve further product market development CPL will need to work closely with others in the sector, as it simply does not have the resources to go it alone in what would be highly capital-intensive developments.

One problem that seems to be hampering harmonious working relationships within the company is that it is widely believed by other employees and indeed by others working in the sector that a number of the most senior editorial staff of CPL are very highly paid in relation to those in other firms. The board of CPL want these senior staff to be at the forefront of the company's move to expand its product development strategy and build on its current excellent work in developing electronic products. The board sees no particular reason to alter their pay arrangements – indeed, their rather *ad hoc* approach to pay has remained virtually the same for about 30 years. There are no pay scales or systems in place and no trade unions are recognised for collective bargaining on pay.

There is however a problem on which the senior management is focused at present. At the company's main production facility – in the Home Counties, near to Gatwick Airport – there is a high rate of staff turnover, as the area is a noted 'hotspot' with very low levels of unemployment, plenty of job vacancies locally and fast connections to central London.

Student review task
You are appointed reward manager to the company and given a very specific brief.

- Consider whether harmonisation of terms and conditions is necessary, and what information is needed before a decision can be taken on any changes.
- Consider the extent to which a regionally based pay structure would be appropriate.

- Determine whether or not trying to implement total reward concepts would be appropriate.

- Identify what form and nature of consultation and communication with line managers and employees would be needed before you can finalise any plans.

- Indicate your preliminary judgements about the market positioning of the current pay packages.

Your initial report back to the board is needed within 10 days.

EXECUTIVES – A GROUP APART

The trend to harmonise terms and conditions in large companies has largely bypassed directors of companies, who are invariably set apart from the generality of employees when reward packages are considered. Amidst the plethora of views expressed on executive pay, some have agreed with Adrian Cadbury (1995), who argued: 'What we want is a consistent policy on salaries, benefits and any form of add-ons that run throughout the company. There has been a divorce between directors' salaries and what happens elsewhere in the company. Quite apart from not being good personnel practice, it leads to dissatisfaction.'

There is little evidence of organisations adopting organisation-wide reward policies – and even reward managers whose role covers the whole company may find their remit does not run to board level. This is in spite of the fact that directors of modern corporations are not usually owners of their respective businesses, but employees, working under employment contracts.

Theoretically this might suggest that, as agency theory provides, directors should be incentivised to perform at their best on behalf of a company they do not own. Shareholders could, in the words of Gregg *et al* (1993), 'monitor the performance of top executives and award them pay increases that are concomitant with their work effort'. Research by Gregg *et al* and others indicates that practice is different, with only weak links at best between directors' emoluments and their company's financial performance.

Setting the contours of the executive pay package

It is not just in recent times that top executive pay has been debated. In the mid-1970s a Royal Commission on the Distribution of Income and Wealth (chaired by Lord Diamond) concluded that 'whilst company size ... and profitability ... influence the level of remuneration of the highest-paid director, the relationship is not a particularly close one'. If not corporate performance, what does set the ever-increasing (PIRC 2003) levels of executive pay? The Monks Partnership (1999), which produced some of the most widely used pay data on executives, said that the three main factors influencing board-level earnings were 'company size, degree of international involvement and function'.

The resulting executive remuneration package can be complex. In essence, as the Greenbury Committee – set up to examine corporate government issues – reported (Greenbury 1995), the following elements are typically included in the executive reward package:

- basic salary
- benefits
- annual bonus

- share options
- other long-term incentives
- pension.

Most executive pay surveys indicate that the basic or base salary is worth perhaps 60 to 70 per cent of total cash earnings – excluding the value of share options or non-cash benefits.

External pay survey data

In the 1970s the Diamond Commission pointed to the influential use of market data (salary surveys) in setting executive pay. A quarter of a century later, the use of pay data remains strong and the remuneration consultants who provide data are still influential. A survey by Watson Wyatt in 1998 concluded that the most important influence on pay movements and pay levels for top executives was market data. For most companies this means comparability with others in the same sector on either a national or international basis.

It is this comparative element that can potentially (though not inevitably) lead to inflationary pay trends. Many, but not all, companies set a level in the market at which they would like to pitch their salary levels. (Watson Wyatt reported in its survey that two-thirds of companies that set a level wanted to pay at median levels in comparison with other companies in the same sector, and a third wanted to be 'upper quartile' payers.)

The Diamond Commission suggested that the market and market pay data logically might be thought to have a greater effect on smaller businesses, which must more often recruit externally at board level. However, the reverse seems to be true.

Two decades after the Diamond Commission, these issues were still being debated by the Greenbury Committee and Hampel Committee (1998), which also made recommendations on corporate government issues. The problem of 'ratcheting up' was addressed in the following terms by Hampel:

> **Remuneration Committees should judge where to position their company relative to other companies. They should be aware of what comparable companies are paying and should take account of relative performance. But they should use such comparisons with caution, in view of the risk that they can result in an upward ratchet of remuneration levels with no corresponding improvement in performance.**

Clarke *et al* (1998) found that 72 per cent of company chairmen in a survey mostly drawn from companies in the FTSE 250 indicated they used data/advice from consultants to set basic salaries at the top. However, the evidence on links between pay and performance at executive level are less clear.

The evidence that market rate data are used does not, of course, indicate the existence of a market. The Greenbury Committee (Greenbury 1995) commented that while 'market forces set a broad framework', '*the market is imperfect*'. In large companies many directors and senior executives '*spend much or all of their working lives with the same organisation*'. Board-level pay is set by remuneration committees which, as Greenbury remarked, '*have quite a wide range of discretion in setting levels and forms of pay*'. It is the judgement of these committees that is called into question.

The dispersion of earnings is now significantly wider than in the 1970s when the compression of differentials was causing problems at senior levels, and the Diamond Commission found that there was a higher differential between the lowest (manual) rate of pay and that of the highest-paid director in the UK than in some other countries. Greenbury's international perspective looked at absolute levels of pay and commented that UK levels lay within the range of European practice, and were substantially below those in the United States. A widening-out in the dispersion of pay has occurred, as higher rates of pay have increased at a faster pace than lower-level pay rates. This trend is more evident in the UK than in many other industrial countries (TUC 1998).

Shareholders and other 'stakeholders'

Greenbury (1995) recommended that those responsible for setting top pay should be 'sensitive' to the wider scene, including pay and employment conditions elsewhere in the company. An example of a sector in which that is done is the mutual societies – which tend, according to Incomes Data Services (1999b), to take a wider range of criteria into account than do plcs in setting the incentive element in top executive pay. At Bradford and Bingley, for example, the executive incentive scheme takes into account both customer satisfaction and employee satisfaction indicators in determining the level of remuneration.

Executive share options are commonly found. The Hempel Committee (1998) recommended that executives should hold shares rather than options. In the United States, William M Mercer (1999) comments that about 40 per cent of companies stipulate that executives should hold a minimum number of shares in the company (enforced by contractual condition). IDS found only five companies in the UK top 350 listed companies with similar conditions – British Aerospace, Rio Tinto, SmithKline Beecham, GlaxoWellcome and BP Amoco. Industrial Relations Services (1999) reported a growth in the use of performance conditions to the circumstances in which options could be exercised by executives.

Links with performance

Long-term incentive plans have grown in popularity following the Greenbury report (Greenbury 1995) and in the wake of criticism of share option schemes. Various executive salary surveys indicate that additional cash payments (including incentive payments) account for a minority of the package in most instances, except in the case of owner-managers of small firms. The influential study by Gregg *et al* (1993) of the links between executive pay and performance in 288 companies during the period 1983–1991 concluded that the growth of executives' compensation was insignificantly related to corporate performance, declining markedly in the recessionary period after 1988.

The basic salary may account for perhaps 60–70 per cent of the total value of the earnings package – not counting non-cash benefits such as pension, car, share option (before exercise) and so on. And it is basic salary that tends to be set in relation to external market pay data. It is therefore perhaps not surprising that purely statistically based academic research looking at links between pay and performance find the data difficult to interpret, since in a year when the market pay rates have gone up executives may receive a substantial basic salary rise, even as poorer corporate financial performance means that bonus payments are down.

The institutional investors are influential in this area and the Association of British Insurers (ABI) guidelines give encouragement to companies to set '*challenging performance conditions*', and for the measures of performance used in incentive schemes to be disclosed.

STUDENT REVIEW EXERCISE

Search out some company annual reports and analyse what is said about executive incentive or bonus payments. Using agency theory (see page 15) as a framework for your analysis, summarise the arguments for and against the use of incentive payments at top executive level. If you consider incentive payments are not appropriate, what do you consider should be the basis for setting executive pay?

Regulation and corporate governance

The public policy debates on executive pay have tended to centre on corporate governance issues. In 1999, the then Secretary of State for Trade and Industry, Stephen Byers, announced the Labour Government's intention to 'modernise company law':

> Corporate governance is a crucial aspect of strengthening national financial systems; and of promoting accountability, transparency, growth and investor confidence in an increasingly globalised business sector.

However, Mr Byers also spoke in favour of strengthening the link between executive pay and performance, using the watchwords accountability, transparency and performance. The Cadbury, Greenbury and Hampel committees' recommendations sought to encourage greater openness and taking a wider view in the setting of pay for directors. There were some indications that, post-Greenbury, some companies were including more information on executive remuneration packages in their annual reports, but this was only rarely related to individual managers.

Many critics of executive remuneration believed there to be a need for some form of regulation of executive remuneration, whether voluntary or compulsory. In 2002, Patricia Hewitt, then Secretary of State for Trade and Industry, passed regulations to enforce greater transparency. The Directors Remuneration Report Regulations 2002 required quoted companies to publish an annual report on directors' remuneration, containing details of:

- individual directors' remuneration packages
- remuneration policy
- the Remuneration Committee and its advisers
- company policy on the duration of directors' contracts, notice periods and termination payments
- any payments made in respect of loss of office, and an explanation of any such payments.

The report must also display a line graph showing company performance. Companies are obliged to put an annual resolution to shareholders on the remuneration report.

Case study – New Age Airline

New Age Airline is one of the new wave of airlines operating in a highly competitive sector. Started by a gifted entrepreneur, New Age has eschewed the no-frills ultra-low-cost market in favour of competing on more conventional terms, primarily in the European and Australasian sectors. The aftermath of the terrorist attack on New York City on September 11 2001 and changes in the regulatory framework in Europe and the United States have contributed to both increased costs and very tight margins. There were significant redundancies in the company as the volume of business dipped. The company is relatively heavily unionised and pay for most staff is collectively bargained with a staff union. Pay for the airline's pilots is decided after consultation with the pilots' union. Managers' pay is set on an individualised basis, with senior executives qualifying for share options. Levels of basic pay in the company are set generally to be in the lower part of the salary market, within the inter-quartile range from lower quartile to median. There is a strong, innovative and performance-oriented culture in this company with a 'young', informal atmosphere. All staff are eligible for performance-based lump sum bonuses, based on corporate profitability. In the last two years performance has not reached the necessary target levels for such payments to be triggered.

The company has decided to appoint a new business development director to spearhead the company's plans to develop and keep ahead of the competition. After a protracted search a most suitable candidate has been identified, with very relevant experience in turning around a struggling US domestic airline, with some international routes across the Pacific. He is American and is very interested in taking a more international role, based in London – a city he is keen on living in. He has, however, been disappointed that, although his title would be director, he would – in line with practice in many UK companies – not in fact be a member of the board of directors. In addition, he is disappointed about the level of share options offered with the post, which are far short of those he would expect in a comparable role in the United States. He and his family have investigated the costs of living in London and he is asking for a basic salary of £200,000, plus share options and annual cash bonuses.

Your role
Your role is as reward adviser to the company, and you are asked by the managing director to consider:

- the market rate for the job
- any implications for reward policy in relation to other employees in the company, and the staff relations and related issues if news of an enhanced package leaked out
- any implications of moves for greater transparency in setting top executive pay.

The MD has made it clear to you that the board will decide on the level of basic pay to be offered, but that your input will be important information for them in reaching a decision. You do not know the exact extent of the remuneration packages of the board members themselves – as this information is held in some secrecy and only known to the MD and the Company Secretary.

You have collected some market rate data, but the job itself does not fit closely with the analysis categories used in the main management salary surveys. You would like to contact the other UK-based airlines to exchange relevant salary information, but confidentiality about the nature of this new post is rather too commercially sensitive to permit a useful exchange.

The surveys you have selected, while rather broad-brush, have the advantage of largish samples, and you consider that this data might be most useful in this exercise. The company's annual sales turnover is approx £700 million.

Survey A shows that for companies with a turnover exceeding £500 million.

Heads of major divisions (below board level) earn:

	Lower quartile	Median	Upper quartile
Basic	£62,000	£80,000	£170,000
Total cash	£63,000	£90,000	£195,000

Top sales posts (including business development and all sales director posts) are shown with market rates of:

	Lower quartile	Median	Upper quartile
Total cash	£88,500	£121,000	£179,000

Survey B shows for companies of a similar size:

Median basic salary – for a 'function head' not on the board £127,000, plus median bonus £25,000.

Your task
Write the outline of a report for the MD dealing with the three aspects he has specified (as set out above). In framing your recommendations/interpretations, consider the:

- implications of the new reporting regime on executive pay
- implications for the general staff (making any reasonable assumptions)
- attributes of salary survey data collection, which are associated with better quality data in interpreting the market rate data to which you have access.

PUBLIC-SECTOR AND PRIVATE-SECTOR CONTRASTS

The Diamond Commission in the 1970s first highlighted a problem that became exacerbated during the years of expansion of executive pay: *'High salaries in the private sector put pressure on public-sector salaries'*. The public sector employs five million people in the UK, a fifth of the workforce. Setting public-sector pay is particularly problematic since there are, of necessity, limited market forces. There is no private-sector equivalent of the army or the police force, for example. There may be competition with the private sector for administrative staff or some other occupations, but for many – especially at very senior or specialist jobs – there are quite simply no directly comparable jobs.

Directly or indirectly the government is instrumental in setting pay for public-sector groups and this process entails as much political as it does economic judgement. R Elliot's (1999) analysis (Figure 8) shows the trends that have been evident for two decades – namely, that, whereas earnings for lower-paid staff in the public sector have tended to be fairly competitive, managerial pay levels have failed to keep pace with the inexorable rise of senior pay levels in the private sector.

The UK Labour Government has embarked on a process of 'modernisation' of public-sector pay. In part, as Incomes Data Services (2003) shows, the focus is on attempts to deliver more equal pay in the public services (many of which are highly vulnerable to legal equal pay claims). In addition, the public sector's pay agenda, across a wide range of organisations, covers:

■ individual performance pay and incentive systems in response to employee feedback that many schemes are ineffective

■ comparative pay rates, which are necessary to enable the public sector to compete in the labour market

■ regional v centralised pay determination systems

■ improved performance management to expedite service delivery

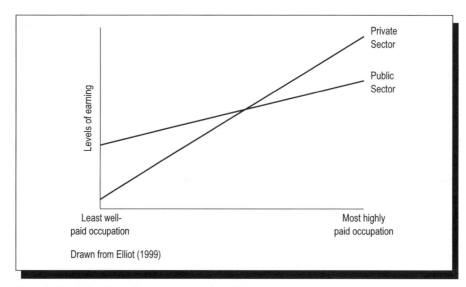

Figure 8   *Trends in public- and private-sector earnings: UK*

■ following the Mackinson report recommending changes in Civil Service pay, potentially greater use of non-consolidated bonus payments to reward performance.

Table 29 illustrates the levels of pay and pay progression potential in well-known public-sector work. With the exception of nurses, most of the other occupations in the table do not receive shift payments. Only police officers and ambulance staff receive overtime pay.

As the Senior Salaries Review Body – recommending appropriate pay and benefits for top civil servants, top brass in the military and for the judiciary – shows in its annual reports, there is a balance to be struck between competing with the private sector and the public acceptability of high pay levels in the public service.

Job	Basic salary after 5 years' service	Max salary	London allowance	Overtime pay	Shift premium levels
Firefighter	21,531	22,491	3,171	No	No
Police officer	23,727	28,905	6,165*	Yes	No
Teacher	22,092	32,217	3,105 (inner)	No	No
Ambulance crews	18,079 (spot rate for qualified staff)**	–	2,135	Yes	No
Armed forces	20,546 (corporal, level 1)	26,280 (corporal, level 7)	–	No	No
Nurse	17,670 (top of grade D)	23,250 (top of grade F)	3,228 (inner) plus 4%***	No	Yes

*For police officers recruited since 1994, who do not receive housing allowances. Officers in post before then receive a lower level of London allowance and a housing allowance.

**Ambulance staff with full paramedical skills receive an additional allowance worth £933 a year.

*** Cost-of-living supplement

Source: www.bbc.co.uk based on Incomes Data Services' data, 2002b

Table 29 *Pay packages for some public-sector occupations, 2002*

An analysis by Hay remuneration consultants (Figure 9, below) showed the senior Civil Service significantly adrift of private-sector pay – the picture worsening progressively at top levels in the Civil Service.

THE VOLUNTARY SECTOR

From the 1980s onwards the voluntary sector in the UK grew as changes in government policy on social welfare provision expanded the role of charities, especially in delivering services that might previously have been provided by the public sector. Increasingly, staff formerly employed by local authorities worked in the voluntary sector, following employment transfer. As Cunningham (2000) points out, the traditional 'rewards' and 'psychological contract' of work in the voluntary sector might be under threat, because some of the staff now in voluntary organisations have been transferred under 'contracting-out' arrangements from the public sector. This might alter the 'psychological contract' because new funding regimes imply stricter performance management regimes.

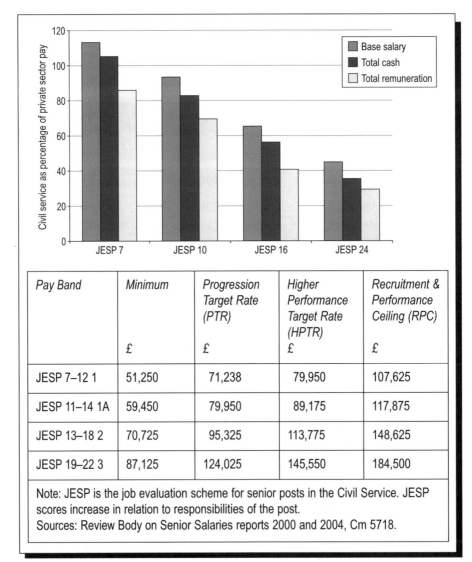

Pay Band	Minimum	Progression Target Rate (PTR)	Higher Performance Target Rate (HPTR)	Recruitment & Performance Ceiling (RPC)
	£	£	£	£
JESP 7–12 1	51,250	71,238	79,950	107,625
JESP 11–14 1A	59,450	79,950	89,175	117,875
JESP 13–18 2	70,725	95,325	113,775	148,625
JESP 19–22 3	87,125	124,025	145,550	184,500

Note: JESP is the job evaluation scheme for senior posts in the Civil Service. JESP scores increase in relation to responsibilities of the post.
Sources: Review Body on Senior Salaries reports 2000 and 2004, Cm 5718.

Figure 9 *Comparisons between senior civil servants' pay and private-sector comparators*

Voluntary-sector employment was traditionally associated with 'intrinsic rewards' such as variety of work and autonomy. If the work environment no longer supports such 'rewards', then more attention to 'extrinsic' rewards might come to the fore. Cunningham's survey of voluntary organisations revealed that one-third of the sample had changed their reward packages in the previous three years:

- breaking established comparability links with public-sector pay
- reducing incremental provisions
- cutting holiday and/or sick pay entitlements
- reducing employers' pension contributions
- increasing the amount of unsociable hours working undertaken by employees.

The main spur to the above changes was related to financial restrictions.

More broadly, the growth in size of many voluntary-sector organisations can – as in the case study below – put pressure on more informal reward structure practices, especially when these draw on the various practices of the public-sector organisations with which they have the closest staffing links. This leads many organisations to seek a firmer and more justifiable base for determining salary and benefits levels that better meet the needs of the organisation. The governance of voluntary organisations may also add pressure for any reward developments to meet what are perceived as the tenets of 'best practice' in industry and to comply with the law.

The following case study of a hospice in the voluntary sector picks up some of these themes – especially the problems for a small, cash-poor organisation looking to harmonise terms and conditions, when a large public-sector workforce provides competition for staff and, effectively, sets the 'going' rates of pay in certain occupational categories. It also illustrates the practical resourcing difficulties in providing a round-the-clock service, when compliance with the Working Time Regulations comes into play.

Case study – St Cares Hospice

St Cares Hospice is expanding the service it provides to its dying patients. For some years it has provided a day care centre where patients can come for palliative care, and it has also provided a limited residential 'respite care' service, so that the families who care for relatives with fatal illnesses can have a few days' holiday. Recently, it has inherited a manor house near its day centre (on the outskirts of London). The house was bequeathed by a former patient, now deceased, to the hospice on the condition that a residential hospice was established there. There are tight time limits within which it has to be converted for such use and staffed.

Currently, the day centre employs just three qualified nurses (at Sister level) who are responsible for the day–to-day provision of clinical care. They manage the health care assistants or nursing auxiliaries (non-qualified nurses) – paid on an hourly basis to look after patients' basic care needs – for example, in bathing, dressing and feeding. The centre finds it is difficult to get enough such staff – especially to cover less popular shifts. When working on night shift, looking after respite care patients, both qualified and non-qualified nurses frequently work through their allotted breaks at difficult times – for instance, when patients are dying. A particular problem for the hospice's chief executive is that he will need to at least treble the number of both qualified and unqualified nursing staff to be able to run a residential service.

The chief executive and his senior team realise that an effective reward system will be crucial in staffing the new set-up, and they recognise that the current approach is haphazard, with people being paid according to the terms and conditions of their work before they were employed by the hospice.

He and the board of trustees of the hospice get together and identify some of the principles they think should underpin their approach to rewarding staff in the future.

- The hospice reward system will be developed with staff involvement.
- Legally the hospice must ensure it provides equal pay for work of equal value and complies with the working time legislation.
- The nature of work at the hospice means that staff must be flexible in responding to clients' needs, while recognising the needs of employees to balance work and home-life needs.
- They need to establish some consistency between the pay and benefits for the staff of the hospice and those in the 'trading' area of the organisation, which includes the 'corporate' fundraisers and managers of the charity shops (which together provide the main source of funding for the hospice).
- The hospice will determine its own salary levels but has to be responsive to salary market pressures, and will have particular regard to the rates and terms on offer in the local hospital, and to directly comparable organisations such as other hospices.
- The hospice intends to retain the bonus payments available in the 'trading areas' of the organisation, as these bonuses are popular with staff – hospice staff have mixed views on performance pay.

Your role and task
The hospice asks you to suggest a practical way forward. Your starting point is to analyse the data you are given on the current pay and benefits of individual members of staff (St Cares Table 1); and to assess some of the market rate survey data the hospice has acquired (St Cares Table 2). You also need to give advice on the legal pay and benefits issues mentioned above.

Write a report for senior management to identify in outline the way in which the hospice could develop its reward system within the given constraints and in line with the facts that you are given. You may make any other reasonable assumptions in arriving at your recommendations.

Any recommended additional expenditure needs to be formally justified and agreed by the board – and cannot be guaranteed. Be mindful of the constraints on finance in such a voluntary-sector organisation.

St Cares Hospice: current salaries and main terms/conditions

Table 1 St Cares Hospice staff annualised salary levels (1999), contractual standard full-time hours (equivalent), retirement dates and holiday entitlement

Job	Salary	Full-time hours	Retirement age	Holidays
Chief Executive	40,750	37.5	65	5 wks+Bankhols
Director Patient Services	36,200	37.5	65	5 wks+stat days
Head of Fundraising &PR	31,500	37.5	65	5 wks+stat days
Day Care Sister i/c	24,403	37.5	State ret age	5 wks+stat days
Area Shops Manager	23,500	35	63	5 weeks
Deputy sisters (qualified nurses):				
(1)	p/t 12,394	n/a	State ret age	5 weeks
(2)	p/t 8,263	n/a	State ret age	5 weeks
Fundraising Co-ordinator	17,000 plus bonus	35	63	5 weeks
PA to Director	16,300	35	63	5 weeks
Fundraising Associate	16,000 plus bonus	37.5	65	5 wks+stat
Shop managers:				
(1)	15,000 plus bonus	35	63	5 weeks
(2)	11,991	37.5	65	5 weeks
(3)	11,589	37.5	65	5 weeks
(4)	11,497	37.5	65	5 weeks
(5)	11,302	35	63	5 weeks
Fundraising Asst	10,815	37.5	65	5 weeks
Deputy shop managers	£5.10 or 5.25 per hour	n/a	65	None
Nursing Auxiliary	£6.17 per hour	n/a	65	4 weeks
Cleaner	£5.80 per hour	n/a	63	16 hours a year

Table 2 Comparative pay data

(a) The local hospital NHS Trust actual pay rates (1999):
Health care assistants – lowest grade
Min £10,760 – Max £12,776
Health care assistants – Grade 2 Must have NVQ level 2 qualification
£12,746 – £13,186
Health care assistants – Grade 3 NVQ level 3 qualification
£13,000 – £13,500 pa
Hourly rates for Nursing Auxilliary staff range from £5.75 an hour on weekdays to £8.91 an hour on Sundays/Bank holidays
(b) Commercial survey data collected from a charities survey, October 1998 – full-time salary levels

Job	Lower quartile	Median	Upper quartile
Chief Executive	39,422	46,539	57,875
Director	32,000	36,000	45,879
Appeals/fund-raising manager	23,633	25,959	29,851
Office manager	n/a	23,018	n/a
Staff nurse/SRN	15,301	18,004	21,110
Enrolled nurse/SEN	12,024	13,500	14,976
Shop manager –large shops	11,817	14,681	18,797
–small shops	8,985	9,134	11,452
Care worker	9,359	10,151	11,273
Cleaner	8,112	8,709	9,750

Salary survey of other hospices – 1998

Job	Lower quartile	Median	Upper quartile
Qualified nurse	14,648	15,593	16,350
Health care assistant	8,984	9,613	9,972
Matron/manager	25,232	27,584	30,333

STUDENT REVIEW QUESTIONS

1. 'Harmonisation and integration of all reward systems from top to bottom across the whole organisation is an unachievable ideal.' Discuss, using company examples.

2. 'It is not just in charity-sector work that employers should consider intrinsic value and motivation in shaping their reward packages.' Discuss this with reference to three different types of work in different sectors.

REFERENCES

Bradley, P, Hendry, C and Perkins, S (1999) *International values in reward strategy*, in Brewster, C and Harris, H (evs) *International HRM: Contempory issues in Europe.* Routledge.

Cadbury, A (1995) as quoted in Littlefield, D, Personnel looks to pay role after Greenbury hint. *People Management*, August.

CIPD (2002a) *Total reward.* Quick Fact Sheet, updated December 2002.

CIPD (2002b) *Total reward: executive briefing.* CIPD.

CIPD (2003) *Managing international assignments.* Quick Fact Sheet, updated July 2003.

Clarke, R, Conyon, M and Peck, S (1998) Corporate governance and directors' remuneration: views from the top. *Business Strategy Review*, Vol 9, no 4.

Cully, M, O'Reilly, A and Millward, N (1998) *The 1998 Workplace Employee Relations Survey: first findings.* Department of Trade and Industry.

Cunningham, I (2000) Sweet Charity! Managing employee commitment in the UK voluntary sector. *Employee Relations.* Vol 23, no 3.

Diamond Commission (1974) – see Royal Commission on the Distribution of Income and Wealth (Chairman Lord Diamond), Report No 3, Cmnd 6383, 1974.

Elliot, R (1999) *Public-sector pay determination in the EU.* Macmillan Press.

Evans, J, *et al* (2000) *Trends in working hours.* OECD Occasional Paper 45.

Gomez-Mejia, L and Welbourne, T (1992) Compensation strategies in a global context. *Human Resource Planning*, Vol 14, no 1.

Greenbury, R (1995) *Directors' remuneration.* Report of a study group chaired by Richard Greenbury.

Gregg, P, Machin, S and Szymanski, S (1993) The disappearing relationship between directors' pay and corporate performance. *British Journal of Industrial Relations*, March, pp1–9.

Hampel Committee on Corporate Government (1998) *Final Report.* Gee Publishing.

Hofstede, G (1980) *Culture's consequences.* Sage.

Incomes Data Services (1999a) Case study: AXA Sun Life: post-merger harmonisation of terms and conditions. *IDS Report* 784. May.

Incomes Data Services (1999b) *IDS Management Review.* June.

Incomes Data Services (2002a) *IDS Employment Europe* 482. February.

Incomes Data Services (2002b) London allowances. *IDS Study* 738. November.

Incomes Data Services (2003) *Public sector pay 2003.*

Industrial Relations Services (1999) Rewarding top managers. *IRS Management Review.* Issue 15, October.

Kessler, I (2001) Remuneration systems, in Bach, S and Sisson, K (eds) *Personnel management: a comprehensive guide to theory and practice.* 3rd edition. Blackwell Business.

London Assembly (2002) *London weighting.* Report of the London Weighting Panel, June.

Mercer, WM (1999) *Research report on share ownership.*

Milkovich, G and Bloom, M (1998) *Rethinking international compensation,* in Mendenhall, M and Oddou, G (eds) *Readings and cases in international human resource management.* 3rd edition. South-Western College Publishing.

Milkovich, G and Newman, J (1996) *Compensation.* 5th edition. Irwin.

Monks Partnership (1999) *Remuneration of directors and managers: United Kingdom.*

Oswald, A (2002) *London's public-sector workers need to be paid 50% more than those in the north.* Paper presented at the House of Commons on 21 March, 2002.

Pay Board (1974) *London Weighting.* HMSO.

Pension Investment Research Consultants Ltd (2003) Directors' remuneration. PIRC evidence to the Trade and Industry Select Committee, June 2003.

Perkins, S and Hendry, C (1999) *The IPD guide on international reward and recognition.* IPD.

Persaud, J (2003) Keep the faithful. *People Management.* 12 June.

Pfeffer, J (1998) *The human equation.* Harvard Business School Press.

Price, E and Price, R (1994) *The decline and fall of the status divide,* in Sisson, K (ed) *Personnel management: a comprehensive guide to theory and practice in Britain.* Blackwells.

Review Body on Senior Salaries reports 2000 and 2003, Cm 5718.

Royal Commission on the Distribution of Income and Wealth (Chairman Lord Diamond), Report No 3, Cmnd 6383, 1974.

Russell, A (1998). *The harmonization of employment conditions in Britain: the changing workplace divide since 1950 and the implications for social structure.* Macmillan Press.

Sisson, K and Storey, J (2000) *The realities of human resource management.* Open University Press.

Trades Union Congress (1998) *Wider still and wider.* TUC.

Walker, R (1999) *Motivating and rewarding managers.* Economist Intelligence Unit.

Watson Wyatt (1998/9) *Executive compensation survey* as quoted in *IDS Management Pay Review* 215. January 1999.

Zingheim, P and Schuster, J (2000) Total rewards for new and old economy companies. *Compensation and Benefits Review.* Vol 32, no 6, November/December, pp20–23.

Zingheim, P and Schuster, J (2002) Pay it forward. *People Management.* 7 Feb, p32.

Useful website
http://europa.eu.int/eurostat

Performance pay

CHAPTER 5

INTRODUCTION

Unlike many other areas of reward, the literature on performance pay is extensive. HR academics rooted in the industrial relations tradition have tended to focus their research efforts in the reward field primarily on performance pay, which from some perspectives is seen to undermine the traditional nature of collective bargaining. There is a notable divide in the literature, with material written by senior managers and reward consultants generally supportive of the move to individual performance pay, while the academic literature is characterised by scepticism.

This chapter assesses this debate, considers practice in performance pay and discusses how performance is measured.

It supports the following CIPD professional standards.

Operational indicators – Practitioners must be able to:

■ analyse the case for or against the introduction of a contingent pay scheme (paying for performance, competence, contribution or skill) and advise on its introduction, implementation and auditing.

Knowledge indicators – Practitioners must understand and be able to explain:

■ the part financial and non-financial rewards play in attracting, retaining and motivating people
■ the principles underlying performance management.

PERSPECTIVES ON PERFORMANCE PAY

Definitions and the nature of schemes vary considerably, but a broad distinction can be made between pay linked in some way to performance that is paid as an addition to basic salary or wages and the type of individual performance pay that is consolidated into and becomes part of basic salary or basic wages, thereby in many cases making the payment pensionable. The definitions of types of performance pay used in some studies use overly restrictive definitions. The typology in Table 30 makes the distinction between additional-to-basic-pay schemes and those that are consolidated into salary. The term used by the compilers of the Government's New Earnings Survey for additional payments related principally to output is '*payment by results*' (PBR). Purely output-related schemes are now much less used than they were in the 1970s, when the term PBR was coined; few organisations now refer to their bonus or performance pay as PBR. Many schemes use a mix of criteria, complicating the picture further. Brown and Armstrong (1996) put forward the term 'contribution-based pay' as an umbrella term, encompassing all forms of performance pay and competency-based pay.

A key difference in both the literature and in practice is seen in schemes that provide one or other of the following:

- an *incentive* – based on a promise of a future reward if performance reaches a certain level
- a *reward* for past performance which may not have been promised or agreed in advance.

Incentive schemes typically provide a bonus payment in return for some improvement in output, profitability or other performance measure. The term 'merit pay' usually describes individual performance payments that are consolidated into basic salary – or possibly paid as one-off payments – based on assessment or appraisal of past performance. The term 'contribution-based pay', though, is less retrospective in nature.

Incidence of individual salary-based performance pay

As Lewis (1991) highlights, the popularity of individual performance-related pay (PRP) grew in *'the 1980s with its emphasis upon individual, unitarist employee relations'*. Wood (1996) describes the annual growth in the number of schemes, which continued during the 1990s, in spite of criticisms of performance pay in practice, with little evidence of schemes being withdrawn (Randle 1997; IPD 1999). The IPD survey of public- and private-sector organisations found that 43 per cent of organisations used individual performance pay. It is possible this and other practitioner surveys overestimated the incidence, as the sample is biased towards large organisations, and the figures tend to include managers, for whom individual performance pay has become an expected part of the package. The main structured sample survey in the UK – the Workplace Employee Relations Survey (WERS) of 1998 – found individual performance pay for non-managerial staff in 11 per cent of

---

There are various types of performance pay. These include those that are:

Salary-based (consolidated):
- individual PRP, possibly related to appraisal or competencies
- some skill-based pay systems may be included in the definition of PRP

Additional to basic pay/salary:
- bonuses – based on output only

Piecework, measured day-work, productivity bonuses:
- bonuses – based on a mix of indicators, eg output and/or profit/group performance, quality indicators

Some executive bonuses, divisional performance bonuses, team bonuses, sales commission/bonuses, quality bonuses are in this category:
- profit-sharing – cash-based, not share-based schemes, eg all employee end-of-year profit bonuses, executive bonuses related to simple profit-based calculations
- gain-sharing – must include strong employee involvement

Table 30   *Typology of performance pay*

workplaces (Cully *et al* 1998). Whatever the most representative figure, it seems fair to conclude that PRP is common for managers and staff groups in a wide range of industries and services, with lesser take-up for manual occupations and in some sectors.

Mixed views on performance pay

Performance pay is controversial and at times it seems that an unbridgeable chasm divides its proponents and its opponents. Although a quantity of research exists on this topic, there remains a polarisation of views – between managers, HR specialists and consultants who 'believe' in what they may regard as the self-evident and practitioner-led case for performance pay, and most of the academic writers who are sceptical of the value of the practice.

Managers' views

Line managers are central to the perceived fairness of PRP and hence its effectiveness (Harris 2001). Cannell and Wood's (1992) survey found that although most personnel managers believed in performance pay, they had no evidence of its effectiveness. Managers and reward consultants have tended to see PRP as essential to motivating people in the workplace and have emphasised the place of individual performance pay in the building of performance cultures. The IPD's (1999) survey found personnel practitioners generally still positive about performance pay – certainly in the private sector. Respondents in the public sector were markedly less supportive of PRP than their counterparts in the private sector – see Table 33 (page 121).

Brown *et al* (1999) voiced the views of many managers who see any problems in implementing PRP as stemming not from fundamental or conceptual weaknesses but poor management – some schemes have unclear objectives, bad design and poor implementation. Brown cites a Towers Perrin 1997 survey, which showed that individual performance was considered the most important factor that managers wanted to see determine pay rises in their organisations. 'Focus and improve, rather than remove' was his message – and he advised practitioners not to rely overly on academic studies that drew on the experience of public-sector organisations.

Academic perspectives

The pervasiveness amongst managers of the notion that 'money motivates' is counterpointed by the work of academics on both sides of the Atlantic who have taken a largely sceptical stance on PRP, stressing both the theoretical deficiencies underpinning the concept and the preponderance of studies showing mediocre effectiveness in practice.

Both expectancy theory and equity theory (discussed below) are potentially relevant to the practice of performance pay. Under expectancy theory it may be assumed that PRP could work if employees:

PRP BELIEVER	NON-BELIEVER

■ believes PRP rewards performance
■ individuals paid according to
  contribution
■ complements performance management
■ is fair and motivates people
	■ PRP equals conformity-based pay
	■ is divisive – not for team players
	■ is unfair and demotivates more than it
	  motivates
	■ has confused objectives and is
	  subjective

Table 31   *Belief and non-belief in performance pay*

> **If one ignores the substantial body of evidence which casts doubt on the links between pay and performance, the case for PRP is very plausible.**
>
> **Sisson and Storey (2000)**

- believe that they are able to achieve the objectives set for them
- perceive that their effort will result in improved performance
- understand that good performance will be recognised and rewarded by managers
- put a value on the reward – and the reward is seen as large enough to justify the effort expended.

Some common failings with PRP – such as lack of transparency, problems in measuring outcomes or setting objectives and/or isolated incidences of favouritism in application of the scheme – could (if expectancy theory were to work in practice) be enough to undermine the whole scheme. More broadly, expectancy theory implies a complex web of individual and organisational relationships. This makes it difficult to rely on in practice.

Under equity theory employees compare their reward in relation to their input with others and perceive they are equitably rewarded, relatively under-rewarded or over-rewarded. Fairness can be considered from two points of view:

- *distributive justice* – or the perceived fairness of the outcome
- *procedural justice* – fairness of how the rewards are allocated or decisions made.

Both of these concepts can be deployed to evaluate the working of any PRP scheme. However, two people with the same pay outcome in an organisation may view fairness differently, because they are comparing their experience with different people. In assessing how important these elements of perceived fairness may be in researching pay attitudes Heneman and Judge (2000) conclude that not enough is known about why people focus on particular 'referents' (ie with whom they choose to compare themselves) to the exclusion of others when they decide if their pay is fair or unfair.

Kohn (1993) expressed more fundamental concerns about the conceptual underpinning of PRP. Prominent among the critics of PRP, he forcefully argues that any form of performance pay 'can erode intrinsic interest ... Higher quality work, particularly in jobs requiring creative thinking, is more likely to occur when a person focuses on the challenge of the task itself, rather than on some extrinsic motivator, and feels a sense of self-determination, as opposed to feeling controlled by praise or reward'. He goes on to argue that PRP is founded on behaviourist psychology notions and is counterproductive to building long-term performance. He says: *'rewards succeed at securing one thing only: temporary compliance. When it comes to producing lasting changes in attitudes and behaviour, however, rewards, like punishment, are strikingly ineffective ... There is no firm basis for the assumption that paying people more will encourage people to better work or even, in the long run, to do more work.'*

The evidence on association between high corporate performance and the existence of performance pay is difficult to interpret. While Pfeffer (1998) and a number of other sources suggest that there is an association, its nature is unclear. In the UK the Workplace

Employment Relations Survey (WERS) 1998 data suggests, in common with Pfeffer, that 'shared compensation' (as distinct from individual performance pay) is associated with higher productivity (see also Conyon and Freeman 2001).

Does PRP work in practice?

If we put theoretical deficiencies to one side for a moment, we can examine studies of PRP in practice. In academic studies, as distinct from practitioner-based research, the perspective of employees is explored as well as that of managers, because as one commentator put it: *'it is the fish which decides what is the bait, not the fisherman'.*

M Thompson's (1993) study found that employees did not perceive PRP as motivational – even for those with high performance ratings. Moreover, the study showed the capacity of PRP to demotivate some employees. The study also cast doubt on claims that PRP helps in staff retention and can promote organisational culture change.

Marsden and French's major (1998) study of public-sector organisations – the Inland Revenue, Employment Service and the NHS – found that for most staff, support for the principle of performance pay did not translate into a positive willingness to work harder or to improve work quality. Moreover, the PRP systems engendered distrust both of line managers and higher management and soured work relations. Some staff felt demoralised and there was jealousy among workers, jeopardising teamworking and co-operation. Only a rather small minority said that PRP had given them an incentive to work beyond the requirements of their jobs, and most believed that it had not.

Not all the research that is critical of PRP has been conducted in the public sector. Randle's 1997 study in a private-sector company – within the UK pharmaceutical industry – found that the case study company had made several changes to its performance pay scheme covering scientists in order to try to get the scheme to operate well. In spite of the revisions the scheme *'remained unpopular with both those who were in favour of, and those who were against, the principle of linking pay to performance, and with those who felt they had gained, and those who felt they had lost from the operation of the system'.*

Pfeffer (1998) argues that the practice of individual PRP is an expensive, time-consuming activity in many organisations: *'individual incentive pay, in reality, undermines performance – of both the individual and the organisation'.* It *'undermines teamwork, encourages a short-term focus, and leads people to believe that pay is not related to performance at all but to having the "right" relationships and an ingratiating personality'.* Pfeffer's case study research (in mostly private-sector US corporations) found examples of organisations in which managing PRP took up substantial amounts of managers' time, cost money and could *'yet make everybody unhappy'.*

Kessler and Purcell's 1993 study in eight UK companies found that problems in managing PRP schemes in practice were linked to:

- objective-setting inconsistencies between the decisions of different line managers in the same organisations, combined with questions about the 'viability' of this process for some occupations – for example, R&D scientists
- performance assessment evidence of managers taking 'easy options', and a 'centring tendency', with managers reluctant to mark people too high or low; labels attached to performance rankings sending 'demoralizing messages to staff'; subjective criteria of some managers

- linking performance assessment to pay encouraged 'tunnel vision' evident as employees concentrated on those aspects of their job linked to PRP, neglecting others

- problems with the traditional linkages of pay rise with cost of living increases which could dilute the performance linkage mismatch between appraisal ratings and pay

- a diversion of PRP budget by some line managers to deal with other pay pressures.

STUDENT REVIEW EXERCISE

Your managing director supports the introduction of PRP, but you are concerned that it may be difficult to manage well. Identify some of the elements that would be included in your plan to design and operate a scheme effectively.

Discuss whether you believe PRP can be made to work well in any organisation if managed skilfully or if there are some organisations or types of job for which it is not appropriate at all.

PRP in the public sector

> Performance pay is an old idea with a lousy record. I cannot understand why the Government is so keen to introduce it into teaching and the NHS. The evidence shows that it simply does not work...
>
> Pay, whilst important, is not the most important moulder of behaviour.
>
> Guest (1999)

Implementing private-sector management practices into the public services gained momentum during the 1980s and 1990s. Performance pay was introduced into most of the UK public sector following the commitments to PRP given in the Citizens' Charter (1991), as the nostrums of private-sector practice were translated into the public services. Wood's (1993) study shows that the introduction of performance pay into the public services in many OECD countries was part of a wider set of reforms of the structure and management of public-sector organisations, loosely described as the 'new managerialism'. The adoption of private-sector techniques and the growing emphasis on managerial skills were part of a move at government policy level to change the basis on which performance was considered, stressing output measures of performance such as service quality and delivery as well as more traditional input-based measures, such as performance against budget. In this context the introduction of PRP into the public sector can be seen as a logical component of reforms aimed at securing a more effective delivery of public services.

The rationale for PRP in the public sector therefore was fairly clear, but the effectiveness of the policy in practice is highly questionable. As the IPD survey (1999) shows, even though there are not many perceptible differences between the practice of PRP in the public and private sectors, 'there are clear and important differences in the extent to which they are perceived to succeed'. On nearly all the indicators offered, private-sector respondents were more positive than public-sector ones (see Table 33, page 121).

Marsden and French (1998) show that there is a particular problem in using PRP in public services, prompting the question as to whether there are different factors at work in the

Advantages	Disadvantages
Motivates staff by providing a direct incentive	Demotivates staff and undermines morale
Rewards employees fairly and equitably	Relies on subjective and arbitrary measures
Provides a tangible means for recognising achievement	Contaminates the developmental aspects of appraisal
Delivers a strong message about performance imperative of the organisation	Used to reward favourites
Improves goal-setting	Undermines teamwork and co-operative behaviour
Focuses employees on improvement and innovation	Divisive and undermines co-operation with management
Rewards those who contribute most to the organisation	Does little to improve organisational efficiency
Bolsters commitment and loyalty	Raises expectations of constant pay-out
Helps retain valuable staff	Encourages employees to focus on short-term quantifiable results
Facilitates change in the organisation	May result in a mismatch between individual and organisational performance
Helps identify poor performance	Undermines performance if unattainable targets are set
Can be self-financing	Little scope for meaningful awards in periods of low inflation
	Relies too heavily on ill-equipped line managers
	Poor value for money
	May prove discriminatory
Source: Adapted from e-reward.co.uk *Performance Pay Guide* (2002)	

Table 32 *Advantages and disadvantages of PRP*

Percentage responses – private-sector responses first in each cell				
	A large improvement	A small improvement	No real change	A small deterioration	A large deterioration
Employee performance	19–4	61–56	20–39	0–1	0–0
Employee commitment/loyalty	10–3	37–25	48–63	5–10	0–0
Rewarding employees in a way they think is fair	17–4	45–44	28–33	9–15	1–6
Employee willingness to stay with your organisation	7–2	34–17	54–75	5–5	0–1
Delivering a clear message about the importance of organisational performance	34–16	38–47	25–31	3–4	0–2
Facilitating change in your organisation	15–6	31–26	50–61	3–5	1–2
Encouraging employees to suggest improvements and innovations	6–2	27–17	64–76	3–4	1–1
Effective team working	4–3	27–18	58–62	10–17	1–1
Curbing trade union influence on pay decisions	5–5	8–11	84–82	2–2	1–0
Your ability to identify and get rid of poor performers	20–4	40–30	39–61	1–4	0–1

Source: IPD (1999)

Table 33 *The effects of individuals' performance-related pay in public and private sectors on various factors*

motivation of employees in the private and public sectors. There is somewhat mixed evidence on the question as to whether public-sector employees are as motivated by financial rewards as their counterparts in the private sector (Brown 2001; Dowling and Richardson 1997; Gould-Williams 2002). One of the key differences highlighted by the IPD (1999) survey is the effect of PRP on 'high performers'. As Table 34 (page 124) shows from the CIPD survey, 'high performers' in the private sector were much more likely to have been perceived as improving their performance as a result of PRP those than in the public sector. Research does not yet address the factors behind such findings.

Brown (2001) summarises some of the special characteristics of public-service organisational contexts for performance pay.

- PRP schemes cannot work when employees do not value the perhaps small increments offered. *'The problem for public sector organisations is to provide meaningful pay increases ... when the amount for distribution is generally very small.'*
- There is a conflict between *'an economic versus a service culture ... public sector organisations need to find a balance between providing adequate economic rewards without destroying the intrinsic needs of public employees'.*

- *'Hiring economically-oriented employees can be detrimental to an organisation with a service culture.'*

- The generally high levels of employee support for the principle of pay for performance are contrasted with concerns about both distributive and procedural justice.

STUDENT REVIEW TASK

Strong views on PRP

Performance-Related Pay, Yes
By Andrew Oswald, Professor of Economics, Warwick University

Would tougher links between pay and performance lead to higher standards in schools? Yes. It has to be done sensibly, however, and individual teachers' salaries should become confidential. To set the scene, the Government is now contemplating ending the automatic incremental rises to all classroom teachers. Teachers' unions are bound to be against this, out of intellectual habit. Yet I am for it. Let us consider arguments and counter-arguments.

Concern 1. The short-term benefits that PRP would bring might be undermined by the effect on morale and retention, thereby fuelling the shortage crisis.
I doubt this. Let's start with data. My research group is one of the few in the world to have looked for statistical links between job satisfaction in workplaces and the existence of performance-related pay. We cannot find any convincing link. This cuts both ways: PRP does not on average seem to make life more pleasant or less pleasant for employees in British establishments. But my side of the argument is helped fractionally more than the side likely to be taken by people such as Doug McEvoy. There is some evidence that performance-related pay does improve productivity in workplaces, so on balance I view the sheer statistical evidence as favouring the pro-PRP case. Now, I accept that much more statistical evidence needs to be gathered, especially in schools. So I suggest the following. There should be an experimental set of 100 schools, chosen randomly, in which strong PRP (we already have in principle weak PRP) is introduced for two years. A control group of 100 similar other schools should also be picked. Then an independent panel should be commissioned to judge, after the two years are up, whether strong PRP has been a success. The panel should consist of those without prior known bias one way or another.

We should have an experiment, in other words. This is, after all, exactly how a drug company would be forced to behave if it wished to market some new sleeping pill. Britain's public sector should start to enforce proper standards of scientific evidence.

Concern 2. PRP would damage collegiality in schools and undermine relations with head-teachers.
Not if salaries were confidential. It is really no-one's business what I earn. The oh-so-British idea that pay should be fixed on some mechanical scale, depending on how old I am, so that my next-door neighbour can look me up, is decades out of date. People should be rewarded on merit and effort.

Concern 3. Lots of headteachers are against PRP in their schools.
Very probably. But it does not cut a lot of ice with me. Headteachers are British. They have been brought up to read the *Guardian*. They have been brought up to be suspicious of meritocratic principles. They have been brought up to distrust the private sector (in life, not just in education). They are prisoners of their own mind-set.

Andrew Oswald *Times Educational Supplement*, August 2002

STUDENT REVIEW QUESTIONS

- In groups, decide if you agree with Andrew Oswald? Give reasons for your opinion.
- How do you respond to the strong views in Concerns 2 and 3?
- How feasible do you consider the research proposed in Concern 1 would be likely to be? Use the model of expectancy theory as a framework for your discussion.

Individual PRP schemes in practice

In general individual PRP is added to basic salary. As Heneman *et al* (2000) point out, most modern reward systems are 'multilayered', with basic pay the largest component. It is important therefore to acknowledge that, even in a performance-based pay system, the major influence determining an individual's pay may be something other than performance. External market relativities and internal relativities (job evaluation) may, in practice, have greater impact, especially at a time when performance payments are low as a result of low inflation. Performance judgements are – in most cases in individual PRP – merely the mechanism by which individuals achieve pay progression within the relevant pay structure. In narrow bands this takes place via a small number of annual percentage pay increases, or via an incremental step structure. However in a broad-banded structure (see page 75), progression may be through zones or sub-sections of the band – in order to control costs. The overall rewards of individual PRP are then, almost by definition, very limited, especially in an era when overall rises in pay and corporate budgets for pay rises are low.

When individual performance pay is to be consolidated into basic pay, a decision needs to be made as to whether the annual salary increase should be based wholly on performance, or made up of a general (cost-of-living) award, with the 'merit' payment being paid in addition to a general element. Splitting the pay award into the two elements was more common in times of higher inflation, but a combined single pay award – reflecting both 'economic' and performance elements – has become more popular as inflation has declined.

Performance judgements are typically based on the line manager's assessment of the individual employee's performance in the previous year. This may be a retrospective view or be based on a comparison of the results individuals have achieved with the objectives they have been set. The review or appraisal process in many, but not all, schemes generates ratings. These ratings or performance assessments then set the percentage pay rise – as in Table 35 (page 124).

The example matrix in Table 36 (page 125) sets out the percentage increase payable for five different performance ratings according to the position of the individual's pay in the salary range.

Percentage responses – private-sector response first in each cell				
	A large improvement	A small improvement	No real change	A small deterioration	A large deterioration
High performers	27–8	44–30	28–62	1–1	0–0
Average performers	6–1	56–45	35–52	3–2	0–0
Poor performers	4–2	38–30	46–62	10–5	2–3
Source: IPD (1999)					

Table 34   *The effect of individual PRP on the behaviour of public- and private-sector employees*

Performance management, performance appraisal and PRP

Schemes for monitoring and measuring individual performance have become commonplace in the UK across public and private sectors. The *Workplace Employee Relations Survey* (Cully *et al* 1998) indicates that 56 per cent of workplaces have systems for performance appraisals of most non-managerial staff. As in PRP there is something of a divide between the perspective of HR practitioners, who may emphasise the positive and developmental objectives of performance appraisal or performance management, and some academic work, which is more negative – viewing the techniques as instruments of control and discipline. See, for example, Newton and Findlay (1996).

In terms of techniques, performance appraisal has given ground to performance management, which may be seen as part of the 'orthodoxy' of management that performance should be measured, monitored and controlled. Unlike appraisal, performance management is conventionally thought to be a broader process in which organisational aims and objectives are used as a starting point for the setting of objectives for divisions, departments, teams and individuals. In practice, at the individual level a performance management review is pretty similar to an appraisal interview, since the process can be used for multiple purposes, principally:

■ employee development

■ performance pay

■ management control of individual performance.

Concerns remain about the effectiveness and nature both of performance management and of performance appraisal; they can be viewed as often time-consuming and controversial, especially when a pay rise is at stake. Part of the problem might be related to the mechanics of systems. Forms are often lengthy, sometimes complex. Managers as well as employees may feel they are asked to pass judgements and make comments in the absence of objective criteria. The setting of objectives, while easy in some organisations for some jobs, can be problematic in others.

Outstanding performance	Very good performance	Good performance	Satisfactory performance	Needs improvement
Pay rises of up to 12%	Pay rise 6%–8%	Pay rise 4%–5%	Pay rise 2%–3%	Pay rise zero to 2%

Table 35   *A basic illustrative model of pay rise and performance assessment*

Range of percentage pay increases – Norwich Union staff

Position in salary range

Rating	80–88%	89–96%	97–104%	105–112%	113–120%	120%+
Outstanding	8.0	7.0	6.0	5.0	4.0	3.0
Very good	6.5	5.5	4.5	3.5	2.5	1.5
Good	5.0	4.0	3.0	2.5	1.5	1.0
Developing well	3.0	2.0	1.5	1.0	1.0	0.0

Not developing acceptably : zero increases
Unacceptable performance : zero increases
Data as at 1999

Adapted from *IRS Pay and Benefits Bulletin* 471, May 1999; E-Reward.co.uk

Table 36 *Norwich Union's salary progression matrix*

There is some evidence that goal- or target-setting can be one way of improving performance. Goal theory (Locke 1968) suggests the following.

- The more specific the goal, the more likely it is to be achieved.
- The completion requirement (finish date) should be specific.
- Goals that are difficult to achieve may be achieved more readily than easier ones.
- Every individual needs feedback on performance to improve.

The SMART concept of setting performance objectives grew from this concept, with the objectives or key results areas or what the individual intends to achieve crafted in terms that are:

Specific
Measureable
Achievable
Realistic
Time-bounded.

While it is possible to see targets in a sales environment as falling easily within this definition, with other jobs this might be extremely problematic.

As Table 37 (page 126) illustrates, there has been some progress (Armstrong and Baron 1998) in the 'engineering' of performance management schemes to ameliorate the top-down, single-rating, reward-driven systems of the 1980s and early 1990s and move towards a more 'democratic process' with emphasis in some companies on inputs (competencies) as well as outputs (performance against targets). Bach (2000), however, comments that some of the same problems occur with the newer approaches – such as 360-degree, self-appraisal or peer appraisal, as with earlier systems. There is little disagreement that assessment of performance must be based on reliable judgements and be consistently carried out. The problem might be that we do not have adequate 'tools' or techniques for this task, or that as Bowey *et al* (1992) found with incentive schemes, there are subtle processes at work in organisations which can undermine managerial plans.

Measuring performance

The assumption that individual performance might be managed by a relatively simple process of identifying overall corporate objectives and then cascading these down a hierarchical organisational structure is a rather over-simplistic idea. Performance at both individual and corporate level is a complex and multifaceted phenomenon, of which an in-depth understanding is necessary to be able confidently and robustly to set pay. IRS (1997) shows how leading companies are exploring the use of measures of performance that move away from the traditional reliance on purely financial elements. Increasingly, companies are incorporating a number of variables that give a wider set of perspectives. Kaplan and Norton (1992) highlighted the widely evident problem that 'what you measure is what you get' – and that the traditional use of performance measures has promoted 'short-termism'. They put forward the concept of the balanced scorecard with a multi-perspective approach. Figure 10 shows that in the original model there were four major aspects of organisational performance – financial, innovation/learning, internal processes and customers. Incomes Data Services (2001) shows that some companies are beginning to use the concept within individual performance management schemes.

From PRP to competency-based pay

Problems with PRP prompted an interest in competency-based pay. The suggestion that it might be possible to identify and define the behaviours that individuals display when they are good performers and that these might be codified and used to predict which individuals would produce superior performance in the future came to prominence in the 1980s (for example, Boyatzis 1982).

The CIPD's 2002 reward management survey found that an individual's pay progression is now commonly linked to an assessment of performance and the skills and competencies that he or she applies in the job. This approach is the most popular method of determining salary rises for middle/first-line managers (63 per cent), non-manual non-management staff (58 per cent) and senior managers (56 per cent). However, the more extreme uses of competencies

From (past)	To (present)
■ System	■ Process
■ Appraisal	■ Joint review
■ Outputs	■ Outputs and inputs
■ PRP-linked	■ Development
■ Ratings common	■ Less rating
■ Top-down	■ 360-degree
■ Directive	■ Supportive
■ Monolithic	■ Flexible
■ Owned by HR	■ Owned by users
Drawn from Armstrong and Baron (1998)	

Table 37 *Developments in performance management*

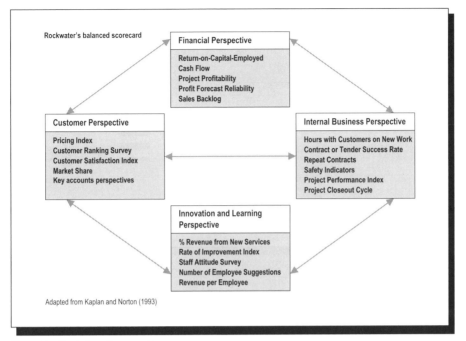

Figure 10 *The balanced scorecard*

propounded by the new pay theorists (see page 3) seem largely not to have translated into practice in the UK. Mostly, competency pay systems provide progression payments based on performance/assessment of competencies in the role. Figure 11 (page 128) shows the rationale for this in relation to the development of individual expertise or competencies. As such, this progression model might be seen as providing a more sophisticated version of the service increment model, in the sense that people are paid for their developing skills and expertise in the organisation. But unlike the service increment model, this is not seen as a function of time but of individual performance and the growth of expertise in the role.

At face value, gearing some part on an individual's pay to skills or competencies may be seen to have the following advantages.

- It could foster a developmental culture in the organisation, albeit placing considerable demand on training and administrative resources.
- It fits with the concept that job roles are now broader and there needs to be some reward for people to progress in their roles.
- It may be seen as a more sophisticated variant of pay progression based on performance.

Under competency systems, the assessed levels of competency may determine an individual's position or pay within a salary band. The assessment might be a qualitative one – the individual has met or exceeded the expected level of each competency that is appropriate for his or her role. Competencies are a mix of skill and behaviour and therefore could veer more towards hard skills or competences – for example using IT. Typically, however (see Incomes Data Services 2000), the competencies used in practice are 'softer' skills such as communication and teamworking. An Industrial Society survey (1997) found that competency-based pay systems were increasingly being used, principally as part of attempts to make

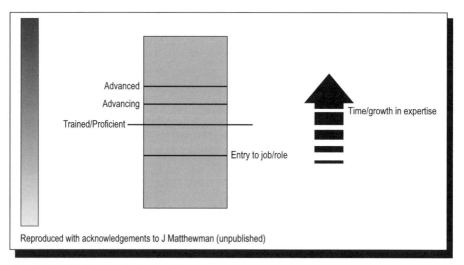

Reproduced with acknowledgements to J Matthewman (unpublished)

Figure 11 *Model of progression in role or job*

performance pay work better. The survey revealed that the majority of organisations with such schemes found they were 'popular with employees' – or at least were not criticised as widely as individual performance pay arrangements. From the HR perspective they had attractions as a mechanism enabling HR practices to be more smoothly integrated, since they could be used for recruitment, employee development and pay. The approach also seemed to fit with the more modern emphasis on broader roles rather than narrowly prescribed jobs.

Was the discovery of competencies and their use by HR specialists 'too good to be true', asked Paul Sparrow (1996)? Clearly indicating that the answer to this question should be 'yes', Sparrow said that using competencies made sense when it was easy to determine the skills needed to deliver each key result, but argued that the concepts underpinning competencies were not sufficiently robust as a basis for constructing pay systems. Some could be too 'vague', some not good enough for all the uses employers want from them. Problems in definition and in measuring competencies were also revealed by the Industrial Society survey (1997). Strebler's (1997) study also questioned whether the use of competencies in constructing pay systems could be discriminatory (see Chapter 6). More broadly, there are concerns that employers' main interest is to control employees and gain compliance – similar to some of the criticisms of performance management – rather than to use competency-based pay systems as an aid to gaining employee commitment.

Individual or 'collective' – does group or team performance pay work better than individual?

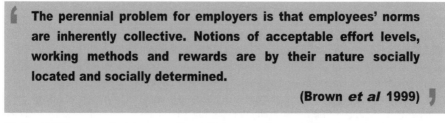

> The perennial problem for employers is that employees' norms are inherently collective. Notions of acceptable effort levels, working methods and rewards are by their nature socially located and socially determined.
>
> **(Brown *et al* 1999)**

Pfeffer (1998) argues that because the achievement of organisational results is a 'result of collective behavior and performance', individual performance pay is essentially misguided.

Other research in the United States of employees' experience of lump-sum bonus arrangements (LeBlanc and Mulvey 1998) suggests that, on balance, employees prefer merit pay based on assessments of their own performance and, critically, prefer payments permanently consolidated into basic pay, rather than paid as a variable addition to basic pay. The views of employees are particularly variable, and may depend on whether or not they have experienced different types of performance pay, whether they are perceived as high performers, the rewards they expect and those that they personally value, and the organisational climate.

The 2002 CIPD reward management survey found that team bonuses are more common for clerical (20 per cent of organisations surveyed) and blue-collar staff (18 per cent) than middle/first-line management (15 per cent) and senior management (8 per cent). Surveys by the CIPD and Institute of Employment Studies (Thompson 1995) stress that team pay cannot work in isolation – it is important for it to be sited within a genuine teamworking culture. Thompson's study for the IES study considered the relative attributes of team pay and individual performance-related pay (see Table 38). The CIPD found some organisations developing reward policies that included both a team bonus and a separate individual skill or competency-based pay scheme. Yet others were beginning to include team work ability as an 'input' factor in competency or performance management schemes.

Team pay	Individual merit pay
Rewards teamwork and co-operation	Creates internal competition between employees
Encourages group to improve work systems	Encourages employees to withhold information
Increases flexibility and ability to respond to changing needs	Individuals' attempts to improve work systems may fail
Not incorporated in base pay	Decreases flexibility within the organisation
Encourages information sharing and communication	Incorporated into base salary
Focus on wider organisation	No focus on wider organisation
Adapted from Thompson (1995)	

Table 38 *Individual and team pay compared*

Advantages of team pay	Disadvantages
■ encourages co-operative work and behaviour ■ clarifies goals and priorities at team and organisational level ■ emphasises a flatter and process-based organisation ■ a lever for organisational change ■ encourages flexible working and multi-skilling ■ a fairer perceived payment system ■ collectively improves performance and team process ■ encourages the less effective to meet team standards ■ develops self-managed teams	■ diminishes individual self-worth ■ masks individual team contribution ■ compels individuals to conform to oppressive group norms ■ results in low output that is sufficient only to gain a reasonable reward ■ causes difficulties when developing performance measures that are fair ■ shifts problems of unco-operative behaviour from individuals in teams to the relationships between teams ■ prejudices organisational flexibility – as cohesive and high-performance teams may be unwilling to change
Source: CIPD (2002)	

Table 39   *Team pay: advantages and disadvantages*

Case study – Teamworking and PRP in the Benefits Agency

The attempts of the Government's Benefits Agency (BA) in implementing devolved teamworking created problems. In particular, it exposed contradictions in the management approach to change, which on the one hand encouraged collective working arrangements but on the other operated an individualised staff reward system. PRP was introduced into the BA in the early 1990s – a development perceived by many managers and employees as an essentially political move. One of its original purposes was to quantify the volume and the efficiency of work being performed by individuals. Relative productivity between the local benefit offices run by BA was measured. This measurement of efficiency was problematic, both in terms of comparing time spent on processing different kinds of benefit and of dealing with different types of claimant. The measurement of individual throughput times linked to the processing of benefit claims and a system of accuracy checks carried out by supervisors was compared by some employees to 'factory piecework'. This mechanical evaluation of work performance was accompanied by an annual appraisal interview with a line manager, a process that elicited criticisms from staff, who felt it was open to abuse and 'highly personalised'. Line managers allocated box markings on a scale of 1–5, which determined the amount of individual PRP awarded: at the top of the performance scale was 1 (excellent) and, at the bottom, 5 (unsatisfactory work). There was widespread belief in the BA that box markings of 2 and 3 were given only to frontline staff, box 1 awards being reserved for managers. Staff believed that PRP was paid out of a small fixed budget and that box allocations were adjusted to correspond to the money available. The hostility and resentment of staff towards the system of PRP was acknowledged by the managers interviewed by researchers, and subsequently led to the development of a new system. The old 1–5 box allocation was replaced with a similar A, B, C, D grading – the key difference being that managers assured staff that A grades *would* be awarded.

Adapted from Foster and Hoggett (1999)

Case study – Public agency no 3

Public agency no 3 is a central government agency set up under the Next Steps programme to deliver a specific service to the public. The agency has offices around the country, with a headquarters in a Midlands industrial town.

Government ministers have set some challenging performance targets for the agency, but its budget for staffing has been frozen because its work is not seen to be a top political priority. Any problems with its service, however, very quickly become a public and political issue – and the relevant minister has to answer any charges of mismanagement.

Staffing cost budgets have been met by using a large number of temporary staff, all paid at the lowest pay grades. Permanent staff and line managers have felt the pressures of extra work as a result of the policy to use large numbers of temporary staff who create demands on their time, additional training requirements and supervisory problems.

In common with the mainstream Civil Service, the staff in the agency have their pay progression linked to annual individual performance assessments, in line with the commitments made in the Citizens' Charter, introduced by the John Major Conservative Government in the 1990s. Following the election of a Labour Government, trade union officials began raising with members of the Government the problems they perceived with performance pay in the Civil Service.

In the case of Public agency no 3, neither the politicians nor the agency's top management are keen on departing from performance pay, since they believe that performance management is essential if the agency staff are to 'keep on message' and meet the challenging performance targets set for them.

Union officials persuade management at least to consider some new ideas and with that in view ask the agency to commission independent researchers to investigate the views of the staff. The union emphasises that the voice of employees has not been heard on performance pay matters in recent years.

The independent investigation uses a methodology based on one-to-one interviews with a 1 per cent sample of the staff and on focus groups with a further 2 per cent of staff. Both of these are structured to gather views broadly representative of those in the agency.

An extract from the results of this research follows.

Participants in the research were asked if PRP is a good idea in principle. A substantial majority said they thought it right for those who work harder/do a better job to be paid more than those who work less hard, and most thought it was right to recognise good performance.

Specific views were typically:

'I have a gut feeling that if one works well one should be rewarded more than someone who does not make the effort'

'Some people are plodders and it is right that others who put in more effort are rewarded in some way. For good work you deserve more than for slacking. It's difficult to argue with.'

'I have worked hard most of my career and others have sauntered through and done enough to get by. And because you make the extra effort you should be compensated accordingly – when promotion is not available.'

'PRP in principle gives individuals some control over their pay and shows that if they do more they can earn more. This is a good idea for me as a manager and for individual members of staff.'

'People who perform better should get recognition as they do in industry ... Promotion opportunities are poor in the Civil Service, so people need to be given recognition.'

'PRP helps to keep standards up ... I have been doing the same job for 20 years and if there was no incentive to keep work standards up they might slip.'

'In the Civil Service a carrot is needed to drive people on. If not people will do no more than is necessary.'

Others took the view that performance pay was fundamentally unfair because they thought line management was not capable of being fair; the process of performance assessment was too subjective and staff had a lack of control over their jobs. Some union members, in particular, also felt PRP was divisive.

Typical views were:

'Everyone should be paid the same rate for the job. If you are given the job you should be able to do it. It's very divisive to give individuals different rates of pay ... It can often pull teams apart as staff begin to see themselves as individuals rather than team members.'

'I can see that from my position as a reporting officer and from being reported on ... We are only human and have our likes and dislikes and prejudices, really. I feel that most people do their best but a lot of time marking is a gut reaction.'

'If you start a new job you earn less regardless of your skills or training. Also if you have the same manager for years your performance marking will go up as you get used to each other and the manager understands your job ... New managers will always give middle-of-the road markings regardless of your performance.'

'I appealed to the next line manager and then to the next one who agreed that I had been under-marked. This does not happen if you are a favourite with the assessing manager.'

'There is no accurate way of measuring performance, so it is done on a subjective basis.'

'Staff are measured against things they have little or no control over.'

'Some people's jobs are more complicated than others. The more complicated the work, the more chances there are of making errors. Under the pay system the errors are penalised.'

'There's not the freedom of action to influence your job, or the freedom to pay high performers enough to make it worth their while.'

Interviewees were asked how the newer PRP system compared with the previous pay system, which had paid a general (cost of living) pay increase each year, plus an annual service-related increment. Many expressed a wish to return to the old system:

'I preferred the old pay system because it was generally accepted as being fair while performance pay is not fair. You were rewarded for your experience and there were ways of dealing with inefficient workers which was considered fair too.'

'The basic principle that if you were working for the organisation you deserved an increment plus cost of living rise is correct. There was no possibility of abuse, favouritism and corruption by management in the old system.'

'The old system was more objective and everyone received the same increase or would have had the opportunity to do so. The performance pay system is too subjective. It is not based on what you do but who you know and how well you get on with them.'

'I preferred the old system of increments because you could guarantee that you would get an increase, which helped with financial planning. Today it is difficult to make commitments and plan. It took a long time to get to the top of your grade with increments, but you knew you would get there.'

'Everyone knew where they were and would be. It was more transparent and fairer.'

There were a few staff who preferred the new performance-related pay system. They said:

'The current system is best for me. I feel that my performance is at its peak and I get rewarded for the extra effort I make.'

'The old system was demotivating for those who worked hard, and performance pay addresses that.'

'It allows effort to be recognised. Even though the money isn't very good it at least gives you the feeling that "you are doing something right".'

Most interviewees who supported the principle of PRP said it was unfair in practice in the agency. The reasons related mainly to: the lack of skills among managers to operate the system properly; favouritism; and inconsistency and inequity in the operation of PRP between different jobs and different parts of the organisation or for some jobs. Typical views were as follows:

'It could be fair, but it depends on the individual line manager. In practice it often is not fair.'

'PRP is better but ... in the Civil Service it causes more unrest than the money is worth. In practice it is unfair ... I see people who are rightly deserving of higher performance markings and others deserving lower marks not getting them so their reporting officers can have a quiet life. We have spineless management.'

'There is too much personality involved in assessing people. I have experienced this personally.'

'Many managers are so aloof from staff that they don't really know what's going on. There is much favouritism on the part of many managers. Many managers tend to mark down people who talk back to them.'

'It is difficult to be fair because you are relying on someone else's view of what is satisfactory performance. Some managers have very demanding standards and others have less. Some managers will only give you a high rating if you clean their boots on top of your job. The system is not applied consistently between individuals or jobs. At a training session on the performance pay system, people had to work in groups to evaluate someone's performance. Everyone came out with different outcomes. The trainer said that "there is no right answer". This made me feel that the guidelines issued to managers are not very good and that there needs to be more steering from the organisation. The training session just highlighted the subjective nature of the pay system.'

'It is often difficult to see how the performance of one individual has impacted on that of another. It is not fair that this feeds into pay. Some people may get rewarded by blowing their own trumpet about targets achieved, while someone who is doing a more reliable, consistent job may not be noticed.'

'Whether people get a good or a bad report depends on the quality of the person doing the report. If your boss is having difficulties holding things together, it will show in your marks. It's simply chance who you end up with.'

'The lack of money makes it unfair and makes people think that it doesn't matter how you perform. Good, improved performance doesn't mean more money under this system.'

Interviewees said that the main reason PRP was not perceived as an incentive was that the amount of money involved was too low. Others said that PRP was irrelevant to their motivations either because non-financial rewards such as promotion were seen as more important or because there was not seen to be a genuine link between effort and reward in current performance-pay systems. Some said PRP acted against people's desire to work harder.

The Agency senior management are concerned by the results of the study and wonder if team-based performance pay might be a better option.

Focus groups of staff discussed this proposal. Managers were perplexed and concerned that after discussing detailed ideas as to how such team bonuses might work, the staff in the focus groups unanimously came down against the idea. One group described the proposal as 'similar to PRP, only worse'.

STUDENT REVIEW EXERCISE

Assess the expressed views of the staff and:

- discuss whether there is any evidence that an effective performance pay scheme could be made to work in the organisational context of the agency
- consider alternatives to individual PRP and team bonuses that might be more appropriate
- consider the managerial challenges in this organisation, in relation to pay management.
- consider the relevance of theoretical perspectives such as expectancy theory and effort-bargain relationships.

BONUSES AND INCENTIVES

A bonus is usually a lump sum payment linked to performance or results in some way. In incentive schemes the targets that must be achieved may be set in advance. A wide definition of bonuses and incentives would also usually encompass individual and group bonuses – from sales staff commission to controversial executive incentives.

Incentives can be difficult to categorise but they typically include the following:

- sales commission or sales incentives, designed to increase the performance of sales force personnel
- bonus payments related to output of a team or business unit
- executive incentives that may be profit-related or based on a number of factors that indicate the performance of the company or business unit

■ piecework or payment-by-results systems in which individual output is measured and remunerated.

The CIPD's (2003) reward management survey shows that just under two-thirds of employers (64 per cent) offer cash bonuses to senior managers, just under three-fifths (58 per cent) to middle/first-line managers, 44 per cent to non-manual non-managers and 34 per cent to manual staff. According to Incomes Data Services (1999), bonus schemes account for a significant part of many employees' pay packages, but the overall number of schemes is declining.

For employers there are perceived cost advantages to paying performance pay in the form of a bonus that is not consolidated into base pay:

■ Bonuses can be paid without inflating the pay bill every year.
■ Bonuses can be viewed as self-financing if productivity in the organisation increases.

In addition, if bonuses are not available there can be difficulty recruiting into occupations for which bonuses have become an expected part of the package. The Industrial Society's (1997) survey found that over half of respondents thought that those employees without bonuses would like to receive them and 70 per cent of organisations with bonuses said that these schemes are highly valued by the staff covered.

The development of bonuses

Individual incentive schemes for manual workers have a long history, and are still widely used. The early incentive schemes were piecework-based, on Taylorist principles. Work tasks were measured and the time taken for standard tasks was set by managers.

Bonuses are paid over and above a standard time per task threshold or per 'piece' of work completed. The survival of such systems in modern organisations (including at one US company, Lincoln Electric, lauded for its reward practices – see page 31) is perhaps surprising. An ACAS report on payment systems (1990) found that the longest-surviving pay system tended to be those that were piecework-based.

Such survival may be related to the clarity of the performance system used to determine the bonus and the clear 'line of sight' between what employees do and what they will get for doing it.

Bowey's (1982) seminal work in evaluating the effects of incentive schemes showed that incentive bonus schemes deteriorate over time and illustrated how significant 'informal' group norms and actions grew up around any system of controls put in place by managers to increase work effort.

Design of bonus schemes

Executives, especially top directors, are usually eligible for bonuses linked either to profits or some other measure of corporate financial performance. The Greenbury Committee recommended their bonus schemes should be designed with the following principles in mind:

■ Performance targets set for executives should be challenging, so as to avoid the bonus in effect becoming a guaranteed part of remuneration.

- An upper limit (a percentage of basic pay) should be set.
- Financial performance measures selected should be those that executives can influence.

In the organisation as a whole 'line of sight' means that employees must see a clear connection between what they do and the bonus payout. Employees must feel they have control over the performance criteria and that:

- there is specific understanding about the behaviour that will generate performance
- it is clear how performance is measured
- different levels of performance link directly to different bonus payments.

Bonus targets must be achievable, otherwise – as expectancy theory suggests – they will not serve as an incentive. This means, for example, that changing targets part way through a bonus period could be counter-productive.

Bonuses may not be assessed or paid on an annual basis – they could be paid quarterly or monthly. Payments made on time and as close as possible to the achievement that gave rise to the bonus are more likely to work as an incentive.

There is something of a paradox on the question of bonus criteria simplicity. Bonus schemes based on simple and easy-to-understand criteria may be more durable, but the inevitable complexities in modern organisations complicates what constitutes performance. Merely acknowledging such complexity could also help to increase the viability of a bonus scheme.

Performance indicators on which bonuses are based include:

- *profits* in schemes covering either all employees or senior executives only (in about two-thirds of organisations in the Industrial Society's 1998 survey)
- *quantity of work or output* (used by 63 per cent of organisations) and/or *quality of work* (used by 47 per cent of organisations) in the case of manual workers
- a *combination of factors*, which Incomes Data Services (2001) suggests is a growing trend.

Multifactor schemes

Some organisations with bonuses have job-specific as well as site-level or company-wide bonus elements. For instance (Incomes Data Services 1999) Autoglass has a job-specific element that focuses on growth and a company-wide bonus element that includes reference to a customer service index; while Bonas Machine has a multifactor scheme based on six customer service targets (for example, customer response times) and on six employee measures (such as attendance).

Some large organisations have set up a central flexible framework for bonus schemes in the organisation, which enables business units or teams to decide on the selection of appropriate performance measures while retaining a common payment system. This has an advantage in equal value terms since, if equal access to an equivalent bonus arrangement can be seen, there is less basis for a successful equal value claim based on one 'gendered' occupational group having a bonus and another, also gendered, not having access to a bonus.

Multifactor manufacturing bonus at IBC Vehicles

The bonus is related to the performance of the whole manufacturing area. Targets are set for four factors: attendance, health and safety, product quality and meeting the set production schedule. The target level of achievement for each of the factors is determined by the parent company, General Motors. The targets are 'hit/miss', with a fixed payment being made for reaching the set level. Each target accounts for a quarter of the potential pay-out.

Factors	Targets	Bonus payment
Attendance	Attendance rate of 96 per cent or above	0.25%
Health and Safety	Fewer than 3.3 work days lost due to accidents per 2,000 hours worked	0.25%
Quality	Reaching 95 per cent of the global delivery survey	0.25%
Schedule	Achieving 100 per cent of the set schedule	0.25%

Drawn from Incomes Data Services (1999)

Table 40 *Example of a multifactor bonus scheme*

Gainsharing

The concept and term 'gainsharing' was coined by the architect of scientific management, FW Taylor, who advocated sharing between a firm and its workers the benefits of any positive margin between actual and expected costs during a given period. Gainsharing is a type of bonus scheme, in which employees share the benefits of increases in productivity. It is typically based on added value concepts and, critically, it has a strong employee involvement element within it.

There are many varieties of gainsharing, but schemes typically involve bonus payments for productivity improvement and/or reductions in costs. The organisation's profit performance is usually of lesser significance within the bonus calculation, since the groups covered by gainsharing plans are frontline or shop-floor workers, who individually are likely not see to see that they have much control over overall bottom line figures. Such schemes are customised to fit the individual organisation's circumstances. There is no definitive gainsharing scheme, but these two older schemes provide reward specialists with something of a model.

- The *Scanlon* plan stresses cost reduction while maintaining output levels. In its simplest form the formula calculates the bonus based on the wage costs of the employees involved as a proportion of the sales value of what they produced. In more detailed schemes, other costs are also included. An important aspect of the Scanlon plan was the employee participation it entailed – it involved the creation of a productivity norm and the setting up of committees in the organisation to facilitate employee involvement in the organisation. Bowey *et al* (1980) argued that much of the success of the Scanlon plan was due to the co-operative atmosphere, and sense of participation, which the productivity discussions promoted.

- *Rucker* plans have a bonus formula based on added value that allows employees to benefit from savings in production-related materials. Added value is defined as the difference between sales revenue and the cost of goods and services bought in; a measure of the 'wealth' created by the company. Rucker showed that labour costs expressed as a proportion of added value remained stable over long periods of time, and therefore could provide a measure of productivity to be used in a bonus formula.

Gainsharing plans have grown in popularity in recent years in the United States (Band *et al* 1994), as employers have sought productivity and quality improvement as well as better employee relations. According to Band, gainsharing has three essential elements: '*a values base, an involvement mechanism and a tangible reward, usually financial*'.

Its advantages are the promotion of teamwork and co-operation in the workplace, including communication of goals, substantial access to performance information and the empowering of employees to identify and resolve impediments to performance. Gainsharing might be seen to suffer from a 'dilution' of the incentive effect, especially when there is a large group of employees covered. But it can create an environment in which productivity issues can be discussed and taken forward in a co-operative spirit.

Proponents of gainsharing approaches argue that they provide managers in a company with a good basis for communicating information, encouraging teamwork and focusing attention on factors such as the quality and usage of materials (IRS 1996).

Profit-sharing and share ownership

Cash results-based bonus schemes are not alternatives to share-based schemes, with many private-sector organisations having more than one arrangement in place (CIPD 2003). Both

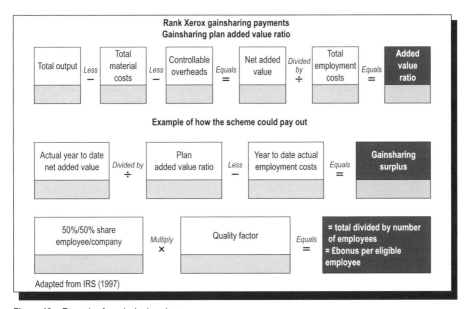

Figure 12 *Example of a gainsharing plan*

Quarterly plant performance is measured against a predetermined standard based on the concept of added value (the value of total output less total material costs and controllable overheads). Payments are generated when a certain level of productivity improvement is exceeded. To maintain quality, product quality targets are set annually and failure to achieve these reduces the gainshare payments. Productivity improvements in each of the first three years of the scheme generated a positive gainshare pool split 50:50 between the company and eligible employees. In 1995, the scheme delivered flat-rate cash payments averaging around 2% of employees' salary but payments in the second year fell to under 1%. There is no upper limit on the earnings that can be achieved.

Source: IRS (1997)

profit-sharing and employee share ownership can provide managers and workers with a sense of common purpose, and are characteristic of organisations viewing relations with employees as unitarist. The DTI (1999) also argues that employee share ownership schemes or equity-based management recruitment incentives have been used successfully by companies to promote the sharing of knowledge in their organisations. This – it is suggested – is particularly important in the sharing of '*tacit knowledge*', which can if utilised lead to 'competitive advantage' for companies.

Various governments have given tax breaks to encourage wider share ownership. The UK Chancellor, Gordon Brown, said in his 1999 Budget speech: '*Share ownership offers employees a real stake in their company ... I want ... to reward long-term commitment by employees. I want to encourage the new enterprise culture of teamwork in which everyone contributes and everyone benefits from success.*'

There is a clear distinction between schemes for top executives that offer an option to buy shares in the company at a future date and all-employee share ownership plans. Encouraged by favourable tax treatment, the number of senior managers covered by share option schemes has nearly trebled since 1979. The take-up for all-employee schemes has been rather more modest. Senior executives' share options are seen as a benefit, since they are potentially worth millions, but the more modest out-turn gained by other employees, typically via Save As You Earn (SAYE) schemes, are seen as a means of providing a sense of common purpose, encouraging employees' understanding of business conditions and providing a valuable point of reference for communicating about corporate performance issues.

Schemes that conform to the rules laid down by the Inland Revenue and obtain approval by that organisation qualify for tax concessions.

- The all-employee share plan (or 'Aesop') allows firms to give free shares (which may be performance-related) to the whole workforce without tax liability. It also gives tax breaks to employees who buy shares and hold them for five years (with smaller tax breaks to workers who hold them for three years).

- The enterprise management incentive programme (EMI) was introduced to help smaller companies with potential for growth to recruit and retain high-calibre employees. A qualifying organisation can grant options under the EMI to up to 15 of its most important people.

- The company share option plan is aimed at senior managers and other high-level employees. The Inland Revenue allows employees to be given options to purchase shares at a predetermined price at some future date, without paying income tax on the grant or on any increase in the market value of shares. Participants pay capital gains tax when the shares are sold. In practice, because there is a ceiling on the amount that can be granted free of tax, most companies provide options in addition to, or instead of, those granted under the scheme.

- Under SAYE schemes employees enter a special savings contract that deducts money from their pay-to-buy options that allow them to buy company shares in three, five or seven years' time, at today's price or at a discount of up to 20 per cent of that price. It tends to be seen as a savings scheme, rather than a share-ownership scheme.

There is some evidence that such schemes do have a corporate benefit. The work of Conyon and Freeman (2001) suggests a positive correlation between company productivity and the existence of shared compensation schemes (profit-sharing and share schemes).

Case study – AutoParts Manufacturing Ltd

AutoParts Manufacturing Ltd is one of many firms in the supply chain for the automotive industry, which used to be the mainstay of the West Midlands industrial scene. During the 1980s and 1990s the company downsized several times – cutting its workforce, which had been 7,000-strong in the early 1980s progressively to just under 500 by early 2001. The company's product range has been gradually whittled down over that same period of time to a handful of specialised automotive components, made to the detailed specifications of just four car manufacturers. Quality initiatives in the car-manufacturing firms have meant that the quality aspects of the product specifications in the supplier company have become more and more exacting.

At the same time the cost base of AutoParts Manufacturing Ltd has been under constant pressure and subject to detailed review by its parent company – International Engineering Co. The parent company has appointed a succession of managing directors to lead AutoParts Manufacturing Ltd during the past two decades. However, most of these top executives have only served as MD for less than two years before being moved elsewhere within the parent company group. Other senior managers, too, have ended up as rather short-term appointees. In marked contrast, the rest of the workforce has an average length of service close to 10 years. Many joined the company when it was generally thought that they were privileged to gain a position with such a well-known and solid company as AutoParts Manufacturing Ltd, with whom they could expect a 'job for life'.

The workforce that remains after the many waves of redundancy is divided as follows:

- 280 machine operators on two separate, but very close, factory sites
- 30 craft and maintenance staff, covering both sites
- 10 production engineers – largely focused on quality work and in meeting customers' specification standards
- 25 administrative and centrally based office staff
- one personnel officer and a half-time personnel assistant
- two senior managers – one production director/manager and one financial director/manager.

Pay arrangements for the manual worker groups (operators and craft) used to follow the national engineering agreement. Since the ending of national pay bargaining in the engineering industry, pay has – in effect – been set by management, albeit after a somewhat perfunctory consultation with the trade unions – principally the T&G. Union membership is still fairly high, but most employees in the company – including the union representatives – believe the unions are weak and ineffective.

For a number of years, manual workers have been paid (for the most part) only basic pay rates – upgraded very marginally each year by slightly less than the rate of inflation – plus a modest set of shift premiums. Overtime payments are now only available in exceptional circumstances.

In addition, for a few years most employees were eligible for inclusion in a profit-sharing scheme, which gained tax exemption under the Government's profit-related pay scheme. This never yielded high payments, but did provide something of a cushion against any erosion of basic pay rates in relation to the market. Once the Inland Revenue terminated the PRP scheme's tax breaks, the company's financial director could no longer see any point to the scheme and ended it.

In January 2002 a new MD was appointed to the company from within the parent company. A dynamic American, he is shocked by the culture he observes in the UK company. He has been briefed to keep the UK company going and potentially to merge it with an Italian company in the group, which has a similar product range. If the two companies could work well together, both of their long-term futures would be more secure. He has, however, also been tasked with keeping the cost base of the UK company under tight control.

As part of his initial discussions with employees in the UK company, he is much influenced by one of the longer-serving trade union representatives. She tells him that following all the redundancies in the company the remaining employees are experiencing 'survivor syndrome', in that many people believe that it is the employees made redundant who were the 'lucky ones' and those who kept their jobs the 'unlucky ones'. This union representative also tells the new MD that staff morale is 'on the floor'.

The MD calls you in as a trusted reward manager with whom he has previously worked in another difficult corporate situation.

Your role
You are given a very specific brief.

- Propose two optional new performance pay schemes that would be suitable for this organisation, identifying the organisational constraints as well as the need for a new scheme. Consider some of the options, given the organisational circumstances – gainsharing, share schemes, individual PRP, or competency-based schemes.

EVALUATING AND MONITORING PERFORMANCE PAY

Monitoring and evaluating performance pay schemes is desirable not just to ensure that the schemes 'work', but also to assess value for money and to minimise equal pay problems. If some groups in an organisation have access to bonus schemes and others do not, the situation can give rise to valid equal pay claims. Equality of access between different occupational groups, particularly those in which one or other gender is much more numerous, is therefore an important aspect to check.

Evaluating any pay system is problematic (see Chapter 1). Thorpe (2000) suggests a multiple-perspective approach, since most studies of performance pay show that managers, especially top managers and senior HR managers, are much more optimistic about the effects of schemes than are line managers and employees. Therefore evaluations need to include research on the views of the senior managers, the line managers who operate the system and the employees.

The research may include an attitude survey conducted at different points in time and at different levels in the organisation. (An example of part of an attitude survey of senior civil servants conducted in 1993 is shown in Table 41, page 144) The evaluation also may include collection of organisation data on the distribution of performance pay, over a period of time. The extent to which other HR data (such as exit interview results) are relevant is questionable. Hendry *et al* (2000) give a useful checklist of points to consider in Table 42, page 145.

STUDENT REVIEW QUESTIONS

1. Bearing in mind all the research on performance pay that has been carried out, should organisations be devoting more or fewer resources to developing and managing performance pay schemes?

2. What do you consider are the organisational circumstances in which performance payments work well? Give reasons and examples in your answer.

SECTION 2	THE LINK BETWEEN PERFORMANCE AND PAY IN THE SENIOR OPEN STRUCTURE					
	strongly disagree	disagree	neither agree nor disagree	agree	strongly agree	no response
17. Since the performance pay scheme was introduced discussions about my performance are more sharply focused on:						
– continuing performance improvement	13.3%	40.3%	29.5%	13.7%	.6%	2.5%
– addressing development needs	16.4%	45.3%	30.1%	5.6%	0	2.5%
– achievement of objectives	11.4%	33.1%	24.1%	26.4%	2.7%	2.3%
18. I have a clear understanding of how my box marking/performance assessment links to performance pay awards	14.6%	32.6%	16.0%	31.8%	4.0%	1.0%
19. I have a clear understanding of how performance pay awards are allocated for my grade in my Department/Agency	17.7%	36.2%	12.5%	28.1%	5.2%	.4%
20. The performance pay scheme encourages better individual performance	23.5%	31.4%	22.0%	20.4%	2.5%	.2%
21. I am satisfied with the process for deciding my performance pay awards	11.6%	23.1%	35.1%	26.8%	2.5%	.8%
22. The performance pay scheme has a negative impact on co-operation and teamwork	5.8%	44.9%	33.1%	11.4%	4.2%	.6%
23. I believe the performance pay awards in my grade are distributed fairly	3.3%	6.7%	68.6%	18.7%	1.2%	1.5%
24. I can expect to receive a performance pay award if I perform exceptionally well	2.3%	6.7%	13.3%	64.4%	12.5%	.8%
25. The performance pay awards under the current scheme are worth striving for	21.6%	37.6%	21.6%	18.1%	.6%	.4%
26. I am motivated in my job by the possibility of receiving a performance pay award	36.0%	36.8%	12.9%	12.9%	1.0%	.4%
27. I can influence my chances of receiving a performance pay award through my own efforts and management of my staff	6.0%	8.5%	18.9%	60.3%	5.8%	.4%
28. Exceptionally good performers should receive significantly higher pay awards than average performers	2.1%	7.7%	8.9%	55.7%	24.5%	1.0%
29. I believe the management of the performance pay scheme has improved over the last two years	7.7%	18.7%	57.6%	13.5%	.8%	1.7%
30. The performance pay scheme rewards teamwork	13.5%	47.4%	31.8%	7.1%	.0	.2%
31. On the whole, the performance pay scheme is well designed	16.4%	31.4%	39.9%	11.0%	.4%	.8%
32. On the whole, the performance pay scheme is well managed	10.0%	23.5%	46.4%	19.1%	.2%	.8%

Table 41 *Example of part of a performance pay evaluation attitude survey questionnaire*

Performance management diagnostic

1. Reasons
What has triggered rethinking the performance management system or rewards at this time?

2. Objectives
What are our strategic business goals for the short, medium and long term?
Who or what delivers critical performance with respect to the business goals?
What kind of performance contract do we want with employees?
What is the performance system designed to do (eg attract/retain/motivate/control)?

3. Environment
External contingencies:
What stage of the business cycle are we in?
What are the effects of the national/societal culture we operate in on attitudes to performance and differentials?

Internal contingencies:
What are the motivational assumptions of the relevant group(s) of employees?
What are the relevant internal employee reference groups and how do they affect attitudes to differentials?

4. Systems
What is the range of things we have to do to support these particular performance/business goals that affect employees' knowledge, capability, and motivation?

5. Design
Content:
What is a reward? How do we define rewards?
What is an incentive? How do we define incentives?
What measures are appropriate (eg in terms of the short, medium, and long term; financial v non-financial measures; individual v group)?
Can we measure performance and design rewards appropriately?
Can people perceive this connection (the 'line of sight')?

Process:
Are there linkages or disconnections through the whole reward structure? Is there 'buy-in' from other managers in the design/management of the performance system?
Is the process manageable or over-complex?
How do we communicate about performance and rewards, including feedback?

6. Outcomes
What is the impact on behaviour (eg does the performance system reinforce the old or motivate new behaviours)?
Retrospectively ... what is the pay-off or success criterion?
Is it possible to define return on investment criteria, taking into account the overall costs of designing and administering the scheme, and paying out rewards?

7. Monitoring
What review process is in place, or needs to be created?

Adapted from Hendry *et al* (1999)

Table 42 *Performance pay diagnostic*

REFERENCES

ACAS (1990) *Developments in payment systems: the 1988 ACAS survey*. Occasional Paper 45, ACAS.

Armstrong, M and Baron, A (1998) *Performance management: the new realities*. IPD.

Bach, S (2000) *From performance appraisal to performance management*, in Bach, S and Sisson, K (eds) *Personnel management: a comprehensive guide to theory and practice*. 3rd edition. Blackwell.

Band, D, Scanlan, G and Tustin, C (1994) Beyond the bottom line: gainsharing and organizational development. *Personnel Review*. Vol 23, no 8, pp17–32.

Bowey, A, Thorpe, R and Hellier, P (1980) *Payment systems and productivity*. Macmillan.

Bowey, A, Thorpe, R, Gosnold, D, Mitchell, E and Nichols, G (1982) *Effects of incentive schemes, United Kingdom 1977–1980*. Research Paper 36. Department of Employment.

Boyatzis, R (1982) *The competent manager: a model for effective performance*. Wiley.

Brown, D (1998) *Rethinking performance pay*. Institute of Personnel and Development's Compensation Forum Ninth Annual Conference.

Brown, M (2001) Merit pay preferences among public sector employees. *Human Resource Management Journal*. Vol 11, no 4, pp38–54.

Brown, W, Deakin, S, Hudson, M, Pratten, C and Ryan, P (1999)*The individualisation of employment contracts in Britain*. Research paper for the Department of Trade and Industry, Centre for Business Research, Department of Applied Economics, University of Cambridge.

Cannell, M and Wood, S (1992) *Incentive pay: impact and evolution*. IPM/NEDO.

Caplan, R and Norton, D (1992) The balanced scorecard: measures that drive performance. *Harvard Business Review*. January–February.

Chartered Institute of Personnel and Development (2002) *Reward management survey: survey report*. CIPD.

Chartered Institute of Personnel and Development (2003) *Reward management survey: survey report*. January. CIPD.

Citizen's Charter (1991) Cmnd 1599, HMSO.

Conyon, M and Freeman, R (2001) *Shared modes of compensation and company performance: UK evidence*. National Bureau of Economic Research, working paper W8448.

Cully, M *et al* (1998) *The 1998 workplace employee relations survey: first findings*. DTI.

Department of Trade and Industry (1999) Our competitive future: building the knowledge-driven economy. Cmnd 4176, HMSO.

Dowling, F and Richardson, R (1997) Evaluating performance-related pay for managers in the NHS. *International Journal of Human Resource Management*. Vol 8, no 3, pp348–366.

Foster, D and Hoggett, P (1999) Change in the Benefits Agency: empowering the exhausted worker? *Work Employment and Society*. Vol 13, no1, pp19–39.

Freeman, R (2001) Upping the stakes: employee share ownership. *People Management*. 8 February, pp25–29.

Gould-Williams, J (2002) 'Rewarding' management practices: the effects on public sector workers. Paper presented at the Performance and Reward Conference, Manchester Metropolitan University, 11 April.

Guest, D (1999) IPD Compensation Forum. 9 February.

Harris, L (2001) Rewarding employee performance: line managers' values, beliefs and perspectives. *International Journal of Human Resource Management.* Vol 12, no 1.

Hendry, C, Woodward, S, Bradley, P, and Perkins, S (2000) Performance and rewards: cleaning out the stables. *Human Resource Management Journal.* Vol 10, no 3.

Heneman, H and Judge, T (2000) *Compensation attitudes,* in Rynes, S and Gerhart, B (eds) *Compensation in organizations: current research and practice.* Jossey-Bass.

Heneman, R, Ledford, G and Gresham, M (2000) *The changing nature of work and its effects on compensation design and delivery,* in Rynes, S and Gerhart, B (eds) *Compensation in organizations: current research and practice.* Jossey-Bass.

Incomes Data Services (1999) Bonus schemes. *IDS Study* 665. March.

Incomes Data Services (2000) Performance pay. *IDS Focus* 96. Winter.

Incomes Data Services (2001) Bonus schemes. *IDS Study* 705. March.

Industrial Relations Services (1996) Rewarding employees in the 1990s. *IRS Management Review.* October.

Industrial Relations Services (1997) *IRS Pay and Benefits Bulletin.* 431. September.

Industrial Society (1997) *Competency-based pay.* Managing Best Practice.

Industrial Society (1998) *Bonus and incentive schemes.* Managing Best Practice. 50.

Institute of Personnel and Development (1999) *Performance pay survey.* IPD.

Institute of Personnel and Development (1999) *Performance pay trends in the UK: survey report.* IPD.

Kaplan, R and Norton, D (1993) Putting the Balanced Scorecard to Work. *Harvard Business Review.* Vol 71, no 5, Sept–Oct, pp134–147.

Kessler, I and Purcell, J (1993) *The Templeton performance-related pay project: summary of key findings.* Templeton College, Oxford, MRP94/93.

Kohn, A (1993) Why incentive plans cannot work. *Harvard Business Review.* September–October.

Kohn, A (1998) Challenging behaviourist dogma: myths about money and motivation. *Compensation & Benefits Review.* March–April.

LeBlanc, P and Mulvey, P (1998) How American workers see the rewards of work. *Compensation and Benefits Review.* Vol 30, no 1, pp24–31.

Lewis, P (1991) Performance-related pay: pretexts and pitfalls. *Employee Relations.* No 1, pp12–16.

Locke, E (1968) Towards a theory of task performance and incentives. *Organizational Behaviour and Human Performance.* Vol 3, no 2, pp157–189.

Marsden, D and French, S (1998) *What a performance.* LSE Centre for Economic Performance.

Newton, T and Findlay, P (1996) Play God? The performance of appraisal. *Human Resource Management Journal.* Vol 6, no 3.

Pfeffer, J (1998) Six dangerous myths about pay. *Harvard Business Review*. May–June, pp109–119.

Porter, L and Lawler, E (1968) *Managerial attitudes and performance*. Irwin.

Sisson, K and Storey, J (2000) *the realities of human resource management*. Open University Press.

Sparrow, P (1996) Too good to be true? *People Management* Dec. 1996, pp22–27.

Strebler, M (1997) Skills, competencies and gender: issues for pay and training. Institute of Employment Studies Report 333.

Thompson, M (1993) *Pay and performance: the employee experience.* Institute for Employment Studies Report 258.

Thompson, M (1995) *Team working and pay.* Institute for Employment Studies Report 281.

Thorpe, R (2000) *Reward strategy*, in Thorpe, R and Homan, G (eds) *Strategic reward systems*. Financial Times/ Prentice Hall.

The Work Foundation (2003) *Restructuring performance-related pay*. Managing Best Practice 105.

Wood, R (1993) *Private pay for public work: performance-related pay for public-sector managers.* Puma Public Management Studies. OECD.

Wood, S (1996) High commitment management and payment systems. *Journal of Management Studies.* January, pp 53.

Equality and reward

CHAPTER 6

INTRODUCTION

Providing reward policies that are genuinely equal between men and women, and between people of different ethnic origin, are issues likely to rank high on the reward practitioner agenda in the future. Fresh impetus to change will probably come through European Union policy initiatives that require the UK Government to take action.

The Government for its part has launched research and taken measures to improve the cumbersome legal process. Reward managers have some very difficult issues to confront and tackle. Within the European context, the UK has a particularly acute problem with pay and gender. Increasing volumes of research in this field have added usefully to existing knowledge, but much of the work is at the macrostatistical level, and application at the organisational level can be problematic.

> **Organisations ... need practical guidance and advice on correcting or avoiding ... unjustifiable gender pay differences.**
>
> **(CIPD 2001)**

This chapter focuses on gender and pay and touches briefly on pay and ethnicity and pay and disability. It reviews the research literature in these areas and then looks more practically at the conduct of equal pay audits, reviewing company practice.

The material in this chapter can contribute to the development of the following CIPD professional standards in reward:

Operational indicators – Practitioners must be able to:

- promote fairness in reward practice
- help to analyse a pay structure to assess whether it contains sex or other discrimination
- suggest ways of ensuring that a job evaluation scheme is free of bias
- conduct an equal pay audit to identify any cases of pay discrimination
- advise on methods of eliminating them.

Knowledge indicators – Practitioners must understand and be able to explain:

- the factors that influence employee satisfaction with their rewards and the reward system – such as equity, fairness, consistency and transparency
- the significance of relevant legislation, including the law on equal pay.

A LONG WAY TO GO, AND FEW SIGNPOSTS . . .

Within the literature on reward there is a notable lack of guidance on what employers should do to reduce the gender pay gap. However, since the causes of the gender pay gap are not fully understood, this reluctance is perhaps explicable. The now growing literature on equality is of limited practical help on pay and gender and could easily give readers the impression that reward systems are nothing to do with the initiatives that many large organisations take to promote greater diversity and equal opportunities among their workforces. Although there are many equal opportunities specialists and managers employed in organisations, their role rarely extends beyond the traditional areas of recruitment/selection and training/development to cover aspects of reward equality. Among the possible reasons for this is that reward may be perceived as a technical area that is the preserve of a few specialists, either in the organisation or in external consultancies, deploying value-free, 'objective' techniques. There is a tendency (as, for example, in Cornelius 2002) to leave unchallenged the techniques of pay determination in a way that seems highly unusual when compared with the manner in which other HR practices are scrutinised.

Government and EU policy

The equal pay problem is evident in other countries but is particularly problematic in the UK, in spite of more than 30 years of legislation prohibiting unequal treatment. The principle of equal pay for work of equal value has, in one form or another, been enshrined in European law since the 1950s. As an EU paper (European Commission, Economic and Social Affairs Committee (2001) commented:

> Governments, employers and trade unions all accept that women should receive the same pay as their male colleagues for doing equal work or work of equal value. However, turning this principle into reality has proved a formidable task.

The Swedish presidency of the EU during the first six months of 2001 launched a set of policy initiatives to address equal pay problems across the Union. The legal framework for this initiative relates to the principle of equal pay for men and women, which is contained in Article 141.1 of the EC Treaty. More details are given on pages 160ff below of the relevant legal framework.

Labour market data show that women are increasingly in paid employment, with many more women working part-time than men. It may be said that self-evidently if women work fewer hours than men they should be paid less than men. Of course, full-time work generates more pay than part-time employment, but there is a deeper problem, since overall average effective pay worked out on an hourly basis is higher for men than women part-timers, and higher for full-timers than part-timers.

Repeated surveys show that when women and men are asked why they work part-time, the most common answer is that they don't want full-time employment. Part-time working is particularly attractive to mothers keen to reconcile parenting with paid employment. The question for individuals and employers is the extent to which part-time work is seen as a benefit in itself, apparently justifying lower effective pay rates – even though this sort of trade-off does not comply with the law.

The gender pay gap

The gap between average earnings (worked out on an hourly basis) for men and women when they work full-time has narrowed from 31 per cent to 18 per cent since the introduction of the Equal Pay Act 1970, but the 39 per cent gap between average hourly earnings of women working part-time and men working full-time has barely moved. In the UK, although a high proportion of women work, differences in their pay compared with that of men persist. After the effects of the Sex Discrimination Act and the Equal Pay Act of the 1970s worked through, there was a slow upward trend in women's relative earnings. There have been some changes to close the gap following the introduction of the national minimum wage (see Chapter 2).

How is the gender pay gap measured?

The overall gender pay gap across the country is measured by comparing the average pay of full-time men and women, worked out on an hourly basis. The best measure is usually thought to be the rate that excludes overtime payments from the reckoning. This most fairly reflects the fact that far fewer women than men work overtime. The survey data used are from the New Earnings Survey, as this is a representative sample survey of the national workforce. In 2003 women's average hourly pay was 82.0 per cent of men's (compared with the 81.0 per cent recorded in April 2002), yielding a pay gap of 18 per cent.

If median hourly pay (excluding overtime) is used instead of the average, the gap between women's and men's hourly earnings (excluding overtime) is 12.9 per cent.

CAUSES OF PAY INEQUALITY

No single cause can explain why the pay gap persists. Uncovering its causes has been likened to peeling an onion – as each layer of causes is revealed the gap narrows but some remain. In some ways the gap is linked to, but not explained by, some obvious differences in employment patterns between men and women (in terms of hours worked, when those hours are worked and so on). There are also differences in education levels – at least historically – and in the length of time women have spent out of the labour market. Other significant factors are occupational segregation and the low pay and status of part-time work. A debatable proportion of the gap is caused by direct or indirect unequal treatment or pay discrimination.

More broadly, the pay gap could be viewed as a reflection of women's less advantageous position within the labour market. Generally speaking, work done by women is valued less highly than work done by men, and this has implications for the use of job evaluation to justify differences in pay (see Chapter 2).

Other reasons include:

- age (women in the workforce are generally younger on average than men)
- education (women may have fewer qualifications than men)
- sectors of work (women tend to work in different sectors and in different occupations from men)
- career breaks for child-rearing
- lack of opportunities for promotion.

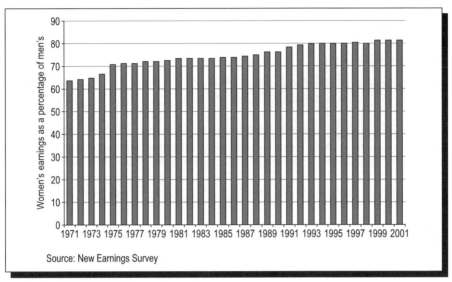

Source: New Earnings Survey

Figure 13 *Trends in the gender pay gap 1971–2001*

But does pay discrimination have a role to play? Many employers say no. Others argue (for example, the EOC Equal Pay Taskforce – see EOC 2001) that at least 15 per cent of the pay gap is caused by direct or indirect discrimination.

Managers may insist (Morrell *et al* 2001) that they do not treat men and women differently. Indeed they may be firmly convinced that their respective organisations have no problem. Morrell's study showed that many managers were complacent or convinced that their pay systems did not discriminate, even though they had not conducted any equal pay audits to assess this. Morrell also comments that 'many HR managers are clearly far more comfortable discussing equal opportunities issues in general than equal pay specifically'. Most of the discrimination in pay systems takes the form of indirect or hidden discrimination. Therefore teasing out all the many causes of gender pay differences can be a complicated quest.

Many managers may simply assume that most of the gender differences are justifiable on grounds other than gender *per se*, because they can see no obvious signs of gender bias in pay systems.

Uncovering the elements of inequality

Looking a little more closely at some of the elements associated with the gender pay split – and using research to help illuminate some of the issues – can help in solving the problem.

Time off to have children and career experience
The career break to have children is often assumed to be a main cause of pay difference. This is partially substantiated, but as research by Rake, Davies and Joshi (2000) for the Cabinet Office found, the gap in earnings for women in comparison with men over a whole career is substantial, even if the women have no time out of the labour market apart from maternity leave. For example, a woman graduate with children can expect to earn just £19,000 less than a women graduate who is childless; however, the gap between women graduates who are mothers and men graduates who are fathers rises steeply to £162,000 over a whole career. There is also a significant pay gap between childless women and men.

Level of education	Man	Childless woman	Woman with 2 children
No qualifications	£731,000	£534,000	£249,000
GCSEs	£891,000	£650,000	£510,000
Graduates	£1,333,000	£1,190,000	£1,171,000 ·
Source: Rake *et al*, 2000			

Table 43   *Estimates of gross life-time earnings for men and women, with and without children*

Dispersion of earnings – higher pay moving faster than lower pay

The dispersion of earnings in the UK widened considerably during the last two decades of the 20th century. Certainly, the main gainers from this were those at the top of the earnings distribution, whose pay moved faster than those on both middle and below-average earnings. This trend, together with the slow moves of women into senior posts, exacerbated the gender pay gap.

The top 10 per cent of women wage earners in the European Union earn on average 35 per cent less than the top 10 per cent of men wage earners, according to the 2001 *Harmonised Statistics on Earnings* (ESTAT 2001). This feature holds true throughout the Union, and is especially marked in France, Italy and the UK. On the other hand, the lowest paid 10 per cent of women have hourly wages that are on average some 15 per cent lower than men. The *OECD Employment Report 1998* commented: 'women, accordingly, would appear to experience more difficulty than men in advancing their careers, at least so far as pay is concerned, no matter what type of job they do. Though the difficulty seems to be more acute among managers, it is also evident for office workers and sales staff as well as manual workers.'

Clouded in mystery

A large part of the gender pay gap evades statistical explanation, leading analysts to suggest that it is attributable to continuing direct discrimination or inadequacies in the analysis – according to econometric research in Australia (Pocock 1999), which has a somewhat better record on equal pay than the UK.

There is widespread lack of knowledge about pay and gender issues. Research for the EOC (2000) showed that when people were given information about gender pay differences they agreed that it was unacceptable for women still to earn less than men.

International dimensions

Yet international comparisons (Figure 14 overleaf) show, on average, that women across the EU continue to earn less than men by as much as 25 per cent. This is despite a small rise in the average earnings of women compared with men since 1995. A disproportionate number of the low-paid are women, while a disproportionate number of those in the highest-paid jobs are men. Women make up an estimated 77 per cent of low-income employees in the European Union.

The comparisons in Figure 14 (drawn from Eurostat data) show that the gender pay problem is not unique to the UK, but the UK has a poor record in Europe on equal pay compared with other countries.

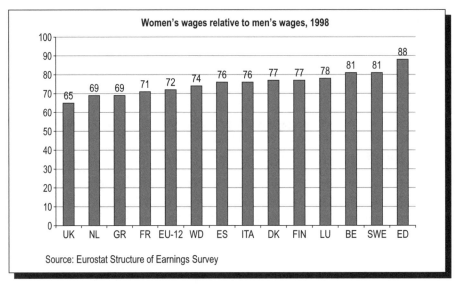

Figure 14   *Gender pay gap in European countries*

Job evaluation and equal pay

Job evaluation is clearly an important tool for employers wishing to defend themselves against an equal pay claim. However, as discussed in Chapter 2, it is important to recognise that a job evaluation scheme implicitly contains the value set of the organisation that uses it. If that organisation has strong job segregation by gender there must be some obvious equality questions about the nature of the job evaluations used. Since the *Bromley* v *HJ Quick* case (see page 161), only analytical job evaluation schemes have been used by the majority of UK employers.

However, no job evaluation scheme is objectively free of gender bias – the lack of testing in the tribunals does not guarantee gender neutrality. Moreover, as the local government sector has found, attempting to implement a job evaluation scheme devised with equality as its principal objective makes it difficult in other respects to set a workable pay structure.

Contribution of EU and UK Government initiatives

Equal pay was the priority theme of the European Commission's programme and received a good deal of attention. The remedying of deficiencies in available data in permitting cross-country comparisons – so as to be able to measure progress in achieving equal pay objectives – is one practical tactic suggested before more substantive guidance could be given.

Just Pay – the report of the Equal Pay Task Force – was published in 2001. The Equal Pay Task Force considered how to eliminate discrimination in pay systems, estimated to account for 25–50 per cent of the total pay gap. It recommended:

- publicising the facts about unequal pay
- improving equal pay legislation, introducing mandatory pay reviews and a streamlined tribunal process
- improved guidance for employers and unions and a Government requirement for pay reviews in the public sector

- opening up discussion about pay, with reporting of pay reviews in employers' annual reports
- various Government actions, using policies such as the National Minimum Wage, the National Childcare Strategy and the National Skills Agenda to help narrow the pay gap.

The report contains a number of recommendations to tackle the three causes of the pay gap. In relation to pay discrimination, the Task Force believes that the most effective measure is to force employers to carry out pay audits of their workforces. This recommendation, however, has caused a great deal of controversy.

While the Government has voiced its commitment to eradicating unequal pay, the Task Force and the Government did not accept the Task Force suggestions about mandatory equal pay reviews.

The Task Force believed that the pay gap could be eliminated entirely within eight years, provided the main barriers to equal pay were addressed. These barriers included:

- lack of awareness and understanding of the issues
- ineffective, time-consuming and cumbersome equal pay legislation
- lack of transparency and accountability for implementing equal pay
- social, economic and policy measures – such as family credit – that have failed to keep pace with women's changing place in the labour market.

Another point that emerges from the report is that any successful attempt to eradicate the pay gap within the eight-year period would require considerable commitment, resources and concerted action by employers, trade unions and the Government. The Task Force also found that occupational segregation and the unequal impact of women's family responsibilities contribute to the pay gap.

The Kingsmill Review (2001) confirmed some of the findings of the Task Force and also found in favour of compulsory equal pay audits in companies.

Age and other contributors to the pay gap

The OECD's 1998 *Employment in Europe Report*, which looked at the gender pay gap, said that age was part of the cause. The gap exists in all age groups considered separately but widens significantly the older the worker. So for women aged 40 to 54 working full-time, average hourly earnings were over 20 per cent lower than men's in all EU countries, except in Belgium (19 per cent lower), 30 per cent lower in France, Italy and Luxembourg, one-third lower in the Netherlands, 40 per cent lower in the UK and almost 45 per cent lower in Greece.

Length of service

Surprisingly the OECD's 1998 *Employment in Europe Report* found that relative length of service seemed to make little difference within age groups. The report concluded that 'the wage gap tends to be wider for those who have been in a job for a relatively long period of time than for those who have been in a job for nearly a year or two'.

Starting salaries

One of the problems perpetuating unequal pay is that of pay history. If women start on lower pay than men in the same job or jobs of equal value, then they are likely to carry this difference as a burden though their time in their current role – and very probably for many years. The evidence from a number of studies is that starting salaries for women do indeed tend to be lower than those of men, in spite of apparently gender-neutral policies on setting pay at recruitment. Women may either be offered less when starting a new job than similarly qualified men – or are appointed at lower points on the relevant pay range or pay scale than men. One possible reason for this is that women do not bargain as strongly as men when it comes to negotiating their pay on an individual basis.

Some studies conducted in the United States – a country with as poor a record on pay and gender as the UK – have shed some light on this hypothesis. Gerhart and Rynes (1991) examined whether women and men are equally likely to negotiate starting salary offers – and, if they negotiate, the extent to which they are successful. When all other relevant attributes were equal (education, experience, number of job offers held by the individual and general labour market conditions) the researchers found there was a statistically significant difference between men and women. However, the research also showed that bargaining paid off more for men than women. Men averaged a 4.3 per cent extra salary return when they negotiated with the potential employer, in comparison with just 2.7 per cent for women.

Economic theories used to explain gender pay differences

Various theories have been used to explain gender segregation in the labour market and gender pay differentials. No one theory, however, offers sufficient explanation as to why women and men face different conditions in the labour market.

Theories both from economics and from the feminist perspective have been used to explain the phenomenon of the gender pay gap.

Human capital theory

Women and men may have different types of human capital depending, for example, on their level of educational attainment. Women and men choose to use their capital in different ways, and they are assumed to act rationally in economic terms, as individuals and as employees. Men choose to pursue full-time careers, while women choose to work part-time in jobs that allow them to fit work around their childcare or domestic responsibilities.

The human capital theory, however, fails to take into account the fact that all such decisions by individuals are made in a social context where there are shared values and ideas about what women and men ought to do. Two other assumptions, which underlie this theory, are, firstly, that people with higher levels of skills or qualifications will effectively have greater human capital; and, secondly, that the use of skills by employees is valued by employers for the gains in productivity it brings.

The theory of monopsony

The theory of *monopsony* argues that where the employer is in a monopoly position, the lack of competition leads to a low price for labour. In the public sector, for example, there are comparatively few employers employing and paying for labour. The education, childcare and health-care sectors employ a large number of women. According to this theory, low pay rates can be set, since this part of the public sector is characterised by extreme gender segregation.

Crowding theory

The basic premise in *crowding* theory is the assumption that an excess supply of female labour leads to low pay. Even men who work in occupations where women predominate are affected by this. Indeed, an excessive supply of female workers may have larger negative effects on men's wages than on women's wages. Conversely, the crowding of men in an occupation or a section of the labour market leads to higher wages, though primarily for men.

Discrimination

Gender pay differentials can also be looked at using the concept of discrimination in the labour market.

- The term *direct discrimination* is used to describe the situation where different wages are paid for the same work.

- *Distribution discrimination* describes the phenomenon by which women and men with similar qualifications have differing chances of finding work in particular occupations because employers prefer to select men to work in those occupations.

- The term *value discrimination* describes the situation in which there is lower pay in occupations where women predominate. Work performed by women tends to be devalued.

Social attitudes and the pay gap

A report by a Swedish research team (Fransson, Johansson and Svenaeus 2001) says that *'in the European Union the idea is still current that it is the man who is the family's principal breadwinner, while a woman's income from work is merely supposed to supplement the man's income. For many women, marriage is the primary labour contract.'* In the Nordic countries, they point out, where almost as large a proportion of women are in paid employment as men, the 'ideal' of the housewife survives, though this is now in the form of an ideal that women should work part-time. Looking at the relationship between men and women in the workforce, it may be seen that to a great extent it is part-time employment by women that enables men to work full-time.

The question of shorter working hours is very much a gender equality issue. It may be argued that pay equality for women will not be achieved unless or until both paid work and unremunerated work within the family are shared equally between women and men.

A study of the attitudes of fathers (EOC 2003) shows that there remains widespread acceptance of traditional gender roles in parenting, the father providing financially while the mother looks after the children and home. Fathers, though, experience some tension between the conflicting demands of the breadwinner role and spending time with the family.

Moves to introduce family-friendly working

The Kingsmill report (2001) amongst others suggest that the implementation of HR policies and practices that ameliorate the effects of the 'long-hours culture' and more effective work-life balance policies will promote greater gender equality in workplaces. However, there is some evidence to suggest that this would only be effective in ameliorating the gender pay difference if men as well as women take up any such opportunities. A study by John Forth and Neil Millward (2000) of the factors determining pay levels showed that women with equivalent levels of education and training who have children earn 15 per cent less than men who have no children. By contrast, fathers with young children earn 8 per cent more than their counterparts without children. This finding mirrors the studies on hours of work, which suggest that it is fathers with young children who work the longest hours.

Education/skill differences

Under human capital theory, we would expect people with higher educational qualifications to earn more than those with lesser skills or education – since the productivity of the more qualified worker is assumed to be higher. Surprisingly there is evidence to show that gender pay differentials increase as the level of education rises. According to Eurostat statistics in the *1995 Structure of Earnings Survey*, women earn a maximum 78 per cent of men's wages at the lowest educational level, whereas when they have gone through higher education they earn 71 per cent of men's wages. This casts doubt on assumptions that if women gain access to senior jobs their pay will be the same as that of men at the same level.

A study by Purcell (2002) shows that male graduates have substantially higher average earnings than female graduates. Through new analysis of the Moving On Survey (a major survey conducted in 1998 of UK graduates three and a half years after graduation), the research reveals that women earn less on average than men even when they have studied the same subjects, achieved the same class of degree or entered the same industry or occupation (see Purcell 2002). The differences between men and women were most apparent in the private sector, and for graduates in law and in engineering.

The effect of occupational segregation

Women are concentrated in certain sectors of the economy that are also the sectors offering the lowest wages. Indeed, some researchers argue that a rise in the proportion of women in an occupation may be associated with a decline in relative pay. This concentration is a major contributor to the overall gender pay gap.

There is a shortage of men in the service sector. There is also clear vertical segregation in the labour market. The relation between women and men in the workplace is essentially hierarchical, with women subordinate to men in most organisations. A common image used to describe this vertical sex segregation is the 'glass ceiling', which acts as an invisible barrier to women's prospects of attaining higher positions.

Women are proportionately less well represented at the top of professions as well as at the top of organisations. In almost every occupation and organisation more men than women hold senior or high-level jobs. The resultant pay gap at the top end of the earnings scale is thus proportionately wider than lower down.

Pay discrimination in practice

Discrimination in pay systems is widespread and occurs in virtually all pay systems. But the evidence suggests that some systems may make gender differences easier to defend than others. Questions are directed at systems in which salary growth is linked to service and to performance or competencies, as well as the issue of market-based pay.

Performance pay

A study by Chauvin and Ash (1994) of business school graduates' pay showed that the principal difference by gender related to the proportion of pay that was based on performance.

The provision of non-consolidated bonus payments may be the cause of inequity of treatment within the area of performance pay. The problem here is that jobs done predominately by men have traditionally attracted eligibility for bonus payments, whereas jobs done principally by women have not. While it may be possible in some organisations to provide a non-gender business reason that justifies such differences, many organisations (including local authorities) have not been able to do so. The problem is reasonably widespread: as New Earnings Survey data show, a significantly higher proportion of men's pay is based on 'payment by results' than is the case with women's pay.

The problem of unequal access to bonus schemes can be reasonably readily solved by employers. This doesn't mean that bonuses (see Chapter 5) cannot be targeted at the appropriate business performance aspect, rather it means that all groups in which there is obvious segregation by gender should have equal access to some form of bonus scheme.

Merit or individual pay progression within salary ranges or scales may be subject to bias but there is as yet little clear evidence that this disadvantages women. Some assessments have found that women do comparatively well from such merit pay or individual performance pay schemes, which reward people for performance in the current job. (Women, of course, do less well than men in gaining promotion to higher grades.)

Other variable pay systems are similarly questionable as to the degree to which they are in practice geared more to the jobs that men typically do – so there are questions about shift premiums and other additions to basic pay as well as performance pay.

Competencies

One study of whether the use of competency-based pay potentially discriminates (Stebler *et al* 1997) did not reach any firm conclusions. However, because in competency-based pay schemes a greater degree of pay decision-making is given to line managers than is the case, for example, under pay progression systems based on service increments, the 'scope for greater discrimination' is potentially there.

Service increments

In December 1999 ACAS lost a tribunal case against its own staff. The staff were complaining that ACAS's service increment scheme discriminated against women, who on average had shorter service with the organisation than men. ACAS has subsequently changed its pay system to make the incremental progression run for a maximum of six years. This limit may become a yardstick for other organisations, too.

Benefits

Pensions and other benefits provision are also covered by the requirements of equal pay – and as I discuss in Chapter 7, the thorny issue of pensions and equality (including pensions for part-timers) has been evident since the mid-1980s.

Do equal opportunities 'employers' have a better record on pay equality?

Both large and small organisations in the public sector and the private sector, organisations with strong collective bargaining on pay and those without, have systematic problems with pay inequality.

There appear to be barriers to the progression of women through career structures, which leads to what has been termed the 'glass ceiling'. The argument is that if there were more imaginative policies promoting part-time working, job sharing and 'family-friendly' working patterns, employers would promote more women and traditional occupational segregation would break down. In its train, it is argued, such a development would naturally promote greater pay equality.

This argument, though, does not bear too much scrutiny. In some organisations occupational segregation seems rife, in spite of some years as equal opportunities employers.

LEGAL FRAMEWORK

Whether differences between women's and men's pay are unlawful depends on whether or not women and men are considered to perform equal work or, more specifically, work of equal value. The persistence of the gender equality problem, though, calls into question the effectiveness of the law.

The law relating to sex discrimination in pay is contained in both UK statute and European Community law. The former is required to conform with the latter and UK legislation is interpreted by domestic courts in the light of European law. Claims for equal pay are taken under domestic law if possible, but in some circumstances claims can be made directly under European law.

The relevant domestic law is contained in the Equal Pay Act 1970, the Sex Discrimination Act 1975 (each as amended), and the Pensions Act 1995.

The Equal Pay Act 1970, as amended by the Equal Pay (Amendment) Regulations 1983, provides for equal pay between women and men in the same employment by giving a woman the right to equality in the terms of her contract of employment where she is employed on:

- like work to that of a man or
- work rated as equivalent to that of a man or
- work of equal value to that of a man.

What constitutes equal pay? 'Pay' under the Equal Pay Act includes not only wages but also other contractual entitlements such as holiday pay, discounts, vouchers and subsidies. In the case of discrimination relating to a discretionary payment or allowance, the claim must be brought under the Sex Discrimination Act 1975.

- 'Pay' under Article 141 covers any benefit – contractual or not – which is received because of the employment relationship.
- The principle of equal pay applies to each separate contractual term.
- Occupational pensions are 'pay' and are covered by the Pensions Act 1995.

Effect of European law on equal pay

European law has considerably extended the scope of equal pay protection. The definition of pay under Article 141 (previously Article 119) includes benefits not covered by the Equal Pay Act. Even if the Equal Pay Act does not provide a remedy, Article 141 may do so. In certain areas, therefore, recourse to Europe has been an option for those pursuing equal pay claims. Moreover, cases in the European Court brought by claimants from another EU country may establish a principle which employers elsewhere in the EU must follow.

Principle of transparency

It is important that pay systems are clear and easy to understand; this has become known as transparency. A transparent pay system is one in which employees understand not only their rate of pay but also the components of their individual pay packets and how each component contributes to total earnings in any pay period.

Following the European Court's decision in the Danfoss case (see page 162) if the system is not clear the onus is on the employer to show that the pay differential is not discriminatory.

Material factor defence

The material factor defence can be put forward by an employer to explain why the applicant in a case is being paid less than a comparable employee who is doing equal work. To be successful this factor must be a significant and relevant reason why there is a difference in pay. To succeed in a defence the employer needs to show that the material factor accounts for the whole of the difference in pay. Where it accounts for only part of the difference, equal pay can be awarded for the rest. For example, if the employer cites skill shortages as the reason for higher pay for the man – but this is not the only cause of higher pay – then a tribunal may award the applicant the difference between the two rates of pay.

Objective justification

In circumstances in which a particular pay practice results in an adverse impact on substantially more members of one or other sex, the European Court of Justice (ECJ) has introduced a test of objective justification. This means that the employer must be able to justify the pay practice in question objectively, in terms unrelated to gender – that is, there must be a compelling business need for it.

Case digest

The following case digest, adapted from eoc.org.uk, details some of the milestone cases in equal pay's 30-year history.

Analytical job evaluation scheme needed
MRS S BROMLEY and OTHERS v H & J QUICK LTD [1988] ICR 47 [1988] IRLR 249

After complaints from some of its female staff that they were being paid less than their male colleagues for comparable work, the respondent engaged Inbucon, a firm of management consultants, to carry out a job evaluation study.

The method of evaluation chosen was the 'direct consensus' method. A panel of managers and employees (including women) produced job descriptions for representative jobs, using six factors. The panel then ranked the jobs by means of paired comparison (ie by looking at the job descriptions as a whole and determining which of the two jobs was more valuable). Benchmark jobs were then selected from the representative jobs and paired comparisons of those jobs were made, both on a 'whole job' basis and by comparing each factor. The factors were then weighted. Pay boundaries were then decided. The next step was for the panel to change the ranking of the benchmark jobs on a 'felt fair' basis, ie in accordance with the general level of expectation as to the value of the jobs. The remainder of the representative jobs were then slotted in to the order of ranking.

Once this process was complete, the remaining jobs (which included those of the applicants and three of their four comparators) were slotted in. No written job descriptions for these jobs were produced and the slotting-in was done by management on an assessment of the whole job in each case, without splitting the demands of the jobs into factors.

Mrs Bromley and her colleagues commenced equal value proceedings at the tribunal. The tribunal dismissed the claim but the applicants appealed.

The Court of Appeal held:
The study was not analytical and could not therefore comply with the legislation. An employer seeking to have an equal value complaint dismissed must show both that there has been a job evaluation scheme that complies with the legislation and that the evaluation was not tainted by sex discrimination. 'Slotting-in' also did not comply with this requirement.

Transparency of pay system
HANDELS- og KONTORFUNKTIONAERERNES FORBUND I DANMARK v DANSK ARBEJDSGIVERFORENING (acting for DANFOSS) [1991] ICR 74 [1989] IRLR 532 (Known as the Danfoss case)

A Danish national collective agreement for staff workers established a basic rate for grades of workers, but permitted individual increments on the basis of flexibility, vocational training and seniority. Flexibility was assessed on the basis of quality of work, volume of work and the employee's keenness and initiative. However, employees had no knowledge of how these criteria were applied to them and so could not compare how their pay was made up. Men received on average 6.85 per cent higher pay than women. The system of individual wage increases meant that a woman could not prove sex discrimination as she could not identify the reasons for any differences in pay. Therefore the applicants argued that the burden of proof should fall on the respondents.

The ECJ held that where an employer applies a pay system that is characterised by a total lack of transparency, and where a female worker establishes that the average pay of a relatively large number of female workers is less than that of their male colleagues, the burden is on the employer to prove that his pay practice is not discriminatory.

Comparisons across different pay structures in the same organisation
ENDERBY AND OTHERS v FRENCHAY HEALTH AUTHORITY AND ANOR [1994] ICR 112, [1993] IRLR 591

The applicants were speech therapists employed by three NHS health authorities. They claimed their work was of equal value to that of male clinical psychologists and pharmacists, also employed by the NHS.

The health authorities argued that there was a material factor that justified the difference in pay. The salary of NHS employees were agreed by the Whitley Council and approved by the Secretary of State for Social Services. Under this machinery, the pay of speech therapists was determined separately from that of clinical psychologists and pharmacists. The health authorities argued they were obliged by regulations to pay those rates and, in any event, that market forces played a significant part, since pharmacists were hard to retain.

Whilst accepting that the relevant regulations were legally valid, the three women argued that the effect of the regulations when read with s.51 of the Sex Discrimination Act 1975 (which permits discrimination where this is necessary to comply with prior legislation) was to deny them legal redress and was thus contrary to European Community law.

The applicants argued that speech therapists were predominantly women, whereas there was a far greater proportion of men in the higher grades in the comparative professions. They accepted that there was no deliberate sex discrimination, but argued that the salaries of speech therapists were artificially depressed because of the profession's predominantly female composition. It was therefore submitted that the employer's pay policy discriminated indirectly against women in that the outcome of the pay negotiations had an adverse effect upon women, and was not justifiable.

The tribunal decided that the separate bargaining structures amounted to a material factor defence that was non-discriminatory. However, it rejected the defence of market forces because it said this could not explain the whole of the difference in pay.

Dr Enderby appealed to the Employment Appeal Tribunal (EAT) and the Court of Appeal, which referred questions to the European Court of Justice (ECJ).

The ECJ made the following ruling:

- Where significant statistics disclose an appreciable difference in pay between two jobs of equal value, one of which is carried out almost exclusively by women and the other predominantly by men, Article 119 of the Treaty requires the employer to show that the difference is based on objectively justified factors unrelated to any discrimination on grounds of sex.
- The fact that the respective rates of pay were arrived at by collective bargaining processes that are distinct, and which in themselves have no discriminatory effect, is not sufficient objective justification for the difference of pay.

Hours and pay comparisons
JÄMSTÄLLDHETSOMBUDSMANNEN v *ÖREBRO LÄNSLANDSTING* [2000] IRLR 421 (known as the Swedish Ombudsman case)

The main issues in this case were as follows:

- What statistics are necessary to show that one gender is disadvantaged?
- In comparing basic pay, should an unsocial hours supplement be included?

The Jämställdhetsombudsmannen is the Swedish Equal Opportunities Ombudsman. The Ombudsman brought an equal pay claim on behalf of two local authority midwives who claimed their work was of equal value to a male clinical technician.

Their basic monthly salary was lower than his but they received an additional inconvenient hours supplement for working rotating shifts. The clinical technician did not work inconvenient hours but he worked 5 hours 40 minutes longer per week than they did.

Questions were referred to the ECJ to determine whether:

- the pay comparison must include the supplement for inconvenient working hours and, if so, what difference did it make that the clinical technician did not work inconvenient hours

- whether the lesser hours worked by the midwives should be taken into account when a pay comparison was made.

The ECJ ruled as follows:

- The unsocial hours supplement should be disregarded when comparing the pay. Genuine transparency was only assured if the principle of equal pay was applied to each element of the remuneration granted to men or women.

- If statistical data showed a difference in pay between the two groups (namely midwives and clinical technicians), and if the statistics showed that there was a substantially higher proportion of women than men in the disadvantaged group (ie the midwives), then Article 141 required the employer objectively to justify the difference.

- Neither the reduction in working time, nor the value of such a reduction, is to be taken into consideration for the purposes of calculating the salary used as the basis for a pay comparison. However, the reduction could constitute an objectively justified reason for the difference in pay. It was for the local authority to prove that it was the genuine reason. Although different working conditions (such as hours of work) may have financial consequences for the employees, that is not sufficient to bring such conditions within the scope of Article 119, which is concerned with the amount of pay an employee receives in respect of services provided.

Can employees transferred to an out-sourced operation be compared with employees in their previous employer?
LAWRENCE v *REGENT OFFICE CARE (ROC) LIMITED AND OTHERS*

The main issue in this case was:

- whether the rights conferred by Article 141 are wide enough to permit an employee of one company to make a comparison with the work done by an employee of another company

- whether an applicant can only choose a comparator employed by another company if her employer is in a position to be able to offer an explanation as to why the comparator's employer pays his employees as he does.

The applicants were employees of ROC Ltd and two other cleaning and catering companies. They claimed equal pay from their employers by comparing their rates of pay with those of male comparators, such as road sweepers and gardeners, employed by North Yorkshire County Council. Most of the women were employed as catering assistants preparing school meals and had originally worked for North Yorkshire County Council, at which time their work had been rated as equivalent to that of their comparators. However, they were made redundant by the Council and re-employed by the cleaning and catering contractors, Regent Office Care Ltd, when the Council contracted out these services.

The applicants argued that they ought to be allowed to use the Council's male employees as comparators as the only thing that had changed was the identity of their employer. They argued that there would otherwise be a gap in the protection that Article 141 provides.

The ECJ decided as follows:

- It is not evident from the wording of Article 141 that the comparison must be confined to the same employer. There are three categories in which an employee can make a comparison with a comparator who is employed outside their specific undertaking: (i) in cases where statutory rules govern the pay and conditions in more than one undertaking, establishment or service eg the NHS; (ii) in cases where several undertakings or establishments are covered by a collective works agreement; and (iii) in cases where a holding company or conglomerate lays down terms and conditions centrally for more than one organisation or business.

- In all those categories the difference in pay between different employees is attributable to a 'single source'. Where the differences in pay cannot be attributed to a 'single source', there is no one body that can be held accountable for any differences in pay.

Employees covered by different pay agreements and terms and conditions – can they compare across?
LEVERTON v CLWYD COUNTY COUNCIL [1989] IRLR 28

This is a case that particularly affected the public sector. The main issue was: could a claimant who is working at a different establishment from that of her comparator be described as *in the same employment* as him?

Mrs Leverton, a qualified school nursery nurse, was employed by the local authority. She claimed that her work was of equal value to 11 potential male comparators, including caretakers, supervisors and administrators. The comparators worked at various council sites. The conditions of service and pay scales for all these employees emanated from the NJC for Local Authorities' APTCS (the 'purple book'). The nursery nurses were on scale 1, while the comparators were on scales 3 and 4.

There were significant differences between the hours of work and holiday entitlements. The nursery nurses worked 5–7 hours fewer per week than their comparators and had 50 days more holiday per year.

The council argued that these differences in hours and holidays meant that Mrs Leverton could not use these comparators. They were not 'in the same employment' as her because their terms and conditions were so different that they could not be described as common terms and conditions of employment.

The House of Lords decided that terms and conditions of employment governed by the same collective agreement represent the best (though not necessarily the only) example of common terms and conditions. Therefore Mrs Leverton could compare her work with her comparators at different establishments, notwithstanding the differences in hours of work and holiday entitlement between her and her comparators.

Market forces and the material factor defence
RATCLIFFE AND OTHERS v *NORTH YORKSHIRE COUNTY COUNCIL* [1995] IRLR 439, [1995] ICR 833

The main issue was: in what circumstances can market forces constitute a genuine material factor justifying a difference in pay between women and men doing equal work? Mrs Ratcliffe and the other applicants in this case worked for North Yorkshire County Council as catering assistants, serving meals in various schools. The school catering service had to be put out to compulsory competitive tender under the Local Government Act 1988. The council decided that it had to reduce its labour costs if its in-house school catering tender was going to succeed against private-sector catering companies. The council therefore cut the women's basic pay and other benefits, leaving them on worse terms and conditions than several groups of men council employees whose work had been rated as equivalent to theirs under the council's job evaluation scheme. The women claimed equal terms with the men.

The tribunal upheld their claims and dismissed the council's defence that the difference in pay was due to a material factor that explained the difference in terms, namely the need to keep the women's wage rates competitive with those paid by commercial catering organisations. The tribunal held that this defence was related to sex. Those organisations employed almost exclusively female workforces, which worked for low rates because it was the only type of work that they could fit around their childcare responsibilities. The council's decision that the burden of cost-cutting should fall on the groups of predominantly women workers arose 'out of the general perception in the UK, and certainly in North Yorkshire, that a woman should stay at home to look after the children and, if she wants to work, it must fit in with that domestic duty'.

Can the law be made effective?

The Equal Pay Task Force believes that the pay gap has been exacerbated by 'ineffective, time-consuming and cumbersome equal pay legislation'. However, despite the Labour Government's stated commitment to eradicating unequal pay, the Task Force's proposal for stronger regulation did not meet with Government approval.

The debate about whether or not more regulation would succeed in enforcing equal pay is finely balanced. As Dickens (1999) has argued, the thorny and complex problem of gender inequality may need much more impetus than can result from regulation alone. Dickens suggests that a combination of more law and demonstrations of the business case for equality, together with social regulation or collective bargaining might – as a combined set of forces – lead to change (if all were driving in the same direction).

The Government's introduction in the Employment Act 2002 of an equal pay questionnaire for use by employees prior to any legal action is one step towards making the legal process easier for applicants – and is a significant measure in potentially increasing transparency.

Part 2: The Complainant's Questions to the Respondent
- Part 2 is a question form to be completed by the person with an equal pay complaint.
- **Please read the guidance in Part 4 before completing the questionnaire.** You may find it helpful to prepare what you want to say on a separate piece of paper.
- If you do not have enough space on the questionnaire continue on an additional piece of paper, which should be attached to the questionnaire and sent to the respondent.

Enter the name of the person to be questioned (the respondent) **To**

Enter the respondent's address **of**

Enter your name (you are the complainant) **1. I**

Enter your address **of**

believe, for the following reasons, that I may not have received equal pay in accordance with the Equal Pay Act 1970:

Please give a short summary of the reason(s) that cause you to believe that you may not have received equal pay.

You may find it helpful to complete this summary after you have completed the rest of your questions and are clear who you are comparing yourself with and what your claim is about.

To claim equal pay you should have reason to believe that a person of the opposite sex is being treated more favourably for doing equal work.

Help in completing this form is available from the Equal Opportunities Commission. See the end of this booklet for contact details or see their website. www.eoc.org.uk

Please give the name(s), or, if not known, the job title(s), of the person or persons with whom equal pay is being claimed. These are referred to as your 'comparators'.

Please provide details of their work location and job titles to help your employer to identify them, especially if you do not know their names.

In order to bring a claim you must compare yourself with a person of the opposite sex who is doing 'equal work'.

See Part 4 (paragraph 3) for further information about comparators.

2(a) I am claiming equal pay with the following comparator(s):

2(b) Do you agree that I have received less pay than my comparator(s)?

(If appropriate)
further deails are provided below:

The concept of 'pay' includes both your pay and other terms and conditions of your contract of employment.

You may wish to specify what element(s) of your pay and benefits package you feel are not equal to that of your comparator. For example, a lower weekly salary or annual salary, no bonus payments, fewer holidays etc.

You may also wish to indicate over what time period you think your comparator has received more favourable terms than you.

See Part 4 (paragraph 2) for further information about comparing your pay and benefits package.

2(c) If you agree that I have received less pay, please explain the reasons for this difference.

Table 44   *Extracts from Equal Pay Questionnaire (DTI)*

ETHNICITY AND PAY

Most ethnic groups are less likely to be in employment and those in work are less well paid on average than white people. Forth and Millward (2000) suggest that differences in educational qualifications account for much of the difference. There is some evidence that the market 'rewards' education by ethnic minorities less well than it rewards similar educational attainment levels by white people (see for example, Blackaby *et al* 2000). Data from the *Labour Force Survey* shows that Black Africans are the best-educated ethnic group in the labour market – they are ten percentage points more likely to have higher-level qualifications than whites. But their employment rate is twelve percentage points lower than the rate for whites.

According to the TUC (2002), educational attainment does not seem to pay off as well for black people as for white employees. The TUC says there is also evidence that performance payments are lower for ethnic-minority employees in central government services.

Occupational segregation is evident on ethnic lines. A study for the Office of National Statistics (Twomey, 2001) shows the following.

- Black Caribbean men are over-represented in transport and communications (18 per cent compared with 9 per cent for all men).
- Black Caribbean women are over-represented in the public health and education services.
- Nearly one in five Indian and Pakistani women are employed in textile manufacturing.
- Black African men are over-represented in service-sector industries, notably in transport and communications (14 per cent compared with 9 per cent for all men).
- Pakistani men are over-represented in textiles and clothing (10 per cent of employment for this group compared with just over 1 per cent for all men).
- Bangladeshi men are over-represented in textiles and clothing (9 per cent of employment for this group compared with just over 1 per cent of all men).

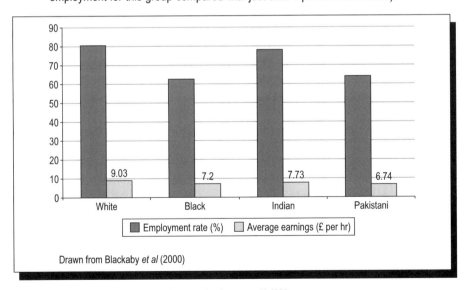

Drawn from Blackaby *et al* (2000)

Figure 15   *Employment and earnings of ethnic minority men, mid-1990s*

White Black Indian Pakistani

Employment rate (%) Average earnings (£ per hr)

Based on Labour Force Survey data for men, 1993–1996.

Earnings are average per hour in 1997 prices, adjusted for local price levels.

Source: Blackaby *et al* (2000).

- 52 per cent of male Bangladeshi employees and self-employed workers are in the restaurant industry (compared to 1 per cent of white men).

- 5 per cent of Indian men were medical practitioners (nearly ten times the national average).

WHAT ACTION CAN EMPLOYERS TAKE TO REDUCE PAY DISCRIMINATION?

The Government envisages that the public sector will be a beacon of good practice in attacking pay discrimination. Among the key strategies proposed are the following:

- reducing the breadth of pay ranges or pay scales – as, for example, in the ACAS example cited above

- centralised monitoring and reasserting a certain degree of central control

- increasing the transparency of the pay system.

Conducting an equal pay audit

Neathey *et al* (2003) show that some progress is being made by leading companies to undertake thorough audits. Auditing reward practices for equality is principally an analytical exercise entailing detailed and sometimes painstaking work. It is not simply a matter just of looking at the average (effective) hourly rates of men and women, but a task that is sensitive to the nature of the specific organisation and its pay systems. In many ways the task is similarly detailed to financial audit trailing processes. Some of the essentials are as follows:

- Assess the pay data that is available within the organisation – not all computer systems hold sufficient data, and some may hold it in a format that is difficult to use.

- Obtain broad-brush data across the organisation (ignoring occupational groupings and so on) of the statistical difference in average or median pay for men and women. To make comparisons between full-time and part-time meaningful, these need to be worked out on the basis of effective hourly rates. Hence information on formal contractual hours of work is needed as well as pay. A study by the author of equal pay audits in companies found that most organisations do have equal pay problems and there were (for example) large, well-known companies, with extensive equal opportunities policies, that had internal gender pay gaps of 30 per cent or 40 per cent (Wright 2003).

- Find reasons for the gap that is shown by the initial analysis. This may entail an analysis of (i) pay differences by grade; (ii) occupational segregation by gender; (iii) comparative rates of pay progression for men and women; (iv) comparative distribution of bonus and other payments additional to basic salary or pay; (v) comparisons of starting pay decisions (by grade or occupational group) for men and women; and (vi) comparative benefit provisions.

It is most important, in doing these analyses, to look for data that shows what is happening in practice – this may be very different from what the policy guidelines say on paper.

The author's 2003 study suggests that managerial views and attitudes need to be examined as part of an equal-pay audit, in addition to focusing on searching out pay practices that discriminate (Wright 2003). This can be achieved by means of qualitative research methods, such as interviews or focus groups.

The typology of organisational stances on equal pay in Figure 16 may be a useful framework in analysing managerial views, which can be a central barrier to developing policy in this area. There may be a few key managers acting as gatekeepers of pay information, controlling the flow of information (or lack of it). In some organisations external consultants may know more about pay than employees. In certain cases consultants have been used to control information, while in others they have been influential in resolving some specific equal-pay problems. In only one organisation studied by the author was there evidence of a challenging equality climate, which Liff (1999) argues is the key to changing equality culture.

Reward specialists may find that monitoring all pay decisions, including promotion, is necessary before progress can be made.

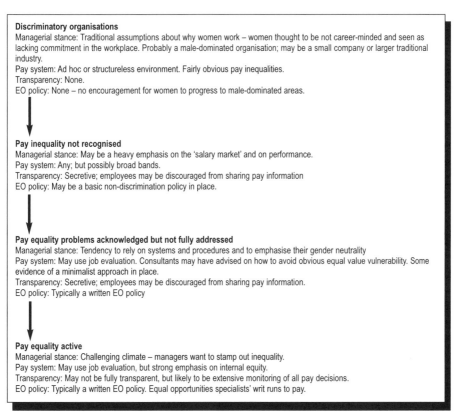

Discriminatory organisations
Managerial stance: Traditional assumptions about why women work – women thought to be not career-minded and seen as lacking commitment in the workplace. Probably a male-dominated organisation; may be a small company or larger traditional industry.
Pay system: Ad hoc or structureless environment. Fairly obvious pay inequalities.
Transparency: None.
EO policy: None – no encouragement for women to progress to male-dominated areas.

Pay inequality not recognised
Managerial stance: May be a heavy emphasis on the 'salary market' and on performance.
Pay system: Any; but possibly broad bands.
Transparency: Secretive; employees may be discouraged from sharing pay information
EO policy: May be a basic non-discrimination policy in place.

Pay equality problems acknowledged but not fully addressed
Managerial stance: Tendency to rely on systems and procedures and to emphasise their gender neutrality
Pay system: May use job evaluation. Consultants may have advised on how to avoid obvious equal value vulnerability. Some evidence of a minimalist approach in place.
Transparency: Secretive; employees may be discouraged from sharing pay information.
EO policy: Typically a written EO policy

Pay equality active
Managerial stance: Challenging climate – managers want to stamp out inequality.
Pay system: May use job evaluation, but strong emphasis on internal equity.
Transparency: May not be fully transparent, but likely to be extensive monitoring of all pay decisions.
EO policy: Typically a written EO policy. Equal opportunities specialists' writ runs to pay.

Figure 16 *Typology of gender pay postures of UK organisations*

STUDENT REVIEW EXERCISE

Consider the practicalities of conducting an equal pay audit in your own organisation or an organisation you know well. What data do you need to obtain to conduct a thorough analysis? What are the barriers to this exercise? The following three case studies (pages 172–5) may help your discussion.

Case study – Small-scale engineering company

An engineering firm has a 40 per cent average pay difference between men and women, with a strong segregation by gender of the workforce. The company has no women above junior management level, except within the HR function.

One of the HR managers – fearful that the company top management are unwisely ignoring a potentially serious equal pay issue – decides she is going to investigate the extent of the problem she is sure exists. Her initial investigation of the computerised personnel system reveals that in each grade in which women are represented women earn an average pay that is less than men. In some grades the differences are very narrow – with the lowest gap just 2 per cent – while in others they reach 30 per cent. She concludes there are systematic pay differences within the grading system, but is unsure what the root causes are. The grades are based on a 20-year-old job evaluation system, which seems primarily to reward technical and managerial attributes. Pay rates for staff and manual workers are agreed following collective bargaining with two recognised trade unions.

To investigate further, the HR manager realises she needs to conduct research within the company, since the HR system does not have sufficiently detailed information.

STUDENT REVIEW EXERCISE

Imagine you are the HR manager and have decided to take this investigation further. This means you will have to persuade both senior managers and trade union officers that the investigation is necessary. Discuss how you will approach this and how you will structure meetings (a) between yourself and senior managers; and (b) yourself and the trade union officers (all men).

Consider in particular issues such as gender segregation, equal opportunities and the nature of the job evaluation scheme.

Case study – Multi-utility Co

A large utilities firm has a nationwide workforce with a growing business, with increasingly diverse services and products. It has many workplaces, with their own traditions and working practices. The company has a high profile and a stated commitment to equal pay. An independent review of equality progress, conducted by academics, has shown that the proportion of women moving into middle management roles has risen dramatically in recent years, there has been substantial progress towards the implementation of 'family-friendly' flexible working policies and these are now perceived by line managers and employees as necessary if the company is to fulfil its desire to be seen as an 'employer of choice'. The academic research, however, revealed two particular problematic aspects – firstly a significant number of male managers, who were full-time, felt they were indirectly 'paying' for the flexible working policy, as they were always there (working very long hours) and able to step in if problems arose in departments managed by part-time, flexibly working women managers. Secondly, an initial assessment of pay data suggested that these full-time male managers earned an average of 15 per cent more (on an effective hourly-pay based comparison) than did the women managers. There was evidence of strong gender segregation within the management pay grades. However, an annual analysis of merit payments showed that these tended to be higher on average for women than for men. While a full formal pay audit had not been carried out, there was some evidence that the reason for this was that women were typically lower in the pay ranges so, although their percentage pay rises have been higher than those of the comparable men, their actual pay is on average lower than men's in every grade.

Senior managers' bonus payments were higher than for middle managers. This meant that grades in which men predominated in practice had a higher percentage bonus eligibility than the grades in which women were in the majority.

STUDENT REVIEW EXERCISE

You have been asked to consider how you might test which aspects of pay and employment policy in this company are unfairly discriminating against women. Consider in particular the differences in merit payments for women and men as well as the significance of the differences in average basic salaries of men and women. What further investigations or data are needed?

Case study – Manu Co

Manu Co is a large manufacturing company based in the West Midlands. It has 2,000–3,000 employees based at various locations. Some locations are manufacturing plants, others are sales-based or research and development centres. The company is proud of its position as a leading company with a widely quoted diversity policy, which is highly supportive of measures to increase part-time and flexible working; the company has a generous maternity leave policy and offers extended career breaks. However, in the main manufacturing operation there continues to be strong gender segregation with a perceptible 'glass ceiling'. Apart from one or two head office posts, there are no women at senior or top management level – with only a handful of women earning more than £45,000 a year.

The company has a highly unionised workforce and a job evaluation system devised in the 1980s and supported by the trade unions. Its pay structures are generally narrow-banded grades with incremental points. The company believes that compared with other companies it has a good record on equality issues and that (also comparatively) its pay systems are fairly transparent. The HR director is becoming increasingly concerned that it may have been lucky in so far escaping an equal value claim and that (in some respects) it may not be able to defend itself against claims of unequal pay treatment of women. He therefore asks the company's compensation manager to make an initial assessment of the degree of confidence he should have in the company's pay systems, in the light of the equal value legislation. A very basic overall analysis shows that (when account of different hours of work is taken) a gender pay gap of just over 30 per cent is evident.

When the compensation manager starts to look more closely at some areas she discovers:

- Amongst the company's 400 mostly men engineers (about 10 per cent are women) women's pay is lower than men's pay in each grade, even when age and length of service are taken out of the reckoning. One of the reasons behind this discrepancy appears to be related to the salary history of the women, who have all been promoted from within the company to their current posts. Because they have generally come from less well paid previous posts than their male counterparts, their salary on promotion was restricted by an overall company rule that on promotion individual salary increases should be subject to an overall limit of not more than 15 per cent of current salary.

- In the head office sales and marketing centre, senior staff are made up of two broad groups – one group of (mainly male) staff who have previously worked as field sales managers. Whilst in the field these sales managers received the benefits of a job-use car, a field allowance worth around 10 pent cent of salary and others benefits and expense allowances. On being transferred back to head office, these staff receive a sum worth almost 20 per cent of salary consolidated into their pensionable basic salary (to reflect these additional field payments). However, the job they do within head office is almost exactly the same as a number of women senior staff, who for various reasons (mostly to do with their wish not to engage in the extensive travel a field sales job entails) have no field experience. The salaries of these staff do not have the extra 20 per cent consolidated.

- In the company-wide middle management grades, women on average earn just 6 per cent less than men, and represent just 12 per cent of the population of middle managers. Company policy is to have broad salary bands at these levels, with a guideline minimum salary set per grade, but no specified maximum. Analysis of the three middle management grades reveals the facts shown in the table.

Grade	percentage of women in grade	Men's average salary	Women's average	Women's as percentage of men's
Middle Mgt 1	8 per cent	£52,000	£57,000	110 per cent
Middle Mgt 2	11 per cent	£40,000	£37,000	93 per cent
Middle Mgt 3	14 per cent	£30,000	£28,000	92 per cent

Closer analysis of the three grades reveals that, the top grade apart (in which there are just two women), the maximum salary earned by men is between £10,000 and £15,000 more than the maximum earned by women. In this context the reward manager also analyses length of service data and finds that the average length of service of men in the middle management grades is 17 years against an average of 14 years for the women.

Before she goes any further with the analysis the reward manager needs to account for the differences already revealed.

STUDENT REVIEW EXERCISE

Identify the aspects of pay in which there appears to be an equal pay problem in this company. In addition, identify the further data that you need to be able to make a judgement as to whether or not there are problems.

Consider whether you agree that the differences described above are the result of gender discrimination.

Consider also whether the corporate pay guidelines in this case are genuinely gender-neutral or whether their practical effect is indirectly discriminatory.

STUDENT REVIEW QUESTIONS

1   Does the market discriminate? If one accepts that it does, then what can the individual employer do to (a) price jobs effectively to maintain competitive pay structures and (b) improve pay equality in the organisation?

2   Has the 'hands off' approach of equality specialists and managers to gender pay inequality meant that potentially valuable resources that could have been brought to bear on the serious and long-term problems of systematically unequal pay have been under utilised?

This code was issued by the Equal Opportunities Commission under the Sex Discrimination Act 1975 s 56A(1), and enacted on 26 March 1997 (SI 1997/131).

Identification of discriminatory elements

Pay systems vary in complexity. Some have more elements than others. In the process of a review, each element will require examination against the statistical data generated at the initial analysis stage.

Basic pay

Problem: Women are consistently appointed at lower points on the pay scale than men.

Recommended Action: Check the criteria which determine promotion or recruitment starting pay. Are these spelt out clearly?

Examine recruitment and promotion records for evidence of criteria that appear to be disadvantaging women. Can these criteria, eg qualification requirements, be justified objectively in terms of the demands of the job?

Check the records for evidence of sex bias in the application of managerial discretion.

Problem: Women are paid less per hour than men for doing virtually the same job, but with different job and grade titles.

Recommended Action: Check whether there are any reasons other than custom and practice for the difference; if so, are these reasons justified objectively?

Problem: Women progress more slowly through incremental salary scales and seldom reach higher points.

Recommended Action: Investigate the criteria applied for progression through the scale. Are these clearly understood? Does any particular criterion, eg length of service, work to the detriment of women more than men? If so, can the use of that criterion, or the extent to which it is relied on, be justified objectively?

Review the length of the incremental scale. Is the scale longer than it need be? Are there good practical reasons for a scale of that length?

Problem: Women progress more slowly through non-incremental salary ranges and seldom reach higher points.

Recommended Action: Check the criteria that applied when the structure was introduced and the current criteria for new recruits/promotees to each salary.

Check whether there is a clear, well-understood mechanism for progressing through the salary range.

Investigate the criteria for progression through the salary range and whether there are performance, qualification or other bars to upward movement. Can these be justified?

Review the length of the salary range. Can this be justified by real need?

Bonus/premium rates/plus elements

Problem: Female and male manual workers receive the same basic pay but only jobs mainly done by men have access to bonus earnings and those mainly done by women do not.

Recommended Action: Check the reason why. Does this reflect real differences – for example, in the value of the work or in productivity? Can it be justified objectively on grounds unrelated to sex?

Problem: Where shift and overtime work is available and paid at a premium rate, fewer full-time women employees have access to this higher-rated work.

Recommended Action: Check that women and men employees have equal access to this work and, if not, that the reasons can be justified objectively.

Problem: A smaller percentage of women employees receive enhanced rates for weekend and unsocial hours work.

Recommended Action: Check the eligibility requirements for this work. Do any of these – for example, those requiring that employees must be working full-time – work to the disadvantage of women? Can these requirements be objectively justified?

Problem: Average female earnings under a variable payment system are lower than average male earnings (even where some women may have higher earnings than most men).

Recommended Action: Review the design and operation of the variable payment system. Do these genuinely reflect the demands of the jobs and the productivity needs of the organisation?

In particular, check how factors such as downtime and personal needs breaks are dealt with in a variable payment system covering men and women.

Performance pay

Problem: The performance pay system is applied largely to employees of one sex only and results in a pay discrepancy to the advantage of that group.

Recommended Action: Investigate the reasons that employees of the other sex are largely excluded from performance pay awards. Are these justified objectively for reasons unrelated to sex?

Problem: Women receive lower performance ratings on average than men.

Recommended Action: Investigate the performance rating system. Is it really likely that women would on average perform less well than men? What are the possible reasons for this?

Review the criteria for performance rating. Do employees and managers know what these are? Do any of these disadvantage women? Do any of these disadvantage ethnic minority women in particular? If so, are these criteria justified objectively?

Monitor the ratings of individual managers. Do the results of the monitoring suggest a stereotypical interpretation of criteria? Are there appropriate controls on managerial discretion?

Problem: Although women and men receive similar ratings, men achieve higher performance pay awards.

Recommended Action: Investigate the reasons for this. Is it linked to managerial discretion? Are potentially discriminatory criteria being applied in the linking of ratings to pay? Can these be justified objectively?

Problem: There is a pay gap between the male and female employees who are assessed in this way.

Recommended Action: Review the competencies assessed. Are women and men assessed for the same set of competencies? Are the competencies being interpreted in a consistent way?

Are potentially discriminatory criteria being applied? If so, are these justified objectively? Monitor the assessment of individual managers.

Can the cause of the difference be justified objectively?..........

Table 45 *Extract from Equal Opportunities Commission Code of Practice on Equal Pay*

REFERENCES

Blackaby, D, Leslie, D, Murphy, P and O'Leary, (2000) *White/ethnic minority earnings and employment differentials in Britain: evidence from the LFS.* University of Swansea Discussion Paper WP-013, December.

Chauvin, KW and Ash, RA (1994) Gender earnings differentials in total pay, base pay and contingent pay. *Industrial and Labour Relations Review.* Vol 47, no 4, pp634–639.

Cornelius, N (2002) *Building workplace equality: ethics, diversity and inclusion.* Thomson.

Dickens, L (1999) Beyond the business case: a three-pronged approach to equality action. *Human Resource Management Journal.* Vol 9, no 1, pp12–19.

EOC (2000) *Attitudes to Equal Pay: Research Findings.*

EOC (2003) *Fathers: balancing work and family.* EOC Research Findings, EOC.

Equal Pay Task Force (2001) *Just pay.* EOC.

ESTAT (2001) *Harmonised Statistics on Earnings.*

European Commission, Employment and Social Affairs Committee (2001) Equal Pay. *Gender Equality Magazine.* No 11.

Eurostat *European Labour Force Survey.*

Forth, J and Millward, N (2000) *The determinants of pay levels and fringe benefit provision in Britain.* Discussion Paper 171, National Institute of Economic and Social Research.

Fransson, S, Johansson, L and Svenaeus, L (2001) *Highlighting pay differentials between women and men.* Report presented by Swedish presidency of the EU.

Gerhart, B and Rynes, SL (1991) Determinants and consequences of salary negotiations by male and female MBA graduates. *Journal of Applied Psychology.* Vol 76, pp252–262.

Incomes Data Services (2002) The equal pay challenge. *IDS Report* 856. May.

Kingsmill, D (2001) *Review of women's pay and employment.*

Liff, S (1999) Diversity and equal opportunities: room for a constructive compromise. *Human Resource Management Journal.* Vol 9, no 1.

Morell, J *et al* (2001) *Gender equality in pay practices.* NOP survey for the Equal Opportunities Commission.

Neathey, F, Dench, S and Thomson, L (2003) *Monitoring progress towards pay equality.* Institute for Employment Studies/EOC.

OECD (1998) *Employment report.*

Pocock, B (1999) Equal pay thirty years on: the policy and practice. *Australian Economic Review.* September, pp279–285.

Purcell, K (2002) *Qualifications and careers: equal opportunities and earnings among graduates.* Working paper series 1, Equal Opportunities Commission.

Rake, K, Davies, H and Joshi, H (2000) *Women's incomes over the lifetime.* Cabinet Office paper.

Stebler, M *et al* (1997) *Skills, competencies and gender: issues for pay and training.* Institute of Employment Studies Report 333.

Twomey, B (2001) *Labour market trends.* January 2001, based on summer 1999–spring 2000 LFS data.

Wajcman, J (1998) *Managing like a man: women and men in corporate management.* Polity Press.

Wright, A (2003) *Equal pay – some missing links – an analysis of equal pay audits.* Performance and Reward Conference, 9 April.

Useful websites
www.e-reward.co.uk
www.eoc.org.uk
www.likestilling.no/genderpaygap

The benefits package

CHAPTER 7

INTRODUCTION

The benefits package has not traditionally been shaped by employers' policies alone, but rather by an amalgam of HR policies and government fiscal or incomes policies. Concerns for employee welfare were important in the early development of benefits, but particularly among large private-sector firms, and in the public sector this motive declined sharply in the latter part of the 20th century. While there is evidence of continuing 'welfarism' in the rationale for some benefits provisions, there is also evidence of a more market-driven approach arising in the late 1990s and the early 21st century.

This chapter discusses benefit trends and issues and contributes to the CIPD professional standards in the following areas.

Knowledge indicators – Practitioners must understand and be able to explain:

- the part financial and non-financial rewards play in attracting, retaining and motivating people
- the significance of relevant legislation, including the Financial Services Act 1986 and the Pensions Act 1995
- new developments in employee reward and their application within the organisation.

DEVELOPMENTS IN THE HR CONTEXT

The UK tradition was characterised by a 'paternalistic' style of personnel management emphasising company-provided occupational welfare benefits policies (Russell 1991). Overlaid on that paternalistic approach – under which employers showed their continued care for and commitment to their employees over their working lives by providing company pensions and sick pay – during the 1960s and 1970s benefits provision grew in response to Government Statutory Incomes Policies. Those enforced policies limited the cash pay rises that employers could make to employees. In response employers turned to non-cash benefits as a way of rewarding employees, particularly those staff and executives whose cash pay was also taxed at very high marginal rates.

When examining the nature of a package, therefore, the history of why the provision came about is an important factor to be acknowledged; this also arises when organisations ask questions about the nature of their packages as a prelude to revamping them. A benefit that was originally provided because the tax regime favoured it over cash may be viewed in a different light from, for example, a pension scheme that has existed for 70 or 80 years and was introduced to meet 'welfare' objectives.

WHAT ARE EMPLOYEE BENEFITS?

Conventionally employee benefits have been defined rather widely as, for example:

> **items in the total package offered to employees over and above salary, which increase their wealth or wellbeing at some cost to the employer'**
>
> **Armstrong and Murlis (1988)**

This wide definition in effect covers all the non-pay elements of remuneration and implies a reaction against the narrower term 'fringe benefits'. The term 'perk' (a contraction of perquisite) is more often used in relation to executive reward; as a term it is not without its pejorative overtones.

A brief history of the 'perk'

In the UK the 1970s saw the growth of non-cash means of remunerating the highly paid, during the era when pay rises were restricted under Government Statutory Incomes Policies, and the marginal rates of tax were high. The late 1970s saw some elaborate, so-called 'fringe benefits' develop as employers increasingly sought to reward executives by non-cash means, such as free suits or the use of a company yacht.

This period (and arguably the rationale for the growth of 'perks') ended with the election of the Conservative Government in 1979 on the strength of policies designed to remove government control of incomes, reduce high income tax rates and tighten up on the taxation of benefits. Many of the more extreme perks did disappear with the ending of pay restraint, but in practice the benefits package (particularly at senior levels) proved remarkably resilient.

With the growth in popularity of 'single status' conditions, some benefits became available to employees in many parts of the organisation, not just at the top. As the moves toward single status have taken place executives have been keen to hang on to any benefits that indicate their higher status (notably, of course, the company car). Cars and the other status benefits therefore give executives a means of maintaining their separateness from other employees, as well as being an expected part of a more market-based executive reward package. The importance of social status within UK society may in part explain why, despite reductions in marginal tax rates, which in theory made straight cash more attractive than benefits, and increasingly stringent taxation of employees' benefits, such benefits remain an expected feature of a market-based package.

Moreover, once employers moved away from the notion that they were providing a benefit as a 'tool of the trade', thoughts about 'equity' meant that some rationale as to who is and who is not eligible was needed.

Typology of benefits

If the definition of benefits is drawn widely then the potential list of what might be included stretches to include sometimes quirky, low-cost provisions that are not in the same ballpark as pensions, cars and holidays – either in terms of their cost to the employer or in relation to the value to the individual employee. The broader definitions would also include share schemes, although these are dealt with separately in this work.

In the analysis of trends within this chapter, the following typology of benefits is used. As well as the more traditional personal security, health and job or seniority-related benefits, the list also includes the newer 'family-friendly' category, reflecting the increasingly diverse nature of the labour market.

From welfare to family-friendly or 'social' benefits

Traditionally the concept of 'welfare' was distinguished from 'security' in that it related to benefits provided for the well-being of employees whilst they were at work, rather than when they were too old or sick to work.

Sports and social facilities also come under the definition of 'social benefits', although it could be argued that because their provision adds to employee well-being.

The newer family-friendly benefits that aim to assist/give rights to all employees or those with current responsibilities as carers include childcare and maternity/paternity/parental leave. Company crèches allow parents with small children to go to work – and so could be viewed as simply as a means to allow the individual access to work. Whatever the categorisation, though, family-friendly benefits are being extended by virtue of both voluntary employer action – for example, at Peugeot Citroën UK (see Iziren 1999) – and by regulation. European legal developments are extending this category of benefits by increasing the requirements of paid maternity leave and by the provision of parental leave.

Is flexible working a 'benefit'?

Since April 2003 employers have been obliged to give employees with young children the right to seek more family-friendly working hours. Employers who refuse such a request must give an explanation.

That there is a demand for such moves is understandable in view of the long-hours culture in many workplaces. But do employees perceive there to be a trade-off between benefits and work-life balance? Many benefits surveys now also cover flexible working options, as if this is a non-cash benefit in the same way as holiday entitlement is.

In this sense it seems the UK is more European than North Atlantic in its views. A study for the OECD – by Evans (2001) – examined a European Commission survey in 1995, which showed that on average for the then 12 countries of the European Community, 38 per cent of

---

Personal security and health
Pensions, sick pay beyond statutory minimum, life cover, medical insurance, long-term disability/permanent health insurance, loans

Job, status or seniority-related
Cars, car allowances, holiday leave beyond statutory minimum, sabbaticals

Family-friendly
Childcare or elder care, extended maternity/paternity/parental leave (beyond statutory minimum)

Social or 'goodwill' or lifestyle benefits
Subsidised catering, sports/social facilities, product/service discounts, massages, aromatherapy, ironing collection

---

Table 46 *Typology of benefits*

employees said they would prefer a reduction in working hours to an increase in pay (56 per cent indicated a preference for more pay, while 6 per cent gave no opinion). A comparison of that survey with an earlier survey of the same type showed a small movement in favour of a reduction in working hours in most countries between 1985 and 1994. Overall, these results are in marked contrast to the United States, where the proportion opting for shorter hours as opposed to higher pay is much smaller, and appears to have fallen over recent years.

Why do employers now provide a package of benefits?

While acknowledging the welfare-based antecedents of many benefits packages, do employers continue to provide them because they still harbour welfare-based notions – or are there other rationales for their continuance?

Among the possible reasons for providing a benefits package instead of just 'clean cash' are:

- welfarism or the wish to provide security for employees
- perceptions about employee motivation
- recruitment and retention issues – or a response to a competitive labour market
- job need or status-related reasons
- employers seeking to minimise taxation.

Employer attitudes as to what an appropriate benefits package is and the range of benefits provided may both vary over time. Little UK-based research has been carried out into the factors influencing employers to adopt certain types of benefits package. There is some research on occupational pensions (for example, Casey 1993; Taylor and Earnshaw 1995) showing that employers' motives could be grouped into three categories:

- paternalism
- labour market considerations – recruitment and retention
- rewarding employees – enhancing motivation.

The above factors might work variously together to determine an individual employer's philosophy as to the provision of employee benefits at any given time. It is also arguable that concepts of welfare or security are less of a driving force behind the provision of benefits than they once were – for example, the increase in the number of employers ending final-salary pension schemes in 2002–3 (see page 190) suggests that security is not as important a factor as it has been hitherto.

Recruitment and retention

Recruitment and retention considerations are frequently cited as the prime reason for now providing benefits (CIPD 2000). Nevertheless, there is some evidence that benefits may be more effective in attracting people to the organisation than in retaining them (for example, CIPD 2002; Taylor 2000). Taylor's survey research into the effectiveness of pensions in retaining employees revealed the following:

- Three-quarters of organisations see employee retention as being one of the objectives of the pension scheme, but only half consider them to be an effective method of achieving such an objective.
- For most employees, except older and more highly qualified employees, the pension scheme acts only as a marginal deterrent against voluntary leaving.

- There is little evidence that pension schemes are sufficiently valued by lower–paid employees in the service sector to influence their decisions about leaving.

- Questions about employee turnover do not play a significant role in decision-making about future occupational pension provision.

While recruitment and retention objectives are foremost among the objectives of employers in setting up pension schemes, Taylor (2000) comments: 'belief in the effectiveness of pensions as a retention tool on the part of most employers can be described as soft and limited'.

How relevant is performance to benefits provision?

Offers of free holidays in the Seychelles for 'sales representative of the year' notwithstanding, there is little evidence of employers providing non-cash 'benefits' only to those who have achieved a commendable level of performance. It is the universality of many benefits – except those associated with the executive package – that has been remarkable. Surveys tend to show that when benefits provision is not the same for everyone in an organisation, it varies by the level of the job or status in the organisation and not by level of performance (CIPD 2002; Croner Reward 2002).

Performance is not a significant determinant, but should it be? Cantoni (1997) argues (in relation to benefits packages offered in the United States): 'non-cash benefits corrupt the employer-employee relationship ... From management's point of view, it is difficult to have true pay-for-performance when employees see 40 per cent of their compensation as an "entitlement"'.

Advocates of reductions in the standard benefits approach may favour employee recognition programmes. The growth of employee recognition schemes, which are an increasingly popular way of acknowledging the contribution of staff who do something out of the ordinary, might also be viewed as part of performance pay (see Chapter 5) and/or as a benefit. Recognition awards are now widely used by employers as a way of acknowledging the special efforts and commitment of valued employees. An awards scheme can generate a great deal of goodwill for a relatively modest outlay (Incomes Data Services 2002c). There may be prizes for the most productive employee or other special achievements; such benefits may be of little monetary reward other than membership of the exclusive 'club' of those who have achieved the highest performance levels. The only tangible 'benefit' may be the recognition or status that that exclusivity brings.

The relevance of motivation theory

Amongst the various motivation theories, both expectancy theory and Herzberg's (1968) 'two-factor theory' can be explored when seeking to examine employee perceptions about the extent to which benefits motivate them. The division between factors that might motivate people and those that are contextual or 'hygiene' factors would probably place benefits as hygiene factors. Recognition, though, *is* a motivator – and so it could be argued that status-based benefits such as cars may be motivational, while security-based benefits such as pensions are not.

Should employers provide benefits as a security 'net'?

The guarantee that employees will have a secure income either in retirement or if they are sick could be provided by the state, and/or the employer and/or the individual via insurance or another purchased financial services product. Who picks up the tab has as, Rousseau and Ho (2000) point out, become 'an increasingly contentious issue, at least in developed nations ... Social critics have referred to the organisational performance of social activities (such as caring for an individual in sickness and old age) as the demise of the civil society … and the rise of the market mentality.'

For the employer, security benefits are a costly item; the critical developments in 2002 and 2003 in reducing company pension scheme entitlements was a response to increased cost. However, during the 1980s, when the stock market was rising, the biggest growth areas in employment benefits were in pensions provision (particularly personal pensions) and in private medical insurance.

In the area of medical insurance, growth was restricted mainly to management and was found to a lesser extent in other staff areas. Relatively few companies extended schemes to all their employees, and as the funding of the NHS has assumed greater political importance, this area of benefits provision is not currently set to grow. In the late 1990s and early 21st century a combination of high 'medical inflation' and the growing number of claims has led to renewed concern about the upward trend in the cost of providing medical insurance cover to employees (Incomes Data Services 2001).

In medical and social insurance benefits the differences between countries in their typical employment benefits packages are shown in greatest relief. Comparisons with US companies, for example, are fraught with difficulty since there is a high premium on employer-provided medical benefits as a safety net in the United States, while in the UK the provision is for a quicker medical/surgical service or a better room while in hospital, and not necessarily for essential medical treatment itself.

The 'job need' benefit

Some 'benefits' are (or were originally) not really intended to be a perk, more a 'tool of the trade' provided so that employees (craft workers typically) could carry out their jobs effectively. Free protective footwear and clothing for various manual workers as well as tool allowances for craft workers are certainly in this category. Company cars for sales reps and other users with high business mileage are also in this category. This kind of benefit is circumscribed by what the Inland Revenue will accept as a 'tool of the trade', which is favourably treated under tax legislation. It may be argued that such provisions are only benefits in the extent to which employees can use the items concerned for social purposes when they are not being used for employment purposes. The number of benefits in this category was reduced in light of measures by the tax authorities during the 1990s. These moves to claw back any favourable tax treatment of benefits culminated in the 2002 move to reduce the tax advantages that were previously conferred on company car drivers with high business mileage.

Which benefit – who is eligible?

Surveys of pay and benefits show consistently that, in spite of moves to harmonise benefits in line with the move to single status, *'UK organisations generally maintain a hierarchy of benefit provisions, with a greater concentration on senior management and with lower levels of provision down the organisation'* (CIPD 2002).

Family-friendly benefits
Increased legal minimum rights to time off for parents were included in the Maternity & Parental Leave etc Regulations 1999 (setting out the detail of the rights to maternity and parental leave included in the Employment Rights Act 1996).

	Percentage of organisations providing benefits to:			
Benefit	Senior managers	Line/middle managers	Non-manual	Manual
Sick pay	93.8	94	92.6	88.8
Holidays (21+ days)	91	90	86	83.1
Private healthcare	74.9	58.7	41.2	31.4
Life assurance	71.1	69.2	66.4	62.4
Company car	65.6	43.4	9.1	2.1
Car allowance	54.7	43	12	6.2
Long-term disability/permanent health insurance cover	44.4	40.1	36.1	30.2
Defined benefit pension	40.8.	39.9	38.2	39.3
Defined contribution pension	30.2	30.3	29.5	29.7
Hybrid (mix of the above) pension	6.8	6.7	6.3	6.5
Group personal pension	32.2	32.9	31	27
Contribution to a personal pension	13.3	9.5	8.4	7.8
Stakeholder pension	22.8	26	30.6	33.1
Childcare vouchers	7.4	7.7	8.4	8.5
Personal accident insurance	27.1	25.2	23.1	21.8
Season ticket loan	33.5	33.5	33.6	28.7
Sports club membership	29	29.1	28.8	27.8
Critical illness insurance	21.7	18.1	15.3	13
Canteen or luncheon vouchers	19.5	19.8	20.2	21
Source: CIPD (2002)				

Table 47 *Who is eligible for which benefits?*

Many firms and public-sector employers were already paying above the minimum for such leave entitlements. Croner Reward (2002) reveal that 43 per cent of firms pay enhanced maternity pay (at levels above the statutory minimum), and mostly these employers pay enhanced full pay for up to 18 weeks. Some large firms and the public sector are more generous – Ford, for example, was already paying 40 weeks' maternity pay, well above the statutory level, but this has been increased to 52 weeks, following a collective agreement.

From 2003 fathers are entitled to two weeks' paternity leave, paid at the same level as statutory maternity pay. As with maternity pay, large firms and the public sector tend to voluntarily improve on these terms, with an estimated one-third of employers (Croner Reward 2002) paying fathers at the rate of full pay for five days' paternity leave.

One of the more expensive items in this category is the provision of subsidised childcare – often critical if both parents are to continue in employment. Balancing (or perhaps juggling) family needs with employment is now a major concern for parents. The growth in part-time employment (see page 150), which enables mothers with young children in particular to combine work and childcare, is just one indicator that women still tend to shoulder the bulk of the responsibility for dependant care. The low level of nursery provision by employers is another factor in the slow movement to equal pay (see Chapter 6). Of course children are only nursery age for a relatively short period of time and various surveys (for example, IDS 2002a) show that the provision of holiday playschemes and out-of-school schemes is somewhat greater than that of nurseries for the under-fives. Employers may not be able to provide nurseries, and some pay cash allowances or give childcare vouchers. Latest estimates suggest that fewer than one in ten employers provide childcare vouchers – about half the proportion of employers who provide luncheon vouchers (CIPD 2002; IDS 2002a).

Holidays

Current entitlements to holiday for all employees are set in line with the minimums specified in the Working Time Regulations 1998, which were drafted to comply with European law. These provide that employers must give a minimum of four weeks' paid leave annually to employees, pro rata for part-time staff. There are no exceptions to the minimums allowed, as they are part of European health and safety law. Employers may include within the four weeks any entitlement to paid leave on bank holidays. Employees do not automatically have a right to paid time off on bank holidays – this is a contractual matter – although if it has been custom and practice for staff to have time off paid on these days, they may have a contractual right to the days (or time off in lieu), irrespective of whether this is in any written terms and conditions.

The pace of change in holiday entitlement generally continues to be slow (Incomes Data Services 2002b). While there has been a trend towards harmonisation of manual and non-manual employees' terms and conditions (including holiday entitlement) in recent years, there are still some differences in treatment. There are, in addition, sectoral variations and IDS shows a spread of standard entitlements from an average of more than 22 days in the hotels and leisure sector to an average of 26.5 days in mining and quarrying. Enhanced entitlements are typically available for managers and there may be service-related enhanced provisions for those with standard entitlements (CIPD 2002).

Company cars

The main growth period for company cars was during the 1970s, when a combination of statutory controls in pay combined with high marginal tax rates gave an incentive to employers to look for 'tax-efficient' non-cash benefits to offer, mostly to their comparatively highly paid managers and professional staff. Many got such a liking for the car that it is only after several moves by the Government to raise taxation on the benefit that there are any signs of a diminution of allocation. The company car remains for many a desirable 'perk', indicating that an employee has 'made it' to the ranks of managers who qualify. As such it is debateable whether it is the tax-efficient past that has helped to maintain the company car or its symbolic value as an indicator of high status.

The picture on company cars may change further as a result of a sea-change in taxation policy, implemented from April 2003. The Government has been lobbied for some years to change the direction of fiscal policy from one that rewards consumption of resources and pollution at the same time as taxing employment, to a more environmentally and employment-friendly approach. The 2003 changes to car tax policy effectively link the level of tax charged to carbon dioxide emissions – and the previous reductions in tax that applied to those incurring high business mileage and to older cars no longer apply. The effect of the change is not evident at the time of writing, but it seems likely that higher marginal tax rate payers with top of the range cars and low business mileage may gain, whereas basic rate tax payers with high business mileage will lose, particularly if they opt for larger cars.

Cost and value of a company car

The cost of providing a car is not the same as its value to the individual. The cost of providing a car for an employee includes not just the nominal price of the car (or the lease cost) but also National Insurance contributions, administrative costs, road tax, motor insurance, depreciation and the cost of maintenance.

The value to the individual employee relates to his/her tax position, the level of business mileage he/she does and the type of car. The estimated value in Table 48 is adapted from Croner Reward (2002). These estimates are likely to be revised in light of the taxation changes introduced in April 2003.

Cost of benefits

The overall cost of benefits as a proportion of cash-based pay are variously estimated at 30 per cent to 40 per cent. Survey evidence may not be very reliable on this question, since few employers seem specifically to count the cost in total, and some benefits – such as sick pay and holidays – are difficult to cost. One of the advantages for employers of moving to flexible benefits plans may be greater control over benefit costs.

PENSIONS – ALL CHANGE?

'Pensions have gone from being anorak territory to something avidly discussed in pubs and taxis' claimed Christine Farnish, Chief Executive of the National Association of Pension Funds (BBC News Online, 20 November, 2002).

While governments may have perceived the basic state provision as a safety-net minimum, with employees and their employers contributing over and above that to fund a liveable income in retirement, individual employees have been less convinced that they should devote some of their current income to savings set aside to pay for their retirement. Large employers, acknowledging the difficulty of 'selling' the concepts of retirement and pensions to younger people, have traditionally shouldered the responsibility for planning pensions on behalf of their employees by providing costly but reasonably secure company or occupational pensions designed to top up the state scheme.

Legislative changes in the 1980s made company pension schemes optional for employees; previously employers could insist on everyone eligible joining. In the wake of this change, and

Cost heading	1,400 cc £	2,000 cc £
Average list price	11,028	21,338
Depreciation (1 year)	2,354	4,242
Loss of interest	346	710
Insurance	504	848
Breakdown cover	53	53
Vehicle excise duty	130	155
Total standing charges	3,387	6,008
Total running costs – servicing/repairs etc (assuming 20,000 miles per annum)	1,198	2,006
Actual estimated cost	4,585	8,014
Less individual tax at 22%	377	1,131
Less individual tax at 40%	686	2,057
Estimated net value of car at 22% tax	4,208	6,883
Estimated net value of car at 40% tax	3,908	5,957

Table 48 *Value of a petrol car at April 2002*

of a wave of scandals in which pensions management by ostensibly 'safe' companies was seen to be anything but safe, the confidence of individuals in pensions began to deteriorate. The lack of confidence was also coloured by individuals' lack of knowledge of pensions – hardly surprising in view of the complexity of pensions law and management. It could be argued that it was a mistake to introduce a 'market' into pensions when employees did not have sufficient knowledge to 'shop around' the complex choice of pensions offered.

Employers, individuals and government have subsequently asked some fundamental questions about pensions, which had seemed like a rather dull technical area until the mid-1980s.

State or private – whose responsibility for pensions?

Who should be responsible for ensuring that individuals have a living income in retirement – individuals themselves, their employers or the state? Since the 1980s UK governments have tried various means of encouraging individuals to take a greater interest in providing for their own retirement income.

The state continues to provide a basic state pension (paid to all who have made sufficient National Insurance contributions over their working lives). This is now uprated each year in line with price inflation, although following protests at the small increase this formula

189

produced, a slightly higher effective rate of increase was given by the Government in 2001/2. Since 1978 the basic pension has declined as a proportion of national average earnings; it is now worth about one-fifth of average earnings.

The State Earnings-Related Pension Scheme (SERPS) was set up in 1978 to provide a second or 'safety net' government-sponsored pension for employees not included in an occupational or personal pension scheme. It is paid for through a taxpayer's National Insurance contributions. The pension amount is based on an individual's earnings and National Insurance contributions during his/her working life. Following changes in the 1980s, SERPS will yield a maximum of 20 per cent of the average earnings on which a person has paid National Insurance contributions over his/her working life.

Employees are able to 'contract out' of SERPS if they contribute to an approved personal pension or join a company/occupational pension scheme.

How many people belong to company or occupational pension schemes?

According to the Government Actuary's Department (2001) and based on a sample of more than 1,500 pension schemes in the public and private sectors, just under half of employees in the UK were in an occupational pension scheme in 1995.

- The number of UK employees in occupational pension schemes in 1995 was estimated at about 10.3 million. This represented around 46 per cent of all employees in employment, including part-time workers and members of the armed forces.

- In the private sector the proportion of employees in private-sector occupational schemes was lower (36 per cent) than in the public sector.

Deferred pay – the development of pensions as pay

It was once argued by some employers that their provision of pensions was at their discretion and not an employee right. Trade unions had argued that pensions were in effect deferred pay and therefore should come within the ambit of collective bargaining. This debate was settled to some extent in 1986, when the European Court decided in the *Bilka-Kaufhaus* judgment (IRLR 317, 317 ECJ, 1986) that pension benefits were in effect deferred pay and moreover came within the requirements of European law on equal pay. The wide-ranging ramifications of this judgment and that in the *Barber* case (see page 191) have been considerable, not least in terms of increasing equality between the sexes in pensions and retirement.

Developments in the concept and nature of retirement

There are suggestions that the age of retirement must rise as the population ages, in order to fund pensions. Company pension schemes can decide the age at which their pensions rest. In practice, though, most pension schemes use the same age as that nominated by the state. Until 1986 it was accepted that state retirement and pension ages for men and women would be different. A sea-change in pension age policy and in the more fundamental nature of pensions flowed as a result of the European Court judgment in the *Barber* case.

Many pensions managers expect the state pension age to be 70 by 2030 (NAPF 2002) and the 'think tank' influential in Labour Government circles, the Institute of Public Policy Research (Brooks 2002), is arguing for the Government to raise the state pension age to 67 from 2030. This is in marked contrast to the trends evident in the 1980s and early 1990s, when employers used their pension schemes to help in shedding employees. Employers enhanced pension terms, luring many employees to volunteer for early retirement as a preferred option to redundancy. During this period a buoyant stock market meant that many pension funds were in surplus, thus allowing early retirement via the pension fund to finance part of the cost of shedding employees, rather than the cost being paid directly from revenue. Both public and private sectors got the early retirement habits. Indeed, a number of studies have shown that this was a European-wide trend, with the age at which men were actually retiring from the labour market being typically in their mid-fifties.

State pension age: phased equalisation for men and women

State pensions are currently paid to women from age 60 and men from age 65. The Pensions Act 1995 provides that from the year 2020 both sexes will receive their pensions from age 65. Women born before 1950 will not be affected by this change, but for those born between 6 April 1950 and 5 April 1955, state pension age will be shifted in monthly steps. Women born on 1 May 1950 will retire on 1 June 2010, one month after their sixtieth birthday, while those born on 1 May 1955 will retire on 1 May 2020, their sixty-fifth birthday.

Equality, retirement and pensions

Pensions were largely excluded from the discrimination laws enacted in the UK during the 1970s, although the Social Security Pensions Act 1975 said that pension schemes must be 'open to both men and women on terms which are the same as to the age and length of service needed for becoming a member and as to whether membership is voluntary or obligatory'. The rationale for the exclusion of pensions from the equality laws was that occupational pensions were not regarded as 'pay'. However, this view has changed because of decisions by the European Court. Regulations made under the Pensions Act 1995 concerning equal treatment for men and women came into force on 1 January 1996 to bring the UK into line with European law. The Pensions Act had the effect of inserting into the trust deed and rules of each pension scheme an equal treatment rule relating to the conditions for membership and the provision of benefits.

The 'equal treatment rule' and other changes were needed as a result of the *Barber* judgment (*Barber* v *Guardian Royal Exchange*, IRLR 240 1990). This was one of the legal cases that has had the strongest ramifications in recent years within pay and pensions – ironically taken by a man using equal pay laws that were framed to advance the cause of equal pay for women. Mr Barber's complaint centred on his employer's policy during a redundancy programme, which allowed women at the same age as him to take early retirement, when he – at the age of 53 years – was made redundant. His complaint succeeded because (eventually) the case went to the European Court, which decided that pensions (including early retirement pensions) came within the definition of pay in the Treaty of Rome, which all signatory European Union member states were legally bound to follow. Article 119 of the treaty says that:

> **Each member state shall ... ensure and subsequently maintain the application of the principle that men and women shall receive equal pay for equal work.**

The treaty defines 'pay' as not just 'wages or salaries' but also 'any other consideration, whether in cash or in kind, which the worker receives, directly or indirectly'. Although the judgment had far-reaching implications, the European Court left a problem for pension scheme managers and employers in that it only required them to provide equal treatment in respect of pensionable service after 17 May 1990.

A number of subsequent cases from the UK and the Netherlands sought clarification on how the equal treatment ruling should be applied – for example *Coloroll Pension Trustees Ltd* v *Russell* (IRLR 586 1994), *Smith* v *Avdel Systems* (IRLR 602 1994) and *Van den Akker* v *Shell* (IRLR 616 1994).

For future service, EU law allowed employers to reduce pension benefits if they did the same for men and for women. However, inequalities existing between 17 May 1990 and the date when the scheme was formally equalised might only be remedied by 'levelling up'.

Part-timers and pensions

Part-time employees were typically excluded from membership of occupational pension schemes in the past. This became an equality issue because the majority of part-time employees are women, and therefore most of the people being adversely affected were women. This indirect sex discrimination was first recognised in a German case in the European Court (*Bilka-Kaufhaus GmbH* v *Weber von Hartz* IRLR 317 1986). A part-time woman employee of a department store argued that the employer, which excluded most of its part-timers from its pension scheme, had indirectly discriminated against her. The European Court said that, although Article 119 of the Treaty of Rome (requiring equal pay) did not mention pensions specifically, occupational pension scheme benefits came within the definition of 'pay'.

In the cases of *Vroege* v *NCIV* (IRLR 651 1994) and *Fisscher* v *Voorhuis Hengelo* (IRLR 662 1994), the European Court clarified that the right to join an occupational pension scheme fell within the scope of Article 119. However, to be successful, claimants in law had to show that excluding part-timers had an adverse impact on women, while in practice most pension schemes moved fairly quickly to remove the barriers to part-timers joining occupational schemes. There were nonetheless unresolved issues about the backdating of part-timers' pension rights further than two years. This issue was finally settled to allow part-timers to claim pension rights as far back as 1976.

Pensions, maternity and paternity

Women on paid maternity leave were given additional rights in the Social Security Act 1989, ensuring that they are given the opportunity to accrue pension benefits and be covered for death benefits at the level that would have applied if they had not been on maternity leave.

Either parent must also be treated equally in respect of pension benefits during leave for family reasons – including paternity leave, adoption leave or compassionate leave taken for family reasons.

PENSIONS – A BASIC (ABC) GUIDE FOR REWARD SPECIALISTS

Accrual rate

Different final-salary pension schemes provide pensions based typically on either 1/60th or 1/80th of the final year's pay for each year of scheme membership. Part-years of membership may or may not count towards pension benefits. This means that in a scheme with an accrual rate of 1/60th, a member with 40 years' service will get a pension of 40/60 of final pay before retirement (ie two-thirds), while in a 1/80th scheme 40 years' service will give a pension of 40/80th (ie one-half) of final salary. (In the mainly public-sector pension schemes based on accrual rates of 1/80th, there are typically more generous retirement lump payments than in 1/60th schemes, to give a roughly equivalent entitlement.)

Added years
Final-salary pension scheme members who will not complete the full number of years' service to achieve two-thirds of salary pension by their normal retirement age may be eligible to purchase added years in their pension scheme by paying extra contributions to make up some or all of the shortfall.

AVC – Additional Voluntary Contributions
These are extra payments made towards a pension by a pension scheme member. They are made in addition to the 'normal' pension contributions paid by the employee. Money-purchase Additional Voluntary Contributions are typically provided under an arrangement with an insurance company. These additional contributions pay for a 'top-up' pension that is provided in addition to main scheme benefits.

Company or occupational pension scheme
A company pension is a pension scheme set up and administered by a company for its employees. It may be contributory – with employees making pre-tax payments direct from their salaries – or non-contributory, in which case the employer makes all the payments on its employees' behalf. In contributory schemes, companies will often match employee contributions.

Contracting out
Around 88 per cent of members of occupational pension schemes were contracted out of the State Earnings-Related Pension Scheme (SERPS).

DEFINED BENEFIT SCHEMES – see final-salary pension schemes
DEFINED CONTRIBUTION SCHEMES – see money-purchase pension schemes

Final-salary (or defined-benefit) scheme
Final-salary schemes have traditionally been seen as the best type of pension. They guarantee to pay a retirement income for life, based on a percentage of the employee's salary immediately before retirement.

The amount of pension therefore depends on both length of service and final salary, as well as on the accrual rate. The amount of pension most people receive in practice is between one-half and one-third of final salary. Under Inland Revenue tax rules, the maximum allowed is two-thirds of final salary.

Lump sum
A tax-free payment normally paid on retirement.

'Money-purchase' schemes

The pension received will be determined by the performance of an investment – for example, the stock market. If your retirement coincides with a rising market at retirement the pension will be much higher than if the market is falling. This risk is borne by the individual, meaning there is a danger that employees have a poor income for the whole of their retirement.

Pensionable age

The normal retirement age for members of a scheme. This is typically set at 60 years of age – although it can be earlier in some schemes, for example those public-sector schemes that have accelerated accrual rates.

Pensionable pay

In a final-salary scheme benefits are worked out on the pensionable pay from (typically) the last year before retirement, or the scheme may use a slightly different formula – for example, the best year of the last three years of service. Additions to basic pay such as allowances and overtime are not normally pensionable, but it is the scheme rules that define what is included or excluded.

Preserved pension

People who leave a final-salary scheme before their normal retirement age may have their benefits held in the scheme until retirement age. Benefits are index-linked to protect them from inflation.

Refund of contributions

Employees with less than two years' pension scheme membership may request a refund of pension contributions. Tax and a deduction to purchase membership of the SERPS scheme (see page 190) will be deducted from the refund before it is paid. Members with more than two years in the pension scheme are not eligible for a refund; in that case a transfer of contributions or membership to another pension scheme may be arranged.

Stakeholder pension

All firms with more than five employees must offer workers access to a stakeholder scheme, a low-cost pension specifically designed for those on low and middle incomes. The measure was designed to improve the coverage of pension provision for groups not typically covered by occupational/company pensions (mainly lower-paid people in smaller companies). The early take-up of stakeholder pensions has been low.

LEGAL NECESSITIES – A BRIEF HISTORY OF THE CHANGES TO PENSIONS LAW/PRACTICE

The Pensions Act 1995

One of the principal objectives of the 1995 Act, drafted in the wake of the Maxwell scandal, in which pension funds were misused, was to tighten up the pensions regime to make it less susceptible to fraudulent practice. In 1997 the Occupational Pensions Regulatory Authority

(OPRA) was given responsibility for ensuring that those who run occupational pensions schemes meet their legal obligations under the Pensions Act. There is also an Independent Complaints Adjudicator who can suspend or disqualify trustees. Scheme auditors and actuaries are obliged to tell OPRA if they think something is wrong. The Pensions Ombudsman's role has also been extended.

The Pensions Act ensures that if funds have been removed dishonestly from a pension scheme the employer must make sure enough money is put back into the scheme to pay future benefits.

Trustees

Under the Pensions Act scheme members have the right to choose at least one-third of the trustees – member-nominated trustees (MNT).

Minimum funding requirement

A minimum funding requirement aims to ensure there is enough money in final-salary schemes to pay pensions if a company goes bust. Each pension fund must be valued every three years and, if the actuaries say there is not enough in the fund to meet liabilities, employers have to increase their contributions to the scheme.

Where a pension scheme invests in the employer's company, trustees have to make sure that no more than 5 per cent of the pension fund's assets are invested in the employer's shares.

Pensions for divorcees

In divorce cases a judge is obliged to look at pensions. The judge will not be able split a pension, but will earmark parts of a pension, parts of the death-in-service benefit and parts of any lump sum payout for the ex-spouse.

Various equality measures

The Pension Act codifies various equality measures that have become necessary as a result of equality judgments in European law (see pages 161–6).

Inland Revenue rules

Inland Revenue rules are important for pension schemes, as they set the maximum benefits that can be provided if the scheme is to gain tax advantages. The main law governing the taxation of pension schemes is the Income and Corporation Taxes Act 1988, as amended by later legislation. The law gives the Inland Revenue some discretion to exempt from tax those pension schemes to which it gives exempt approval. The Inland Revenue's rules are in its *Practice Notes*, which, in essence, provide as follows.

- The maximum pension that can be paid at normal retirement age is two-thirds of the scheme member's final pay.
- The maximum lump sum that can be paid by exchanging pension for cash is 1.5 times the member's final pay.
- The maximum contribution on which a member can receive tax relief is 15 per cent of taxable pay.

The above limits apply at normal retirement age for a full (40-year) career. Early retirement and transfer rights from other schemes are also covered by the rules.

Financial Services Act 1986

The aim of the Act was to protect investors and to establish that those who offered advice on matters such as personal pensions should be registered. Advisers who have 'independent adviser' status must offer 'best advice' – that is they must also not be influenced by the prospect of commission payments on the product their client eventually buys. HR or personnel specialists must therefore not give advice on the choice of a specific pension or AVC.

HR staff can, however:

- publicise the advantages of the company's pension scheme
- give general information on pensions
- answer specific questions about the company scheme or about state pension entitlements.

Closure of final salary pension schemes

Research by the Association of Consulting Actuaries in 2002 found that more than half of all final-salary pension schemes were closed or closing to new recruits – or to all members of staff. Many UK employers – including British Airways, BT and Marks & Spencer – have closed final-salary schemes. In contrast, Ford, whose pay and conditions deals have traditionally been seen as a benchmark for UK manufacturing, has agreed not only to retain its final-salary scheme for employees but to enhance benefits paid out to members.

Incomes Data Services (2001) noted a '*gathering momentum*' in the move from defined-benefit pension plans to defined-contribution schemes. The National Association of Pension Funds' 27th annual survey (NAPF 2002) showed a jump in the number of schemes reporting that they had switched from final-salary provision to money-purchase schemes in the previous year. The IDS research illustrates the cumulative impact of the changes. It logs details of more than 50 companies which have launched defined-contribution pension schemes since 1996 and, in most cases, closed their final-salary schemes. The results point to a quickening pace of change. While IDS monitored only a handful of employers closing final-salary pension plans in 1996, by 2001 the list of companies with closed schemes was reading like '*a roll call of traditional blue chip employers*'.

The number of companies closing their final-salary pension schemes to new members nearly doubled in 2001/02, according to the NAPF. In 2002, some 84 companies had closed their final-salary scheme to new members – compared with 46 in the 2001 Annual Survey. The survey also shows that average contributions to money-purchase schemes are only half those for final-salary schemes – the average contribution by private-sector employers to a final-salary scheme is more than 12 per cent, compared with 6 per cent in money-purchase schemes. Around 92 per cent of the NAPF's pension scheme managers expected the trend of increased costs to continue over the next five years. Nevertheless many schemes continue to be well funded – 24 per cent had taken contribution holidays in 2002, though this is down from 34 per cent in 1997.

Why are companies ending final-salary schemes?

There are a number of reasons why companies are increasingly closing their final-salary pension schemes, all broadly related to increased costs or the prospect of rising costs to employers. The average long-term cost, including employee contributions, of providing a typical 1/60th final-salary scheme is often put at around 15 per cent of pensionable payroll. However, average employer contributions during much of the last 20 years have been under half this level as a result of the booming stock market. Specifically the reasons for closure relate to the following points.

- Lower stock market investment returns have meant that final-salary scheme employers are being asked by the scheme actuaries to increase their contributions to fund the shortfall between the scheme assets and its liabilities.

- Longer life expectancy of employees now, compared with the past, also adds to cost pressures, as pensions in payment are paid for a longer period of time and hence cost more.

- The effect of the cost increases now has been compounded by the anticipated effect of an accounting standard – FRS17 – which means that employers must report more clearly on their liabilities. Some 86 per cent of schemes (NAPF 2002) said the accounting standard, FRS17, would make it less attractive to employers to offer a final-salary scheme, while just 2 per cent thought it would make it more attractive.

- The switch from final-salary schemes reduces costs because average contributions to money-purchase schemes are only half those for final-salary schemes (NAPF 2002).

In effect the move from final-salary to money-purchase schemes transfers the risk of poor investment performance from the company to the individual. Critics of this move argue that many companies took advantage of stronger stock market performance in the 1990s to take 'contribution holidays' from their final-salary schemes. This reduced corporate costs at that time, but as investment returns look much less promising, some companies have decided to close their schemes.

Are final-salary schemes the best option?
A switch from final-salary to money-purchase schemes invariably reduces the amount the employer contributes towards the pension, but if the investment market is favourable at the time employees retire they may not necessarily be worse off. The crucial difference is that the retirement income an employee can expect to receive is much more uncertain. The employee, in effect, shoulders all the investment risk, rather than the employer.

IDS (2001) research challenges the argument sometimes put that employees prefer defined-contribution schemes to final-salary schemes. IDS says that in the few companies in which employees have genuinely had a free choice the majority have often opted to stay with the final-salary plan.

Are public-sector pensions better than those in the private sector?
The closure of some final-salary pension schemes has prompted questions about the relative pension benefits available in the public and private sectors. While almost all public-sector schemes are of the final-salary type, their main benefits are generally comparable to those in the private sector, except in the uniformed services (police, fire service and armed forces) and for Members of Parliament.

Some public-sector schemes have a different structure from those in the private sector. For example, in local government and a number of other schemes, the pension builds at an accrual rate of 1/80th of final salary for each year of service. This means that for a 40-year career a public-sector employee in these schemes will achieve a pension of half of their final salary, compared with the standard maximum of two-thirds of final salary in a 1/60th scheme.

However, the overall pension benefits that public-sector employees in these 1/80th schemes receive is equivalent to a 1/60th scheme when the tax-free retirement lump sum is included in the reckoning. Public-sector schemes are subject to the same Inland Revenue limits as those in the private sector.

They may, however, not be funded. Rather, the government pays the cost of paying pensions benefits from taxation.

The uniformed services (police, firefighters and armed forces) have a normal retirement age lower than the standard 65 in the local government and similar schemes and the 60 years of age applicable in the Civil Service pension scheme. In the firefighters scheme, for example, there is a compulsory retirement age of 55, with the first 20 years' service pension benefits accruing at the rate of 1/60th per year of service. For firefighters with more than 20 years' service the rate of accrual rises to 2/60th per year of service after the 20-year threshold has been reached. Contributions from employees to their pension are therefore higher, at 11 per cent of salary a year, compared with a standard 6 per cent of salary in local government, for each year of service.

The main Civil Service Pension Scheme is non-contributory for employees and allows a maximum 1/60th-based pension at age 60. (Some large private-sector companies, such as BP, have similar schemes.)

MPs probably have the best public-sector pension – with an accrual rate of 1/40th of salary for each year in Parliament.

The perspective of employees on pensions

People's concern with pensions varies with age. Young people may feel they want to spend their disposable income on what seem like more immediate items such as mortgages and holidays. While public opinion polls may show pensions rising up the priorities that people feel the government should tackle, there remains a great deal of ignorance and misunderstanding about pensions and this is not difficult to understand in light of the complexity of the field. The Goode Committee Report commissioned research to assess what might be the 'triggers' to get people thinking more about pensions (Goode 1993). These were:

- consciousness of ageing
- access to a pension scheme
- life changes such as taking on a mortgage, getting married or becoming a parent
- having disposable income available
- perceiving the state pension to be inadequate or under threat
- observation of current pensioners' financial struggles.

Sue Ward (1995) comments: *'few people are interested enough, at least under the age of about 40, to take positive action about their pension. If they have the opportunity presented to them, however, they take it.'*

Communicating on pensions

In the mid-1980s, when employers were no longer able to make membership of their company pension scheme a condition of employment, many employers organised extensive communication exercises to persuade people to stay in their scheme.

The CIPD (2002) finds that there are 'large gaps in communication about reward programmes generally, not just on pensions'. Ward (1995) says that the image of the pensions staff or department in a large organisation is of vital importance. All the nostrums of good 'customer care' are suggested, with the following points being of particular importance:

- accessibility of pensions staff
- reaction of specialists when individuals do get through
- accuracy of the information and the speed with which it is given
- visibility of those in the company with responsibility for pensions
- taking the message to employees – for example via roadshows or question and answer sessions
- what key 'opinion formers' such as trade union representatives know and think about the quality of the pension scheme(s) in the company.

An Internet-based 'Pensions Calculator' jointly produced by the Association of British Insurers and the Financial Services Authority can be helpful in explaining pension contributions needed for the benefit to be provided. It is available at www.pensioncalculator.org.uk.

What is the role of personnel specialists on pensions?

Unless personnel staff are registered advisers under the Financial Services Act 1986 they must not give advice on the choice of a specific pension or AVC. They can, however, communicate the advantages of the company's pension scheme and answer general questions on pensions, so that employees can build up their own knowledge as 'intelligent customers'.

NHS ROADSHOWS

NHS pensions specialists produced an Internet-based resource – Pensions on Line (POL). The NHS Pensions Agency took to the road to demonstrate the powerful uses of this tool in producing redundancy cost information or pension forecasts for employees staying on and demonstrating the financial difference of leaving work at, say, 55 rather than at 60 or 65. POL is a very fast way to get pension forecasts and model changes to retirement benefits. The initiative was intended as a tool for HR officers at a local level: it was not intended that they should become pensions experts, just more aware of how to use the Internet resource. The NHS Pensions Agency continues to provide detailed expert help to individuals and HR officers.

STUDENT REVIEW QUESTIONS

Are benefits now outmoded in a more market-driven reward environment? Would the money spent on benefits by employers be better used on increasing basic pay?

In Western countries pensions are becoming increasingly expensive to provide. Why? What should be the response of employers? Give reasons for your answer.

Case study – Retail Giant Co UK

The Retail Giant Company UK is a subsidiary of one of the world's largest retail multinational corporations. It is US-owned and the parent company is considering extending its operations further in the UK. The parent board of directors perceives that although there may be some contraction of business in the short term, the long-term business prospects are good.

The board has decided to limit its commitments on pensions in light both of rising pensions costs and of advice from the group finance director that in future he will have to account in the company annual report for its final-salary pension scheme in a more stringent way – which could make the overall financial picture seem poorer than it might otherwise have been. Since the company needs both to reassure shareholders and to raise finance for its expansion plans, the finance director recommends that either the existing pension scheme be closed altogether or that it is closed to new entrants, in order to limit liability in the future. At the decision-making board meeting, the head of personnel is asked to give her view and argues strongly in favour of closure to new entrants plus the start-up of a money-purchase scheme, with employer contributions of twice that of employees.

In the meantime the head of personnel and the pensions manager realise that some work will need to be done amongst existing employees to boost confidence and security in the final-salary scheme if that is going to remain viable. They are also in receipt of representations from trade union representatives, arguing that it is an 'outrage' that the employees now being asked to suffer 'poverty' in retirement are those who survived a wave of early retirements and redundancies during a period of business cutbacks in the 1980s. They also point out that some of their members were only induced to 'volunteer' for early retirement because the pension scheme funded what would otherwise have been a costly redundancy programme. They say that as the company used the pension scheme to finance part of the cost of 'de-manning' and took advantage of pension contribution 'holidays' until recently, it should now be prepared to fund a funding shortfall.

STUDENT REVIEW TASK

You are asked by the head of personnel to prepare a response both for the board and for the trade unions. In framing your response, consider:

- the business-based arguments for keeping a final-salary scheme going
- the evidence on the recruitment and retention impacts of pensions
- the significance of any changes in the 'psychological contract'.

REFERENCES

Armstrong, M and Murlis, H (1988) *Reward management: a handbook of remuneration strategy and practice.* Kogan Page.

Association of Consulting Actuaries Survey (2002) as reported in No new recruits for 50% of final salary pensions, *Personnel Today.* 19 November.

Brooks, R (2002) *A new contract for retirement.* Institute for Public Policy Research.

Cantoni (1997) The case against employee benefits. *Wall Street Journal.* 18 August 1997, as cited in Rynes, S and Gerhart, B (eds) (2000) *Compensation in organizations: current research and practice.* Jossey-Bass.

Casey, B (1993) *Employers' choice of pension schemes: report of a qualitative study.* HMSO.

Chartered Institute of Personnel and Development (2002) *Reward management survey: survey report.* January. CIPD.

Croner Reward (2002) *Employee Benefits Report* 2002/2003.

Evans, J (2001) *Labour market and social policy – trends in working hours in OECD countries.* OECD Occasional Paper No 45.

Goode, R (1993) *Pension Law Reform.* HMSO.

Government Actuary's Department (2001) *Occupational pension schemes 1995: Government Actuary's report on the tenth survey of occupational pension schemes in the public and private sector.*

Herzberg, F (1968) One more time: how do you motivate employees? *Harvard Business Review.* Vol 46, no 1, pp53–62.

Incomes Data Services (2001) *IDS pensions bulletin* No 151.

Incomes Data Services (2002a) Childcare assistance. *IDS Study* 731. June.

Incomes Data Services (2002b) Hours and holidays 2002. *IDS Study* 736. September.

Incomes Data Services (2002c) The growth of employee recognition schemes. *IDS StudyPlus.* Autumn.

Incomes Data Services (2003) Private medical insurance. *IDS Study* 745. March.

Iziren, A (1999) Age concerns. *People Management.* 20 May.

National Association of Pension Funds (2002) *28th Annual Survey.*

Rousseau, D and Ho, VT (2000) *Psychological contract issues in compensation* in Rynes, S and Gerhart, B (eds) *Compensation in organizations: current research and practice.* Jossey-Bass.

Russell, A (1991) *The growth of occupational welfare in Britain: evolution and harmonisation.* Gower Publishing.

Taylor, S (2000) Pensions and employee retention. *Employee Relations.* Vol 22, no 3, pp253–259.

Taylor, S and Earnshaw, J (1995) An exploration of employer objectives in the provision of occupational pension schemes in the UK. *Employee Relations.* Vol 17, no 2, pp38–53.

Ward, S (1995) *Managing the pension revolution.* Nicholas Brealey.

Useful websites

www.opas.org.uk

Opas is a non-profit-making organisation that offers help to people who have a dispute over or complaint about an occupational or personal pension. It also provides very useful (and independent) general information and advice about entitlements and rights.

www.napf.co.uk

The National Association of Pension Funds provides information on company pensions.

www.dialspace.dial.pipex.com/town/road/xoq83/index.htm

This site primarily provides information about pensions in local government, but also some useful general material.

www.nhspa.gov.uk/nhspaonline

This is the NHS pensions site – it contains a good 'jargon-busting' section.

www.fsa.gov.uk/consumer

This site offers useful information for consumers about pensions and investments.

www.pensioncalculator.org

Flexible benefits

INTRODUCTION

The traditional approach to employee benefits, particularly in respect of the costly pensions and other security benefits, was predicated on traditional assumptions about the nature of households. It is only recently that pension schemes have begun providing equal benefits for men and women. However, the benefits package remains largely predicated on an assumed male breadwinner lifestyle.

This chapter discusses the value and construction of flexible benefits plans. It contributes to the following CIPD professional standards:

Operational indicators – Practitioners must be able to:

■ advise on the management of change when introducing or modifying elements of the reward system, including the case for introducing flexible benefits.

Knowledge indicators – Practitioners must understand and be able to explain:

■ the basis on which flexible benefit systems work.

DIVERSITY AND CHOICE

Data from the Office of National Statistics (Table 49, page 204) show that the traditional nuclear family is now in the minority as households and families become much more diverse in nature. Rises in the number of mothers in work, the increase in part-time work and the gradual extension of work opportunities to both older people and to those with disabilities mean that the social context for reward is changing radically.

Flexible benefits

The standardised one-size-fits-all approach, particularly in respect of benefits, is therefore called into question. Flexible benefits are a means by which employers can offer a more 'employee-centred' approach. Under flexible benefits schemes, employees are offered a choice of benefits, or perhaps a choice between different benefits or in relation to the level of benefit. This principle means that in a diverse labour market, employees choose the benefits that they decide are most suitable for them and their lifestyle.

The notion of flexible or 'cafeteria' or 'menu' benefit packages has its origins in the United States, where a number of these company schemes were established – particularly in the 1980s. Such arrangements grew from only a handful of companies offering flexible benefits in the early 1970s to an estimated 70 per cent of the Fortune 1000 list of companies with plans in place – the United States' largest companies (Heneman *et al* 2000; Barringer and Milkovich

People in households: by type of household and family

Great Britain					Percentages
	1971	1981	1991	2001	2003
One-family households					
Living alone	6	8	11	12	13
Couple					
No children	19	20	23	25	25
Dependant children	52	47	41	39	38
Non-dependant children only	10	10	11	8	8
Lone parent	4	6	10	12	12
Other households	9	9	4	4	5
All people in private households (=100%) (millions)	53.4	53.9	55.4		
People not in private households (millions)	0.9	0.8	0.8		
Total population (millions)	54.4	54.8	56.2	57.4	57.6

Source: Census, Labour Force Survey, Office for National Statistics

Percentage of dependant children living in different family types

Great Britain					Percentages
	1972	1981	1992	2001	2003
Couple families					
1 child	16	18	18	17	17
2 children	35	41	39	38	37
3 or more children	41	29	27	25	24
Lone-mother families					
1 child	2	3	4	6	6
2 children	2	4	5	7	8
3 or more children	2	3	4	5	6
Lone-father families					
1 child	–	1	1	1	2
2 or more children	1	1	1	1	1
All children	100	100	100	100	100

Source: General Household Survey, Census, Labour Force Survey, Office for National Statistics

Table 49 *Nature of families and households*

1998). Flexible benefit plans grew in popularity in the United States in part because of the favourable tax treatment given there to companies' insurance-based benefit plans. In the UK, fiscal policy has gradually been increasing the tax on benefits, so that they are taxed at something like their true value.

Slow developer

There has been a slow growth in interest in such schemes in the UK. In 1994 a Hay Management Consultants survey found that flexible benefits tend to be limited to middle management and above. The Wyatt Company found in its 1994 survey that only 5 per cent of respondents operated a flexible benefits scheme – although a further 40 per cent were actively thinking about introducing one.

Finally in 2002 there were some definite signs of a lift in the number of schemes. Employee Benefits/MX Financial Solutions' (2003) survey showed that about 19 per cent of employers surveyed had flexible benefits, up from 9 per cent in 2002. Survey samples can vary, of course. Lower proportions for the take-up of flexible benefits were given in the CIPD (2002) survey – between 6 per cent and 9 per cent had flexible benefits, depending on the category of employee.

Why flex?

There are a number of different factors encouraging employers to begin what can be a complex process – the development of flexible benefits. The limited evidence on allowing choice in benefits suggests that costs may be reduced while employee satisfaction is increased. Some of the main 'driving forces' prompting the move to flex are as follows.

Diverse labour market

Employers may want to respond to the demographic and labour market changes, recognising that different reward packages may be needed for people with different lifestyles within the workforce. The increased numbers of mothers in the workforce and the continued growth of the dual-career family are some of the trends that underpin the growth in demand for flex.

Controlling benefit costs

Because of the need to identify benefit costs more precisely than employers often do, this exercise alone can help in maintaining control over costs.

Communication with employees

As the CIPD (2002) report finds, the level of communication by employers with employees about reward matters is generally low. Improving communication on benefits can therefore pay dividends in terms of the overall perception employees have of the reward package. Moreover, in comparison with some more sensitive reward areas this is relatively easy to tackle, though it is not without its costs and difficulties.

Increased perceived value from the organisation's 'spend' on benefits

Under expectancy theory, the element of choice itself could be thought to lead to greater employee satisfaction with the benefits package provided, when employees are 'empowered' to select those with a particular value for them.

Employer 'branding'

Branding is a key concept in marketing and some organisations are beginning to develop their own employment 'brand'. Some of those introducing flexible benefits have seen the development in this light – paying almost as much attention to the name or logo for the flexible benefits plan as its contents. Martin and Beaumont (2003) show that 'brand reputation' amongst employees and the extent to which what the brand promises is in keeping with what it delivers are significant factors.

Adding benefits choice as one element in a move from a final-salary to a money-purchase pension scheme

Integrating other benefits with major changes in occupational pensions provision, for instance a move from a final-salary to a defined contribution or money-purchase scheme, may take the sting out of an otherwise unpopular move.

Harmonisation of benefits practices

There are two situations in which harmonisation tends to lead to flexible benefits – firstly, in moves to implement single status between staff and manual groups, and secondly in bringing together and reducing differences in benefits treatment between groups of employees when companies merge.

Cultural change

Flexible benefits could be part of a wider culture change initiative aimed to give employees more individual responsibility or empowerment – for instance, when setting up self-managed teams or other HR innovations.

Perceived value – the relevance of expectancy theory

Expectancy theory may have special relevance to flexible benefits. The concept of valence is particularly worthy of consideration in planning flexible benefits. People at different stages of their life cycle are likely to be motivated by different types of reward, because, for example, younger people may place a lower value on pension benefits than cash, whilst older people might wish to do the reverse. It is not just age that might be a significant factor here but also the lifestyle of the employee.

The fact that employees may value different benefits differently – at different stages in their life, or if their family situation or lifestyle changes – is the principle underpinning flexible benefits. But why employers should respond is a key question. To study this aspect, other theoretical perspectives may be needed.

Other theoretical perspectives

Barringer and Milkovich (1998) discuss some other theoretical perspectives that can be of value in understanding the development of flexible benefits.

Institutional perspective

Organisations may adopt an initiative like flexible benefits, even if it is 'technically' inefficient for them to do so, in order to gain legitimacy or to conform to accepted standards of 'best practice'. By adopting the initiative managers feel they or their organisations will be seen as 'modern' or 'professional'.

Resource dependence

The institutional model might be more convincing when integrated with other theories, such as resource dependence theory. This assumes that management decisions are heavily influenced by internal and external agents, who control critical resources. This theory sees organisations responding more strategically to external pressures than does the institutional model. For example, some studies using this model found that resistance to pressures to adopt family-friendly policies varied with the percentage of women in the organisation's workforce.

Agency theory

The implication of the agency theory is that reward packages should be designed to motivate employees to act in the best interests of the principal (company owners). It might be argued that the concept can be extended to benefits.

Matters of design

Flexible benefits schemes tend to be structured in one of the following ways, according to Coopers & Lybrand (1993).

- *A 'core plus' benefits approach* – in which employers offer a core range of benefits requiring no flexible contribution, plus a further range of options from which an employee can choose, up to a set spending limit.

- *Modular benefits* – this is a choice of predefined benefit packages (Mode A, Mode B etc) without further flexibility, designed to appeal to different employees with different lifestyles.

- *Free choice* – this offers a free choice for individuals to select a preferred package of benefits up to a predefined maximum cost.

Core elements

Core benefits are usually those seen by employers as essential and are typically security benefits such as pensions. The argument put forward by proponents of the core approach is often a paternalistic one. Equally it might be a reflection of the employer practically not wishing, as the Employee Benefits/MX Financial Solutions (2003) survey report puts it, *'to risk employees being able to flex out of the pension'.* Spectres of the potentially destitute dependants of a former reasonably paid employee demanding they receive dependants' benefits, when the deceased ex-employee had flexed them all away, haunt some managers. Hence the pensions elements included in the flexible package may be a choice of a more or less generous pension scheme and/or of AVCs. Often, though, the pension scheme will be excluded from the flexible options.

Another core element now has to be a minimum of four weeks' paid leave, under the Working Time Regulations 1998 – as employees may not flex away leave below the legal minimum. Most schemes are based around the principle that certain benefits will be 'core' and others will be flexible. A minority of schemes are fully flexible in the sense that all benefits in the package can be flexed.

Which benefits are usually included?

Several elements in the benefits package can be 'flexed'. The Employee Benefits/MX Financial Solutions (2003) survey found that the benefits most frequently found in the flexible package were private medical cover, buying/selling annual leave and dental insurance.

Benefit	% age of respondents
Private medical insurance	61
Buy/sell annual leave	58
Dental insurance	52
Critical illness insurance	51
Additional death-in-service cover	48
Life cover	45
Alternative to car	43
Health screening	43
Company cars	40
Health cash plan	38
AVCs	37
Income protection	37
Childcare vouchers	36
Personal accident insurance	32
Leisure/retail vouchers	30
Travel insurance	30
Equipment	29
Financial advice	28
Final salary pension	28
Money purchase pension	28
Group personal pensions	25
Stakeholder pension	25
Gym membership	22
Season ticket loan	22
Source: Employee Benefits/MX Financial Solutions (2003)	

Table 50 *Which benefits are flexed?*

Costing and 'pricing' benefits

A system is invariably needed to price each benefit that is going to be offered under the flexible benefits scheme. Actuarial advice will be necessary at this stage to price any pensions elements included and some other insured benefits, too. Otherwise a good starting point will be the cost to the organisation of providing these benefits. Of course the actual cost in relation to individual employees will vary, some in relation to salary and some in relation to personal factors such as age. Some benefits will be cheap to provide and others much more expensive, and this will probably vary according to employees' age, seniority/grade and salary.

The flexing process therefore may well mean accepting that in terms of costs there will probably be some winners and some losers. Coopers & Lybrand (1993) describe ways in which benefits may be priced in order to set the 'spend' that each employee can make on his/her chosen package. Only once pricing is complete will the employer be able to decide the 'spend' on benefits and how this is to be administered.

Flexible benefits 'spends' are typically expressed either in terms of cash or points credits. Each benefit has a price and each employee a set spending limit, either in points or in 'cash credits'. The advantage of expressing these as cash is that the value is clearly communicated. Using a points credit system has the advantage that the points total can be adjusted to encourage or discourage take-up – for example, to encourage take-up of certain benefits for which low levels of take-up would adversely affect employer costs; points can remain constant over time, whereas actual costs are likely to change.

A few schemes do allow employees to use benefits cash credits to 'buy' actual cash.

Perceived effects by employers:	
Showing employees the value of benefits	62%
Aiding recruitment	53%
Improving retention	46%
Harmonising benefits	45%
Reinforcing company culture	43%
Improving/maintaining motivation	38%
Making organisation an 'employer of choice'	37%
Removing/reducing status symbols	31%
Reducing/containing the cost of reward	24%
Source: Employee Benefits/MX Financial Solutions (2003)	

Table 51   *The benefits of flexible packages*

Communication

This is, according to the Incomes Data Services (2001) study, *'the key to successful implementation of any scheme ... As one employer put it: "You can never explain benefits clearly enough".'* Employees will need detailed information on the range of options, and it can be challenging to communicate details when these are complex. IDS (2001) research shows that the companies that have introduced successful schemes have spent a considerable amount of time, effort and money on communication with employees. They used a range of communication methods – posters, newsletters, presentations, videos, road shows, and one-to-one meetings – and all these require 'management time'.

Evaluating effectiveness

The experience of organisations with flexible benefits schemes indicates that they are popular with employees and lead to employee satisfaction with employer-provided benefits packages (Barringer and Milkovich 1998; Industrial Society 1997). However, the take-up of certain benefit options may not be thought satisfactory. Most organisations offering benefit options monitor the detailed take-up of benefits. Many also use regular employee attitude surveys to gauge employees' views on the package as a whole, its communication – and the views of employees on particular benefits.

As Table 51 indicates there is some evidence that flexible benefits may be more effective in terms of the attractiveness of the employer in recruiting employees than in retaining them.

Drawbacks and disadvantages of flexible benefits

Administrative complexity is the concern most frequently cited in surveys about the downside of flexible benefits. Potentially, more flexibility in benefits provision will lead to greater administrative costs – and case studies have tended to support this. However, the Institute of Manpower Studies (1992) research showed that this was sometimes overstated by managers, who might not be as keen on a flexible benefits plan as they are on a flexible pay system.

The development of software packages to help administer the scheme has proven a distinct advantage in overcoming administrative costs.

Opting out of benefits can be a problem. The problem arises in the case of, say, an insurance-related benefit in which the costs of the benefits are based on age and gender profiles of the whole workforce. If sufficient employees opt out it may change the cost of providing the benefit to the remainder. In addition, employees may make poor choices – for instance ending up with inadequate pension provision.

There is some evidence (Industrial Society 1997) that flexible benefits schemes can help to control benefit costs.

Examples of organisation practice

Senior managers' scheme at British Home Stores (BHS)

BHS established a scheme for its top 50 managers and directors. Under this scheme, flexible benefits are divided into 'fixed-sum elements' (eg company car) and 'percentage of salary elements' (those benefits that vary according to the salary of the individual). The two together make up a cash credit amount that can be spent on various benefit options. Managers may spend against their credit, and any unspent entitlement is paid as a monthly cash allowance. They may also exceed their credit allowance, resulting in monthly payroll deductions.

Available options are:

- choice of car
- life assurance from one to four times salary
- any level of private medical cover
- choice of permanent health insurance policies
- choice of varying lengths of holiday entitlement.

Adapted from Incomes Data Services (1992).

Middle managers' scheme at the Burton Group

The Burton Group operates a flexible benefit scheme for its 1,200 middle and senior managers. Core benefits cannot be traded, and these include pension, personal accident insurance, staff discount and holidays. The flexible benefits include:

- company cars
- fuel cards
- medical insurance
- dental insurance
- financial counselling.

Adapted from Incomes Data Services (1993a).

Senior executive scheme at Scottish and Newcastle

Scottish and Newcastle has a flexible benefit scheme for its top senior executives. This allows salary to be flexed from 75 to 125 per cent of the norm salary, by taking up or not taking up a wide range of flexible benefits options, including:

- various pension arrangements
- varying levels of private medical cover
- different lengths of holiday entitlement and other benefits.

Adapted from Incomes Data Services (1993b).

Employer branding at the Royal Bank of Scotland

The Royal Bank of Scotland set out in 1997 to improve its reward system in a bid to strengthen its 'employer brand'. The Royal Bank of Scotland wanted to be seen as an employer of choice, so as to reinforce its attractiveness to and retention of skilled staff. In 1998 the bank launched RBSelect, a 'total reward' benefits package giving employees a wide choice of benefits and almost complete flexibility in how they allocate the overall value of their remuneration package. The scheme covers more than 18,000 people in 700 locations.

The scheme establishes a 'value account', which includes basic salary and benefits, plus regional allowances, as a fund to be used flexibly, with no limit on the amount that can be spent on any benefit.

211

All employees from the chief executive downwards are included. In the initial selection, one-fifth of the workforce chose new preferences. Employees were sent a 35-page information booklet to help them with their calculations. The company produced a video explaining the scheme, while the internal television network provided briefings and bulletins.

The scheme is divided into six groups:

- private health cover
- insurance, including life assurance for spouses and partners
- savings such as voluntary contributions to pension schemes
- 'lifestyle features', which include the manager's company car, childcare vouchers and retail vouchers for use at Whitbread and Safeway
- basic salary
- holiday.

Innovative features include the facility to buy or sell up to three days' leave, the provision of a legal rights helpline and the availability of an additional car-leasing scheme to all employees. Even the Christmas bonus can be traded in for a different benefit.

There are still some core benefits that are not part of the value account, although their worth is still included in the total reward statement that everyone receives each year. These are the basic pension scheme, the group profit-share scheme, death-in-service benefit and any performance-related bonus. Eligibility for loans, the bank's Sharesave scheme and the house-purchase scheme are also not included on the flexible menu.

Employees can change their benefits package once a year. Apart from the total reward statement, which sets out the value of each of the benefits they currently receive, they receive a preference worksheet each year to work out a new benefit selection for the year ahead. They then alter their options via the telephone, using the outsourced consultancy help-line voice message system. Using this automated method, no paperwork or computer inputting needs to be done, although people can speak to an operator if they prefer to. They then receive a statement confirming their choices, which come into force a month later.

There are only eight specific circumstances in which options can be changed at other times. These 'qualifying lifestyle events' are: promotion giving eligibility for a company car; a reduction in working time to less than 21 hours a week; a change in salary as a result of ill-health; the start or end of maternity leave; the birth or adoption of a child; the death of a dependant; relocation; and repatriation.

Adapted from Trading in options. *People Management*. 6 May 1999, p42.

Post-merger harmonisation: PriceWaterhouse Coopers
PriceWaterhouse Coopers (PwC) used flexible benefits in harmonising employment terms and conditions for its post-merger organisation, which had 150,000 employees in 150 countries.

It was considered at the outset that there was a good 'cultural fit' between the two firms Price Waterhouse (PW) and Coopers & Lybrand (C&L) before they merged in July 1998. Flexible benefits were considered appropriate because the HR policy encompassed a recognition of 'individuality and diversity', and of the variety of benefits needs this generated. In addition, in a competitive recruitment market a flexible benefits plan was thought to represent an important selling point. And a new benefits structure was also seen to be the best way to align the two firms' existing arrangements and create a unified policy. Cost-cutting was not a motive on the part of the company, although some savings on bulk purchases and, in the short term, on National Insurance contributions (where people chose vouchers in place of cash) were made.

The flexible benefits plan was called Choices. The Choices menu comprises:

- holiday (staff must take between 20 and 30 days a year)
- car
- childcare vouchers
- retail vouchers
- travel insurance
- medical insurance
- dental insurance
- permanent health insurance
- critical illness insurance
- personal accident insurance
- life assurance
- pension and cash.

But what distinguished Choices from other employers' policies was the breadth of choice within each option. For instance, the company car list features more than 3,000 models, ranging from a Ford Fiesta to an S-class Mercedes. More significantly, all members could choose any car, subject to using no more than the value of their benefit fund (up to 20 per cent of base salary). Funds were computed for each employee to reflect the value of benefit entitlements from previous schemes and to enable people to reselect existing benefits if they wished.

The company promised that employees would not lose out financially through the introduction of the flexible scheme. Indeed, some gained as the firm enhanced some of the C&L pensions arrangements, while former PW staff found that they were paying less for extra holiday entitlement.

A system of cash-based protected benefit values (PBVs) equivalent to the value of the lost benefits was used when some people would otherwise be 'losers' under the new arrangements.

Communication events included two-hour roadshows – more than 200 in all – held at every major PwC location in the UK over a six-week period. These were said to act as a 'lightning conductor' for some strong views.

In response to feedback from these events, a number of changes were made, emphasising that communication was a two-way process.

All eligible PwC employees became members of the new plan from 1 April 1999, but they could choose to retain their existing benefits within the Choices framework. More than three-quarters of them actually changed one or more of their benefits.

Adapted from Franks and Thompson (2000).

Case study – High Street Travel Ltd

HST is a high street travel agency in an increasingly competitive business environment. Through its retail outlets it sells its own package tours and those of other specialist tour operators – for which it earns commission on sales. The outlets each employ a team of sales consultants. These staff are paid a fairly low basic pay rate compared with other retail organisations. Senior management have not been able to raise basic pay by more than the inflation rate for many years, as the profit margins on the business are very tight and product competition is tough.

The sales consultants are eligible for non-financial rewards in the form of free exotic holidays for an individual high level of sales achieved over the previous quarter. The other main benefit is discount on the company's holidays and flights, worth about 50 per cent less than the brochure price. The company has a severe staff turnover problem. Each year after staff have taken their discounted holidays, the turnover rate rises dramatically.

A newly promoted HR manager is tasked by senior management with finding a solution to the turnover problem. She is a working mother with two small children and finds herself 'time poor'. She has an idea that the company might improve retention of staff by introducing a flexible benefits plan, integrating the existing benefits with a range of low-cost options to provide 'lifestyle benefits'. She has read how companies in the City of London popularly provide benefits such as ironing collection and dog-walking services. The HR manager asks you to research this proposal and make an initial recommendation as to whether or not it is worth pursuing.

STUDENT REVIEW TASK

Consider how you might research this further within the company. Compile an initial recommendation as to whether a lifestyle benefits programme should be developed.

Case study – Mortgage Co Ltd

Mortgage Co Ltd is a small, wholly owned subsidiary of a large financial services corporation, a group of companies that has businesses covering most aspects of retail banking and finance. In many ways Mortgage Co Ltd is rather an oddity within the group of companies. While retrenchment and maturity of business is evident in other parts of the group, Mortgage Co Ltd is a young and thriving concern. It has its own distinctive style and culture, very different from the traditional, rather bureaucratic organisational culture evident within the rest of the group.

Mortgage Co Ltd has a predominately young staff, with an increasing proportion of women in senior management roles. Although it has only 200 staff based at its pleasant offices in Milton Keynes, it is proud of the fact that it provides one – of only two – day nurseries for the children of staff in the whole group of companies. An increasing number of staff use the employer-subsidised nursery and a high proportion of women employees return to work following maternity leave.

In most respects the management of Mortgage Co Ltd have freedom to set pay and benefits for their staff, within overall budget constraints set at group board level. The one exception to this company level of decision-making on pay and benefits is the group-wide pension scheme. After many years of stability in the provision of a good final-salary pension scheme, the group board has decided that it no longer wants to run a final-salary pension scheme for the employees of the group. The board has secretly discussed this option for the past two years, but its recent decision has been informed by research from Incomes Data Services (2001) that has 'shown a jump in the number of schemes reporting that they had switched from final salary provision to a money purchase scheme in the past 12 months'. The research detailed more than 50 (mainly 'blue chip') companies that launched defined-contribution pension schemes in the five years after 1996 and, in most cases, also closed their final salary schemes.

The prime driver of the board's decision is the prospect of rising costs in running the final salary scheme. The annual cost, including employee contributions, of providing the 1/60th final salary scheme is 15 per cent of pensionable payroll. Although the scheme is not now more generous in terms of the benefits it provides than in the recent past, the actual costs to the company are now much higher than they have been for much of the previous 20 years. Several favourable trends over the past two decades, including a booming stock market, helped the group to limit the severity of the costs of the scheme. The board has decided that it can no longer maintain this level of cost and is proposing to close the final-salary scheme to new entrants across the group, offering instead a new, defined-contribution pension scheme. It proposes to pay a 5 per cent employer contribution into the new scheme, in contrast to the 10 per cent it has paid into the final-salary scheme (employees are required to pay 5 per cent at present).

The board is aware that this decision may not be popular among employees. It is also keen to limit any potentially damaging publicity.

Your role and task

The managing director of Mortgage Co Ltd calls you in as her reward manager and seeks your advice. She has been advised by the group board that she could (exceptionally) continue to provide final-salary scheme membership for new members of staff provided she pays the balance of cost from her budget for staff benefits. The other big-cost item in the company benefits 'spend' is the day nursery. She can see the popularity of that benefit with staff, and has anxieties about the potential effect on recruitment and retention of staff if the nursery were to be closed or the subsidy withdrawn in order to fund the pension scheme payments.

Your brief is to consider this problem and to suggest an optimal and practical way forward.

Write an outline report for the senior management of Mortgage Co Ltd, identifying the way in which it could develop its benefits system within the given constraints and with the facts that you are given. You may make any other reasonable assumptions in arriving at your recommendations.

STUDENT REVIEW QUESTIONS

Are employers who are now adopting flexible benefits merely following a fashionable trend set by innovative organisations? Discuss this using company examples and theoretical concepts.

Does the 'employee-centred' approach to reward evident in flexible benefits schemes presage a more extensive future move to consider the needs, wants and choices of employees more generally in the design of other parts of their reward package? Would this be a good idea? Why? What are the drawbacks?

REFERENCES

Barber, A, Dunham, R and Formisano, R (1992) The impact of employee benefits on employee satisfaction: a field study. *Personnel Psychology.* Vol 45, pp55–75.

Barringer, M and Milkovich, G (1998) A theoretical exploration of the adoption and design of flexible benefit plans: a case of human resource innovation. *Academy of Management Review.* Vol 23, no 2, April, pp305–324.

Bright, D (1995) International flex. *Benefits and Compensation International.* Vol. 24, Dec. 1994.

Chartered Institute of Personnel and Development (2002) *Reward management survey.* CIPD.

Coopers & Lybrand (1993) *Flexible benefits: motivation and cost control.* CCH Editions Ltd.

Crabb, S (1995) Adding value with better benefits. *People Management.* 13 July.

Employee Benefits (1998) Does flex point to success? *Employee Benefits, Strategic Reward Supplement.* April, pp10–12.

Employee Benefits/MX Financial Solutions (2003) Flexible benefits research 2003. *Employee Benefits.* April, pp4–9.

Franks, O and Thompson, D (2000) Mix 'n' match. *People Management.* 17 February, p40.

Hay Management Consultants (1994) *Employee benefits report.*

Heneman, R, Ledford, G and Gresham, M (2000) *The changing nature of work and its effects on compensation design and delivery*, in Rynes, S and Gerhart, B (eds) *Compensation in organizations: current research and practice.* Jossey-Bass.

Incomes Data Services (1992) Flexible benefits at BHS. *IDS Top Pay Review* 141. November.

Incomes Data Services (1993a) Burton Group introduces flexible benefits. *IDS Top Pay Review* 144. February.

Incomes Data Services (1993b) Flexible benefits scheme at Scottish and Newcastle. *IDS Top Pay Review* 147. May.

Incomes Data Services (2001) Flexible benefits. *IDS StudyPlus.* Summer.

Industrial Relations Services (1998) Flexible benefits evolve at Cable & Wireless. *IRS Employment Review: Pay and Benefits Bulletin* 658, June, pp2–4.

Industrial Relations Services (2000) The joy of flex. *IRS Employment Review: Pay and Benefits Bulletin* 710, August, pp6–9.

Industrial Relations Services (2003) Lloyds TSB develops a taste for flexibility. *IRS Employment Review* 768, 24 January, pp24–28.

Industrial Society (1997) *Flexible benefits.* Managing Best Practice. 34.

Institute of Manpower Studies (1992) *Introducing flexible benefits: the other side of the coin.* IMS Report 231.

Martin, G and Beaumont, P (2003) *Branding and people management: what's in a name?* CIPD.

People Management (1999) Trading in options. *People Management.* 6 May, p42.

Wyatt Company (1994) *Company Cars and Flexible Benefits.*

Index